ZEN
and the Successful Horseplayer

How to Win and Find Calmness in Horse Wagering

Zen and the Successful Horseplayer
by Frederic Donner
Copyright © 2005 Frederic M. Donner

Published by: Ashcor Publishing
100 Easy Street #903
Carefree, AZ 85377
First Printing, January 2005

ISBN: 0-9743333-5-2
Library of Congress Control Number: 2003103323

Printed in the United States of America

Zen and the Successful Horseplayer will provide the beginner, the advanced, and even the professional horse gambler with specific resources to become a winning player. This book will also demonstrate the applicability of Zen and Eastern philosophy to handicapping, betting, and winning.

Frederic Donner is an eighteen-year veteran Special Agent with the Federal Bureau of Investigation. He has primarily worked in anti-narcotic and counterterrorism efforts in undercover capacities in many cities around the United States and the world. He has been responsible for a number of major investigations and is a Special Weapons and Tactical (S.W.A.T.) Team Leader. He has been wagering on horses successfully for more than twenty-five years, and has been able to incorporate his discipline as an FBI Agent and utilization of a Zen stylized approach to secure significant wins at the track.

ZEN
and the Successful
Horseplayer

How to Win
and Find Calmness
in Horse Wagering

Frederic Donner

This book is dedicated to Kathy,

the shooting star of my life,

the true Secretariat of my world!

Contents

Introduction

"The first springs of great events, like those of great
rivers are often mean and little."
— Jonathan Swift

Zen exists in our everyday lives. Zen and other related Eastern philosophies and disciplines, indicate how order functions without specific conscious effort. Zen quite literally means awaken. To those unfamiliar with Zen and similar philosophies, it might appear that one needs to first simply "wake" to be awake or aware, but to successfully incorporate Zen we need only "be." We do not force awakening, we allow it, we feel it, we exist, and awareness comes with it. We are.

Initially, a link between the way of Zen and horse wagering may seem at odds (pardon the pun), but the ability to incorporate Zen into "playing the ponies" makes infinite concrete sense. As an example, when we look at a horse on the track, any good bettor is immediately looking for strengths (a good shoulder, excellent conformation—

conformation being a horse's overall body, set-up, etc.), and weaknesses (excessive sweating, newly added front wraps, etc.). Being more in tune with one's world (more "Zenned," so to speak) will allow us to see this horse more clearly in a holistic way, and more accurately access its chances in the race. Analyzing or better yet feeling through all the data in the past performances in the *Daily Racing Form* is easier and more accurate if there is greater Zen/awareness.

> **"Learning, is finding out what you already know.**
> **Doing, is demonstrating that You know it."**
> **— Richard Bach,**
> **from *Illusions, The Adventures of a Reluctant Messiah***

The purpose of this book is to make anyone who reads it a more successful horseplayer. Successful is an important term here, and it means more than just winning more or losing less. Wins versus losses are an important dynamic in determining success, yet success also involves how you feel after a horserace experience: Did you enjoy yourself or perhaps more importantly, did those around you enjoy you? Will you be a better handicapper after this particular trip to the track or the OTB (Off Track Betting)? What did you learn?

There is much more to success than wins/losses, but by any gambler's definition, wins, and losses are an important part of horseracing success. If you use the specific handicapping tools discussed in this book, and incorporate the way of Zen into the overall way you approach your horse wagering, you will, by all definitions be more successful. This is true if you are a novice, a seasoned handicapper, or even the rare professional gambler. We can all learn to be better, and when being better can fatten our wallet, we all have incentive.

> **"What is success?**
> **To laugh often and much;**
> **To win the respect of intelligent people and the**
> **affection of children;**
> **To earn the appreciation of honest critics and endure**
> **the betrayal of false friends;**
> **To appreciate beauty;**
> **To find the best in others;**
> **To leave the world a bit better, whether by a healthy**

child, a garden patch, or a redeemed social condition;
To know that one life has breathed easier because you
have lived;
That is to have succeeded."
— Ralph Waldo Emmerson,
as quoted in the *Harper's Book of Quotations*

This book is divided into two sections. The first section will delineate basic skills and techniques you must have within your repertoire to be a winning bettor. Zen is not about guessing; guessing is for losers (at least as far as the track goes). Zen will only work if you have acquired the basic skills needed to understand the reams of information you have at your disposal. Once you are able to locate the data you need, you will be able to utilize Zen to help feel your way to winning play. The second section will deal with Zen and other Eastern philosophies, and how they can be indispensable in helping you pick winners, and be more successful (in its fullest definition) at the track.

To provide some personal background, I have been a Special Agent with the Federal Bureau of Investigation for more than eighteen years. Most of that time I have worked undercover in drug operations. I am also a Special Weapons and Tactical (S.W.A.T.) Team Leader. My background has relevance as to how Zen can work in daily life and at the track. If I am going in to secure an undercover drug purchase of say five ounces of heroin, I do not simply go in with a wad of cash and my cap turned sideways, not unless I have a death wish or am incredibly stupid (and contrary to some of the FBI's bad press of late, the "stupid" FBI Agent is relatively rare). Before I make the buy, I do my homework (read the case file, talk to others who know these bad guys, determine the likely quality and type and cost of the heroin, etc., etc., etc.). In essence, I do all I can to prepare; then, and only then, do I go to initiate meetings with the bad guy and discuss specifics and "feel him out." Feel is a key word here (and a Zen word). If the deal, as set up by the bad guy, does not feel right, I don't do it that way, or more importantly, maybe I don't do it all.

How much does that FBI undercover talk I have sound like wagering on the horses? It is exactly, exactly the same (though a bad wager just lightens your pocket book, it doesn't get you a 9mm in the head). It is the same with your betting: you prepare, you read, and you study. Then with the skills of Zen, after the preparation, you can feel/sense the likely best wager, or if it feels wrong, you can bail out of the wager all together. Some of the best decisions I ever made were not to make a bet.

So read this book, prepare, study, know the tools available to you, and then use the way of Zen to pick those winners.

"Light a candle instead of cursing the darkness"
— Richard Carlson Ph.D.,
Don't Sweat the Small Stuff

I would like to note that at the end of every chapter I provide the reader with an additional book that should assist him/her with the subject matter of the previous chapter. The book icon will identify this book selection. For this introduction I would like to note that two of the principal foundations of Zen are Zazen (sitting mediation) which we will discuss later, and SanZen, or visits and conversation with a Zen Master. One of the primary keys to SanZen is the Wen-Ta, or question and answer "Zen Story." The Wen-Ta is an aid to enable the student to achieve greater clarity and enlightenment. Examples of "Zen Story" would be, "Can you hear the sunset?" or "Can you see a thunder clap?" Many are humorous and inventive. I personally love quotes and scoured hundreds of horse publications, Zen writings, poems, etc., for quotations that could be included in this book and loosely be interpreted as Wen-Ta for horseplayers. I have tried to use quotes to inspire reflection in the reader. I found a wonderful book titled "The Quotable Horse Lover," edited by Steven D. Price. Many of the quotes in my book were discovered (or rediscovered) in Price's anthology.

The Quotable Horse Lover
Ed. Steven D. Price

Section 1
Basic Handicapping Skills

1
What Type of Player Are You?
(Plus Stupid and Lazy Gamblers)

"I started playing the horses and trying to comprehend
the mysteries of the game, I thought I was searching
for great immutable truths. I thought there must be a
set of principles that governed the outcome of races
and was waiting to be discovered... I (eventually)
realized that there were no such timeless verities—
but I wish that there were."
— Andrew Beyer, *The Winning Horseplayer*

The quote by Andrew Beyer is an amazing statement, not because all horseplayers do not feel similarly, but because of its author. Mr. Beyer is a talented, and well-respected professional handicapper, author, and founder of Beyer Speed Figures. If someone of Mr. Beyer's stature thinks it is a hard game, those lesser mortals among us should be darn well prepared!

Before we go into detailed discussions of handicapping techniques in chapters two through eleven, I would like you to think about what type of handicapper you currently are. Are you a novice, a speed figure person, a trainer/jockey person, etc.?

> **"Knowing ignorance is strength.**
> **Ignoring knowledge is sickness."**
> — Lao Tzu, *Tao Te Ching*

While you are accessing your own handicapping style, I would like to provide a brief interlude dealing with my small effort to help a very small category of gamblers: stupid gamblers and lazy gamblers. Most of you reading this book do not fall into these two categories, and you could probably skip to chapter two, but you may find the reading here interesting. Most people will purchase this book because they have a desire to be more successful at horse wagering, and this is true regardless of experience level. Previously, I mentioned Andrew Beyer, the man who popularized Beyer Speed Figures. Even after he developed that successful technique he was not satisfied; new continued success was dependent on "trip handicapping" and other more advanced skills. If he feels the need to improve, we can all benefit from a total look at handicapping.

Oh yes, not all of us can be helped. There are a few stupid and lazy gamblers, and so, while most of you are making the assessment of, "I need more assistance with turf handicapping", or "Wow, a chapter on how horses look at the track," here is my effort to help the stupid and lazy gamblers reading this book (you probably received it as a gift from some kindhearted soul).

> **"A fool takes no pleasure in understanding,**
> **but only in expressing his opinion"**
> — *Proverb 18:2*

STUPID GAMBLERS

Stupid gamblers buy a program so they can find out who the favorite is, and then do not care because they just bet the race time favorite (the odds when the horses are at the gate). Examples of this moronic behavior are legend at tracks and OTBs nationwide. I actually saw one of these "chalk" (favorite) players bet $100 per race on each favorite at an OTB in Phoenix, and he lost five times in a row. In the sixth race there were two favorites, Horse A (which I liked) at 2 to 1, and Horse B at 5 to 2 (2.5 to 1). He obviously bet $100 on Horse A, but just before race time, Horse B became the race time favorite, so he cancelled his bet on Horse A, and then wagered $100 on Horse B. Horse A won by five widening lengths, I had him keyed in a pick 3 and Samuel the Stupid had another "throw away" (losing ticket).

Okay, okay, I said I would help the stupid gambler (though it may hurt mutual pools worldwide). Gamblers like Samuel the Stupid do not handicap. So, the rest of the book will be useless for them, and one knows that they have no Zen or Karma capabilities. So, here goes my try at assistance: Favorites win approximately one in three races and you will never come out ahead in the end (or in most cases in the short run) betting win money exclusively on the favorites. *So stop!*

Instead, try one of the three following options (it does not matter which); you will still lose almost all the time *because you do not handicap,* but there will be rare days when you actually *win,* a concept I know is foreign to you.

OPTIONS

Number One: Bet the second choice to win.

Number Two: Take the favorite and "back wheel" it in the exacta. Take every other horse believing that they will beat the favorite, and hope the favorite runs second.

Number Three: Key your favorite in the "pick 3" with all in the the next two races (attempting to select the winner of three consecutive races). If your favorite wins you can at least hope for long shots in the next two races (and you *still* do not have to handicap).

I do not guarantee you will win very often, but at least you can now have a small chance to win. You may now stop reading this book if you are like Samuel the Stupid and pass it along to someone who you believe will receive legitimate assistance from it. I can provide you no further support.

> **"I never play horse shoes 'cause mother taught us to**
> **not throw our clothes around."**
> — Mr. Ed [The "Talking Horse" of the 1960s TV series]
> as quoted in *The Quotable Horse Lover*

LAZY GAMBLERS

"I did not have time to handicap the entire race card. Who do you like in the fifth?" Does that sound familiar? If you do not have time to handicap, do not bet the race. I just saved you money right there. Instead, make a commitment to fully handicap one race—then just bet that race. You will find the positive reinforcement from your more frequent wins will create incentive to handicap more races next time.

Okay, enough with helping the hopeless. Let's talk some techniques to help you handicap.

My additional recommended reading is to obtain some knowledge concerning the history of horse racing and in particular the amazing high level thoroughbreds that have raced in the past century. The Blood-Horse Magazine® has come out with an outstanding volume titled *Thoroughbred Champions, Top 100 Racehorses of the 20th Century*. This book rates the top 100 thoroughbreds and provides extensive descriptive information and photographs concerning these incredible champions. Just the nature of why the magazine picked Man o' War number one will stir up arguments among horseplayers. This volume provides wonderful background and history concerning the beauty, style, and winning qualities of the nation's finest thoroughbreds.

Thoroughbred Champions,
Top 100 Racehorses of the 20th Century

2
Reading and Understanding the Daily Racing Form

**"Secretariat is blazing along. The first three-quarters
of the mile in 1:09 and 4/5. Secretariat is widening now.
He is moving like a tremendous machine."**
— Announcer Chic Anderson calling Secretariat's
thirty-one-length victory in the 1973 Belmont Stakes.

The *Daily Racing Form* (DRF) is the horse handicapping Bible.
Any serious handicapper knows that without the use of the DRF
(which is also available for use from the Internet), any likely possibility of winning at the races is minimal. Many serious handicappers
and horseplayers reading this book will already know how to use the
DRF to its fullest potential. The purpose of this chapter is for those
who have not used the DRF, or for those who are already followers of
Zen and have decided to review this book as a skills-type test, much
as one would with swordsmanship or archery.

For initial reviewers, the DRF appears to be a series of words,
numbers, and other verbiage that is virtually incomprehensible. In

truth, the DRF is not particularly complex; it is full of information that is essential for handicapping and wagering.

One of the features of the DRF that is often lost on the most hard-core horse bettors is the excellent analysis and articles that are included at the beginning of the form. Often there are outstanding articles regarding breeding, track surfaces, specific races, and bias at various tracks. Unfortunately, the most able handicappers sometimes skip reading these articles, proceed directly to the past performances (PPs), and miss important information that could be of assistance when handicapping races. This is particularly true with major complex races, including Grade I's, Grade II's, and Stake and Allowance races.

One of the most fascinating and artistic aspects of the DRF is that often the caricature artist Pierre Bellocq (known universally in racing circles as "PEB") provides artwork for the cover. This artwork is insightful, almost universally humorous, and is a wonderful respite from handicapping. Often during the course of difficult handicapping sessions, such as those involving the Breeders Cup and Triple Crown races, I will handicap and then refer back to the artwork on the cover page, which always brings a smile. Even the most hardened players do not miss the humor and beauty in PEB's work.

For those of you extremely astute and familiar with the DRF, I will take no offense if you proceed directly to chapter three. For all others, here is a brief run down on how to use the DRF.

"Thou shalt have no God before me."
— GOD

As stated previously, the DRF is each individual horseplayer's Bible, and many horseplayers treat it with such respect. For those new to the sport, do not assume that every horseplayer at the track or OTB will allow you to review his or her racing form. Many players have individual notes, figures, etc., that they write on their forms, and are extremely reluctant to allow others (even the uninitiated horseplayers) to review this. My first suggestion to anyone who wishes to be successful at the racetrack is to buy a DRF and learn how to read it.

I do not mind allowing other people to look at my racing form, and I will relay one brief story that will show how reserved, calm, and centered I am (most of the time). I was working hard at handicapping a race at an OTB, and had completed my notations and handicapping, when an older, well-dressed man asked if he could look at my racing form. "Of course", I responded, handing him the racing form, and watched in abject horror as he took a marker and scratched out various horses and sections from the race I had just handicapped. I will state to all readers, that it took all the anger management control that I possess not to perform an Eastern ritualized killing on this individual.

> **"A knife keeps its edge only with honing and proper cutting. A warrior's virtue is readiness. A sage's virtue is awareness".**
> — **Deng-Dao, from *365 Tao***

Concerning utilization of the DRF, one of the most important informational pages is the front page and the internal pages, which have articles regarding various tracks, trainers, jockeys, etc. Before handicapping any of your races, scan these pages to see if there is information of value about the particular track of which you are handicapping. Due to the extensive amount of simulcasting in the U.S., most racing forms contain information from various tracks. As will be discussed later, it is suggested that individuals focus on one individual track and become familiar with that particular oval. In regards to the analysis found in the DRF, after reading the articles or at least scanning them, the horseplayer should turn to the section at the relevant track upon which he/she is to handicap. Generally, the first page of that track's information contains more valuable information concerning trainer and jockey standings, as well as information concerning which win from which post positions based on certain types of races (sprint, distance, and turf).

Also, in this area is a handicapper analysis provided by various contributors to the DRF. For most major tracks there are four separate handicappers who provide "picks" for the various races. Generally, I will review this information, but believe my own individual handicapping will be more than sufficient to outweigh the information and content provided by these paid handicappers.

> **"The race is not always to the swift, nor the battle to the strong, but that's the way to bet."**
> — **Damon Runyon**

Ok, now let's do a brief analysis of one horse competing in a race at Santa Anita Park on Sunday, February 24, 2002, to see what information the DRF typically contains.

Set out below is Diagram A, which shows a portion of the chart for the fourth race at Santa Anita on Sunday February 24, 2002. Subsequently, various items will be broken out and highlighted and will be explained later.

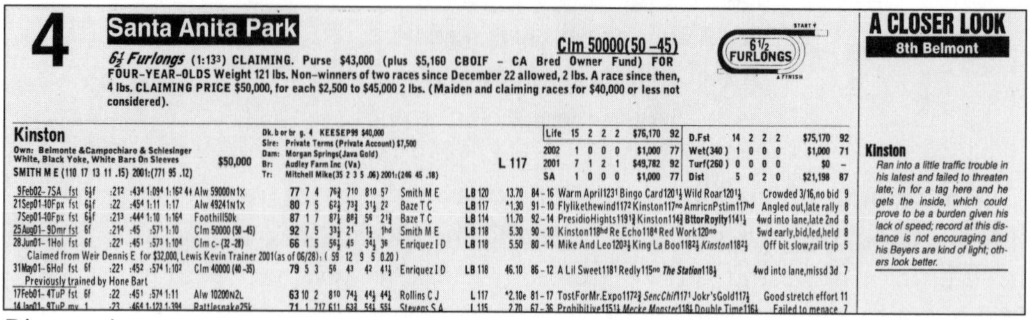
4 Santa Anita Park

Clm 50000(50 –45)

6½ Furlongs (1:13³) CLAIMING. Purse $43,000 (plus $5,160 CBOIF - CA Bred Owner Fund) FOR FOUR-YEAR-OLDS Weight 121 lbs. Non-winners of two races since December 22 allowed, 2 lbs. A race since then, 4 lbs. CLAIMING PRICE $50,000, for each $2,500 to $45,000 2 lbs. (Maiden and claiming races for $40,000 or less not considered).

START
6½ FURLONGS
FINISH

Kinston
Own: Belmonte &Campochiaro & Schlesinger
White, Black Yoke, White Bars On Sleeves $50,000
SMITH M E (110 17 13 11 .15) 2001:(771 95 .12)

Dk. b or br g. 4 KEESEP99 $40,000
Sire: Private Terms (Private Account) $7,500
Dam: Morgan Springs(Java Gold)
Br: Audley Farm Inc (Va)
Tr: Mitchell Mike(35 2 3 5 .06) 2001:(246 45 .18)

L 117

Life	15	2	2	2	$76,170	92	D.Fst	14	2	2	2	$75,170	92
2002	1	0	0	0	$1,000	77	Wet(340)	1	0	0	0	$1,000	71
2001	7	1	2	1	$49,782	92	Turf(260)	0	0	0	0	$0	-
SA	1	0	0	0	$1,000	77	Dist	5	0	2	0	$21,198	87

9Feb02- 7SA fst 6½f :21² :43⁴ 1:09⁴ 1:16² 4↑ Alw 59000N1X 77 7 4 76¾ 710 810 57 Smith M E LB 120 13.70 84-16 Warm April123¹ Bingo Card120½ Wild Roar120½ Crowded 3/16,no bid 9
21Sep01-10Fpx fst 6½f :22 :45⁴ 1:11 1:17 Alw 49241N1X 80 7 5 62½ 73¾ 31½ 22 Baze T C LB 117 *1.30 91-10 Flylikethewind117² Kinston117no AmricnPstim117hd Angled out,late rally 8
7Sep01-10Fpx fst 6½f :21³ :44⁴ 1:10 1:16⁴ Foothill50k 87 1 7 87¼ 88¾ 56 21¾ Baze T C LB 114 11.70 92-14 PresidioHights1191¾ Kinston114¾ BttorRoylty1141½ 4wd into lane,late 2nd 8
25Aug01- 9Dmr fst 6f :21⁴ :45 :57¹ 1:10 Clm 50000 (50-45) 92 7 5 33½ 21 1½ 1hd Smith M E LB 118 5.30 90-10 Kinston118hd Re Echo118⁴ Red Work120no 5wd early,bid,led,held 8
28Jun01- 1Hol fst 6f :22¹ :45¹ :57³ 1:10⁴ Clm c-(32-28) 66 1 5 56½ 45 34½ 36 Enriquez I D LB 118 5.50 80-14 Mike And Leo1203½ King La Boo1182½ Kinston1182½ Off bit slow,rail trip 5
Claimed from Weir Dennis E for $32,000, Lewis Kevin Trainer 2001(as of 06/28): (59 12 9 5 0.20)
31May01- 6Hol fst 6f :22¹ :45² :57⁴ 1:10² Clm 40000 (40-35) 79 5 3 56 43 42 41½ Enriquez I D LB 118 46.10 86-12 A Lil Sweet118¹ Redly115no The Station118½ 4wd into lane,missd 3d 7
Previously trained by Hone Bart
17Feb01- 4TuP fst 6f :22 :45¹ :57⁴ 1:11 Alw 10200N2L 63 10 2 810 74½ 44½ 44¼ Rollins C J L 117 *2.10e 81-17 TostForMr.Expo1172¾ SencChif117¹ Jokr'sGold117½ Good stretch effort 11
14Jan01- 9TuP my 1 :23 :46⁴ 1:12³ 1:39⁴ Rattlesnake25k 71 1 717 611 63¾ 54½ 55¼ Stevens S A L 115 2.70 67-36 Prohibitive1151¼ Mecke Monster118½ Double Time116½ Failed to menace 7

A CLOSER LOOK
8th Belmont

Kinston
Ran into a little traffic trouble in his latest and failed to threaten late; in for a tag here and he gets the inside, which could prove to be a burden given his lack of speed; record at this distance is not encouraging and his Beyers are kind of light; others look better.

Diagram A

Interestingly, it should be noted that on the far right side there is a comment line and analysis regarding the horse Kinston. Kenny Peck did the analysis very professionally in this case. It pays for all handicappers, experienced or novice, to review this information to insure that when they conduct their own analysis they do not miss anything. Additionally, I would like to note that at the top where it says "A CLOSER LOOK" "8th Belmont", this is a typographical error on the part of the DRF. I have universally found that the DRF is probably the best edited news publication in the United States, with the possible exception of *The Wall Street Journal*.® However, the point of this brief side note is to point out that even a publication as accurate as the DRF can make mistakes. All bettors should insure that before making a wager they purchase a program from the relevant track to insure that all numbers, names, etc. are accurate for wagering purposes.

From Diagram A, various areas have been highlighted so that it will be easier to observe what these numbers and data mean.

4 Santa Anita Park Clm 50000(50 –45)

1. This area designates that this is the fourth race at Santa Anita Park; immediately to the right of that is a designation that this is a claiming race "Clm" 50,000(50-45). Claiming means that other horse

owners can, in essence, purchase these horses for $50,000, but only if this election is made before the race beginning. Obviously, in the claiming ranks if there is higher monetary value ($50,000 vs. $25,000), this is indicative of greater ability in the horses.

2. This area, which is next to the claiming amount (Clm), is a chart showing that the race will be run at 6½ furlongs (one furlong = ⅛ of a mile). This chart also shows the start and finish lines for the race.

6½ Furlongs (1:13³)

3. This designation of (1:13³) is the current Santa Anita track record for the race distance of 6½ furlongs.

Purse $43,000 (plus $5,160 CBOIF – CA Bred Owner Fund)

4. This section shows that the purse is $43,000 (plus $5,160 CBOIF— CA Bred Owner Incentive Fund). This is a designation of what the prize money is for the horses when they compete. In this particular case the purse is $43,000 plus an additional $5,160 for California Breds.

> FOUR–YEAR–OLDS Weight 121 lbs. Non–winners of two races since December 22 allowed, 2 lbs. A race since then, 4 lbs. CLAIMING PRICE $50,000, for each $2,500 to $45,000 2 lbs. (Maiden and claiming races for $40,000 or less not considered).

5. This section discloses the condition or requirements for a runner to be eligible to run in the fourth race at Santa Anita. In this particular race the horses must be four-year-olds, and carry 121 pounds (which includes the jockey). This section also discloses that if individual horses have not won in certain time periods they are allowed to decrease the weight they carry accordingly. Additionally, if they run for the decreased claiming prices of $47,500 or $45,000, they may have their weight reduced by two or four pounds respectively.

Kinston			Dk. b or br g. 4 KEESEP99 $40,000		Life	15	2	2	2	$76,170	92	D.Fst	14	2	2	2	$75,170	92
Own: Belmonte &Campochiaro & Schlesinger			Sire: Private Terms (Private Account) $7,500															
White, Black Yoke, White Bars On Sleeves			Dam: Morgan Springs(Java Gold)		2002	1	0	0	0	$1,000	77	Wet(340)	1	0	0	0	$1,000	71
		$50,000	Br: Audley Farm Inc (Va)		2001	7	1	2	1	$49,782	92	Turf(260)	0	0	0	0	$0	–
SMITH M E (110 17 13 11 .15) 2001:(771 95 .12)			Tr: Mitchell Mike(35 2 3 5 .06) 2001:(246 45 .18)		SA	1	0	0	0	$1,000	77	Dist	5	0	2	0	$21,198	87

(L 117 appears between the two blocks)

The above area that we will look at is the specific background of the animal Kinston. I will further break down this information as follows:

Kinston

1. Kinston (in bold letters) is the name of the horse.

**Own: Belmonte &Campochiaro & Schlesinger
White, Black Yoke, White Bars On Sleeves**

2. Underneath the horses name is the ownership of the horse. Kinston owners are Belmonte & Campochiaro & Schlesinger. Just below the owner is a description of the silks that the jockey is going to be wearing (White, Black Yoke, White Bars On Sleeves).

SMITH M E (110 17 13 11 .15) 2001:(771 95 .12)

3. The name SMITH M E (110 17 13 11 .15) is the designation that Mike Smith will be the jockey on Kinston in this particular race, and that his current statistical record as a jockey for 2002 is 110 mounts that produced 17 wins, 13 places, and 11 shows. The .15 is the breakdown of his win percentage. Additionally, for the year 2001, Smith had 771 mounts that produced 95 wins for a .12 percentage.

$50,000

4. Just to the right of the jockey's information is the dollar amount of $50,000. Kinston can be claimed for this eligible amount.

Dk. b or br g. 4 KEESEP99 $40,000

5. This section highlights the color of Kinston as dark bay or brown (Dk.b or br), g. denotes his sex as a gelding (castrated male horse) who is four years old (4) and that was purchased at the Keeneland sale (Kee) in September (SE) 1999 (99) for $40,000.

Sire: **Private Terms (Private Account) $7,500**
Dam: **Morgan Springs(Java Gold)**
Br: **Audley Farm Inc (Va)**
Tr: **Mitchell Mike(35 2 3 5 .06) 2001:(246 45 .18)**

6. Below Kingston's information is his lineage history. The Sire: Private Terms is Kingston's father. Private Account is Private Terms sire (father) which would make him Kingston's grandfather. The amount of $7,500 is the purchase price that was paid for Private Terms. The Dam: Morgan Springs is Kingston's mother. Java Gold is the sire (father) to Morgan Springs, which in turn makes him the grandfather, to Kinston, on his mother's side. Br: represents the location where Kinston was born/foaled. (VA) states that Audley Farm Inc. is located in Virginia. Tr: is the current trainer (Mike Mitchell). The statistics of Mike Mitchell that follow are the same format as the jockey's statistics.

Life	15	2	2	2	$76,170	92	D.Fst	14	2	2	2	$75,170	92
2002	1	0	0	0	$1,000	77	Wet(340)	1	0	0	0	$1,000	71
2001	7	1	2	1	$49,782	92	Turf(260)	0	0	0	0	$0	–
SA	1	0	0	0	$1,000	77	Dist	5	0	2	0	$21,198	87

7. This is the record that Kinston has run in his lifetime. This is also broken down by year (2002, 2001) and includes races run only at Santa Anita (SA). To the right the DRF also includes under what types of racetrack conditions this horse has run—tracks that were fast on dirt (D.Fst), Wet, Turf races, and Distance races (races over one mile). The numbers next to the Wet and Turf races are the Tomlinson Ratings that you will learn about in a later chapter. The sets of numbers to the far right 92,77,92,77,92,71,87 are the calculated speed figures for this horse. The number provided is the highest speed figure in the various categories for that animal. In other words, in five distance races in its lifetime, Kingston's highest speed figure was 87. In 2001 Kingston's highest speed figure was 92 and was run on a dirt fast-track (D.Fst), which corresponds to his highest speed figure in his life. The dollar amounts are the total earnings for Kinston under the various categories of races. The nature and derivation of speed figures will be explained in a later chapter.

L 117

8. To the left of Kinston's race record, you see L 117. What this means is that this horse is running using Lasix. Lasix is a bronchial dilator medication that is used by a large number of horses in the United States. The 117 means that the horse will be ridden at a weight of 117 pounds (which includes the jockey).

9Feb02-7SA	fst	6½f	$:21^2$	$:43^4$	$1:09^4$	$1:16^2$	4↑	Alw 59000N1X	**77**	7	4	$7^{6\frac{3}{4}}$	7^{10}	8^{10}	5^{7}	Smith M E	**LB 120**	13.70	84-16	Warm April123^1 Bingo Card$120^{1\frac{1}{2}}$ Wild Roar$120^{1\frac{1}{2}}$	Crowded 3/16,no bid
21Sep01-10Fpx	fst	6½f	:22	$:45^4$	1:11	1:17		Alw 49241N1X	**80**	7	5	$6^{2\frac{1}{2}}$	$7^{3\frac{3}{4}}$	$3^{1\frac{1}{2}}$	2^{2}	Baze T C	**LB 117**	*1.30	91-10	Flylikethewind117^2 Kinston117^{no} AmricnPstim117^{hd}	Angled out,late rally
7Sep01-10Fpx	fst	6½f	$:21^3$	$:44^4$	1:10	$1:16^4$		Foothill50k	**87**	1	7	$8^{7\frac{1}{4}}$	$8^{8\frac{3}{4}}$	5^{6}	$2^{1\frac{3}{4}}$	Baze T C	**LB 114**	11.70	92-14	PresidioHights$119^{1\frac{3}{4}}$ Kinston$114^{\frac{3}{4}}$ **BttorRoylty**$114^{1\frac{1}{2}}$	4wd into lane,late 2nd
25Aug01-9Dmr	fst	6f	$:21^4$	:45	$:57^1$	1:10		Clm 50000 (50-45)	**92**	7	5	$3^{3\frac{1}{2}}$	2^{1}	$1^{\frac{1}{2}}$	1^{hd}	Smith M E	**LB 118**	5.30	90-10	Kinston118^{hd} Re Echo118^4 Red Work120^{no}	5wd early,bid,led,held
28Jun01-1Hol	fst	6f	$:22^1$	$:45^1$	$:57^3$	$1:10^4$		Clm c-(32-28)	**66**	1	5	$5^{6\frac{1}{2}}$	4^{5}	$3^{4\frac{1}{2}}$	3^{6}	Enriquez I D	**LB 118**	5.50	80-14	Mike And Leo$120^{3\frac{1}{2}}$ King La Boo$118^{2\frac{1}{2}}$ *Kinston*$118^{2\frac{1}{2}}$	Off bit slow,rail trip
Claimed from Weir Dennis E for $32,000, Lewis Kevin Trainer 2001(as of 06/28): (59 12 9 5 0.20)																					
31May01-6Hol	fst	6f	$:22^1$	$:45^2$	$:57^4$	$1:10^2$		Clm 40000 (40-35)	**79**	5	3	5^{6}	4^{3}	4^{2}	$4^{1\frac{1}{2}}$	Enriquez I D	**LB 118**	46.10	86-12	A Lil Sweet118^1 Redly115^{no} ***The Station***$118^{\frac{1}{2}}$	4wd into lane,missd 3d
Previously trained by Hone Bart																					
17Feb01-4TuP	fst	6f	:22	$:45^1$	$:57^4$	1:11		Alw 10200N2L	**63**	10	2	8^{10}	$7^{4\frac{1}{4}}$	$4^{4\frac{1}{2}}$	$4^{4\frac{1}{4}}$	Rollins C J	L 117	*2.10e	81-17	TostForMr.Expo$117^{2\frac{3}{4}}$ *SencChif*117^1 Jokr'sGold$117^{\frac{1}{2}}$	Good stretch effort
14Jan01-9TuP	my	1	:23	$:46^4$	$1:12^3$	$1:39^4$		Rattlesnake25k	**71**	1	7^{17}	6^{11}	$6^{3\frac{3}{4}}$	$5^{4\frac{1}{2}}$	$5^{5\frac{1}{4}}$	Stevens S A	L 115	2.70	67-36	Prohibitive$115^{1\frac{1}{2}}$ *Mecke Monster*$118^{\frac{1}{2}}$ Double Time$116^{\frac{1}{2}}$	Failed to menace
31Dec00-6TuP	fst	1	$:24^2$	$:48^4$	$1:13^3$	$1:38^2$		Suprise21k	**66**	8	$3^{1\frac{1}{2}}$	$3^{1\frac{1}{2}}$	2^{1}	$2^{2\frac{1}{2}}$	$3^{4\frac{3}{4}}$	Stevens S A	L 115	2.00	74-25	Resolve$120^{4\frac{1}{2}}$ Polished Act117^{nk} Kinston$115^{3\frac{3}{4}}$	Bid 1/4, outfinished
17Dec00-10TuP	fst	6½f	$:22^1$	$:44^3$	$1:09^1$	$1:15^3$		ChristmasFty75k	**64**	10	4	$9^{4\frac{1}{2}}$	$7^{3\frac{1}{4}}$	5^{5}	$4^{6\frac{3}{4}}$	Stevens S A	L 120	3.40e	85-15	Top Hit$120^{3\frac{3}{4}}$ Jakes Corner$120^{1\frac{3}{4}}$ Daunting$120^{1\frac{1}{2}}$	Strong stretch rally
1Dec00-8TuP	fst	6½f	$:22^1$	:45	$1:10^1$	$1:16^4$		Alw 5700NC	**69**	5	5	3^{1}	$2^{\frac{1}{2}}$	2^{hd}	$5^{3\frac{3}{4}}$	Stevens S A	L 120	4.00	82-20	*TopHit*$120^{1\frac{3}{4}}$ CrownConnction$117^{\frac{3}{4}}$ TostForMr.Expo120^{nk}	Vied 5/8, empty
Previously trained by Lewis Kevin																					
25Oct00-3BM	fst	6f	:22	$:44^1$	:56	$1:08^2$		Alw 32080N1X	**59**	4	6	$6^{4\frac{1}{4}}$	$6^{7\frac{1}{2}}$	6^{12}	$6^{12\frac{1}{4}}$	Schvaneveldt C P	**LB 118**	8.00	85-10	I'madrifter118^2 Justnowayofknowin'$118^{4\frac{1}{2}}$ Lil'Country118^{no}	3w, no factor

WORKS: ●Feb19 Hol 5f fst :59 H *1/39* Feb4 Hol 5f fst 1:01 H *2/13* ●Jan29 Hol 5f gd $1:00^3$ H *1/5* Jan24 Hol 5f fst $:59^3$ H *2/25* Jan19 Hol 4f fst $:47^1$ H *2/34* Jan14 Hol 4f fst $:49^1$ H *17/26*

TRAINER: Dirt(213 .17 $1.73) Sprint(153 .17 $1.97) Claim(173 .15 $1.12)

In this portion of the diagram, the statistical figures on the races that Kinston has participated in are discussed. Starting with the very first horizontal line you see the date (9Feb02), the date of the last race that Kinston ran. (7SA) indicates the race number, and the two letters that follow are the abbreviation for the track (i.e., the seventh race at Santa Anita on February 9, 2002). The track condition is stated by the (fst), meaning it was a fast track the day of the race. (6½ F) represents the distance of the race. The "fractional splits" are $:21^2$ $:43^4$ $1:09^4$ $1:16^2$ (final time). In races that are less than one mile, the fractional times are ¼ mile, ½ mile, ¾ mile, and the final time. It should be noted that these times are for the lead horse in that race, not for Kinston. Next, you will see that he ran in an allowance race of $59,000. The "N1X" means the conditions of the race were for non-winners of more than one race. The number 77 is a speed figure that Kinston received for that race.

The next set of numbers stands for Kinston's position throughout the race. The first number (7) is the postposition that the horse was given. The second number is after the break; in this case Kinston broke fourth. The third number reveals that after the turn, Kinston was in the 7th position but 6 and ¾ lengths from the leader ($7^{6\,3/4}$). Then he was 7th and 10 lengths from the leader, then 8th with 10 lengths behind. Finally, the last number is his finish: Kinston ran 5th, 7 lengths behind the winner. These positions are in direct correlation with the fraction times given. In other words, at the ¼ mile he was 7th, at the ½ mile 7th, 8th at the ¾ mile and 5th at the finish.

The jockey was Mike Smith, the LB indicates that this horse was on both Lasix (L) and Butte (B), under 120 pounds, went off at 13.70 to one (almost 14 to one) and had a speed figure of 84. It should be noted that there are two separate speed figures provided on most DRFs, the 77 and the 84.

The next section discloses three horses—Warm April, Bingo Card and Wild Roar—the names of the first, second and third place finishers in Kingston's last race. These names are followed by the weight amount they carried, and directly following is the number of lengths ahead they were of their closest pursuer.

The final section is the comment line followed by how many horses were in the race. The comment line usually contains information about how the horse ran (Did he have trouble? Did he run erratically?).

WORKS: ●Feb19 Hol 5f fst :59 H *1/39*   Feb4 Hol 5f fst 1:01 H *2/13*   ●Jan29 Hol 5f gd 1:00³ H *1/5*   Jan24 Hol 5f fst :59³ H *2/25*   Jan19 Hol 4f fst :47¹ H *2/34*   Jan14 Hol 4f fst :49¹ H *17/26*
TRAINER: Dirt(213 .17 $1.73) Sprint(153 .17 $1.97) Claim(173 .15 $1.12)

Toward the bottom of the Kinston statistics is the works and training for this horse from January 14th, 2002 through February 19th, 2002. This area can simply be described by referring to the first reference. Kinston on February 19th, 2002 (Feb19), at Hollywood Park (Hol), trained or worked 5 furlongs (5f), on a fast track (fst), at a speed of :59 seconds. The fraction ⅟₃₉ represents the comment that of all the 5 furlongs works for this day, Kinston returned the fastest time of 39 works (⅟₃₉). The TRAINER: shows various statistics for Kinston's current trainer (who we know is Mike Mitchell) at different distances and surfaces at tracks in the United States in 2002. This information discloses that Mike Mitchell has run 213 horses on the dirt, winning .17 percent and returning an average of $1.73 for each two dollar (win) wager, and the same information is given for Sprint and Claiming races. As will be discussed in later chapters, this section can be extremely valuable in accessing a particular trainers' ability concerning different surfaces and different levels.

The above information demonstrates that the volumes of information contained in the DRF are there at your disposal. Continual review of various races will make you extremely familiar with the usage of the DRF, and will enable you to very quickly extract information that will be essential in handicapping winners. One of the standing jokes among most horseplayers when asked who will be the winner today is to reply "He is right in there," and point to the racing form. Familiarity with the DRF will provide the horseplayer with easy access to the information that will be essential when individual areas of ability are discussed in subsequent chapters.

> **"A horse! My kingdom for a horse!"**
> —**William Shakespeare, *King Richard III***

All successful horseplayers are familiar with the nuisances of the DRF. The articles, the analysis, and PPs (past performances) are what enable you to be knowledgeable enough to successfully handicap. Successful handicapping will enable you to have the information that will then allow you to utilize the force or way of Zen to be successful.

There is no particular book or reference material that will allow you to be familiar with the DRF unless you repeatedly review the DRF to acclimate yourself to its usage.

Reprinted (at the end of this chapter) with permission from the DRF are three pages explaining some of the lexicon used in the DRF. Still, even with this "go-by" it is using the form constantly that will breed familiarity and comfort. My reference for a book that will make learning about the racing form interesting, is a book that deals with the caricature and artwork of Pierre Bullocq (PEB), which has adorned the DRF for more than 50 years. I guarantee if you purchase this book for a seasoned, or even novice horseplayer, he or she will greatly enjoy its content.

Forty Years of PEB.
The Racing World in Sketch and Caricature.

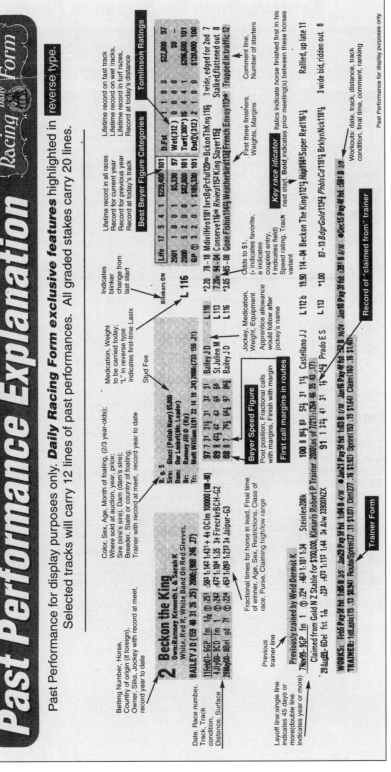

Past Performance Explanation

Racing Daily Form

Past Performance for display purposes only. ***Daily Racing Form exclusive features*** highlighted in reverse type. Selected tracks will carry 12 lines of past performances. All graded stakes carry 20 lines.

Past Performance for display purposes only

Abbreviations for Types of Races

Alw 15000N1x	Non-winners of one race (or more, depending on the number after N) other than maiden, claiming or starter. Used for non-winners of up to 5 races "other than"
Alw 15000N1y	Non-winners of one race (or more, depending on the number after N) in, or since, a specified time period.
Alw 15000N2L	Non-winners of two (or more) races lifetime
Alw 15000N$y	Non-winners of a specific amount of money in a specified time period
Alw 15000N1m	Non-winners of one (or more) races at a mile or over in a specified time period
Alw 15000N$my	Non-winners of a specific amount of money OR races at a mile or over in, or since, a specified time period
Alw 15000N1s	Non-winners of one (or more) stakes lifetime
Alw 15000N1T	Non-winners of one (or more) turf races
Alw 15000NmT	Non-winners of one or more turf races at a mile or more
Alw 150000NC	Allowance race with no conditions
Alw 15000c	Allowance race with multiple conditions or restrictions
Alw 15000s	Starter allowance (number indicates minimum claiming price horse must have started for to be eligible)
CLM 10000/9000	**Claiming race (entered to be claimed for $10,000)**
Clm 10/9000N2L	Non-winners of two races (or more, depending on the number after N) lifetime
Clm 10/9000N2x	Non-winners of two races (or more, depending on the number after N) other than those described in the conditions of a race.
Clm 10/9000N1y	Non-winners of one race (or more) in, or since, a specified time period.
Clm10/9000N1my	Non-winners of one race (or more) at a mile or over in, or since, a specified time period
Clm10/9000N$y	Non-winners of a specific amount of money in, or since, a specified time period
Clm10/9000N$my	Non-winners of a specific amount of money OR races at a mile or over in, or since, a specified time period
Clm10/9000B	Beaten claimers
Clm Stk 10000	Claiming stakes (number indicates claiming price)
OClm10/9000	Optional claiming race. Entered to be claimed
OClm10/9000N	Optional claiming race. Entered NOT to be claimed
Hcp 10000s	Starter handicap race. Number indicates minimum claiming price horse must have started for to be eligible
OTHER CONDITIONS	
Md Sp Wt 8k	Maiden Special Weight race (for non-winners), purse value
Md 32/30000	Maiden Claiming race (entered to be claimed for $32,000)
Handicap 40k	Overnight handicap race (purse of $40,000)
Ky Derby–G1	Graded Stakes race, with name of race (North American races are graded in order of status, with G1 being the best)
PrincetonH 40k	Ungraded, but named Stakes race (H indicates handicap) Purse value is $40,000

Symbols

- ⊡ = Inner dirt track
- Ⓓ = Disqualified (symbol located next to odds and in company line)
- DH = Dead-Heat (symbol located in company line if horses are among first three finishers)
- ♦ = Dead-Heat (symbol used next to finish position)

- 3↑ = Race for 3-year-olds and up
- ♦ = Foreign race (outside of North America)
- Ⓢ = Race for state-breds only
- Ⓡ = Restricted race for horses who meet certain conditions
- Ⓕ = Race for fillies, or fillies and mares
- Ⓣ = Main turf course
- T = Inner turf course
- ⊗ = Race taken off turf
- * = About distance
- + = Start at infield chute

Workout Line

- ● = Best of day/distance
- B = Breezing
- D = Driving
- (d) = Worked around dogs
- E = Easily
- g = Worked from gate
- H = Handily
- tr.t = Training track
- TR = Training race
- 3/25 = Workout ranking
- (W) = Wood Chips

Equipment & Medication

- b = Blinkers
- f = Front bandages
- B = Butazolidin
- L = Lasix (furosemide)
- r = Bar shoe

Track Condition

DIRT TRACKS

- fst = Fast
- wf = Wet-Fast
- gd = Good
- sly = Sloppy
- my = Muddy
- sl = Slow
- hy = Heavy
- fr = Frozen

TURF & STEEPLECHASE

- hd = Hard
- fm = Firm
- gd = Good
- yl = Yielding
- sf = Soft
- hy = Heavy

NOTES:

3

Owners, Jockeys, and Trainers

"Everyone has talent. What is rare is the courage to follow the talent to the dark places where it leads."
— Erica Jong, in *Harper's Book of Quotations*

Without question, the favorite thing for all horseplayers to do is to talk about the great winning horses they have handicapped. The next topic of conversation is the incredible bad rides that jockeys give horses causing them to lose. Often times it does not necessarily have to do with the amount of money bet on the horse (though sometimes it does), but more importantly that the ride was so spectacularly bad that even the most casual horseplayer could see how incredibly inept the jockey's ride was. Some older (and particularly jaded) horseplayers will say that the race was "fixed." However, this is clearly not so, in that the rides were so poor that they stood out, and would have created immediate questions from the owners and trainers of the particular animal. Unquestionably, with the exception of the fitness of the horse, the capability of the jockey and the specific tactics that are employed are the second primary function of whether or not a horse will do well in any particular race.

JOCKEYS

The ideal jockey seems to always know the correct pace of the race, the particular needs of the animal on which he or she is riding, and seems to get that little bit extra at the end of his or her mount. These jockeys enable the horse to pull away, or close and win by a nose or a head. Such jockeys seem to be far above the others in their particular areas of racing. When I say "areas of racing," many horseplayers know that certain jockeys are better at certain tracks, on certain surfaces, or in certain types of races (sprints vs. route racing).

Certain jockeys will win a disproportion number of races, and this is true even with animals that on paper may seem inferior to the others in the race. A classic example of this phenomenon on the West Coast is Russell Baze at the Golden Gate and Bay Meadows tracks. Baze has consistently won more than 400 races per year riding primarily in these two venues, and horseplayers who follow the northern California tracks have a love/hate relationship with Russell Baze. It appears that he is always on the favorite, and this is so whether or not this favoritism seems to be deserved by the horse's form on paper. Still, Baze seems to be there at the finish on the winning horse in a disproportionate share of races; Baze is a rider who gets a little more from the horse each time he is in the irons. The negative horseplayer would say that the reason for this success is the lack of similar skill in the rest of the riding colony in northern California. While I feel that Russell Baze would be an extremely successful jockey in whatever series of venues he attempts, he knows the tracks of Golden Gate and Bay Meadows so well that there is no reason for him to leave. Additionally, it is clear that in Baze's case, he is likely chasing the record for most wins (currently held by Laffit Pincay Jr.), and remaining in the northern California area will insure his eventually eclipsing this record.

The ideal riders seem to have quicker reflexes, better judgement, and specific skills that are useful in particular types of races. Each individual horseplayer, at whatever track he/she is playing, should pay particular attention to the jockey standings in relation to the percentage of wins and "in the money" finishes. Often, particular jockeys will have a disproportionate number of wins, because they secure a large portion of the mounts at any particular track, but the actual number of wins is not as definitive of the jockey's ability at that track as is the percentage of wins. At various highly competitive tracks such as those in New York, Florida, and Southern California, there are a number of highly competent and very able jockeys, and they may secure up to eleven to twelve percent of wins from all the mounts they have. At each particular track, the track program will list the percentage wins for each jockey at the track, and this can be broken down into sprints, distance rides, and turf rides via the program itself or other publications available at the specific tracks.

Jockeys generally have egos in inverse proportion to their size. Many jockeys believe that it is their particular riding skills that will enable any animal to secure a photograph in the winner's circle. In reality, it cannot be over emphasized that it is the ability of the animal that will most likely decide the race. As an example, on a Saturday in 2001, a horse named Starrer ran in the Gazelle handicap at Belmont Park. I wagered on Starrer largely based on her previous races. She had run well in California in the Railbird and Princess stakes at Hollywood Park, and I disregarded the previous race in July at Belmont in the Coaching Club American Oaks. The comment line for the horse Starrer is included in Diagram A. In the Coaching Club

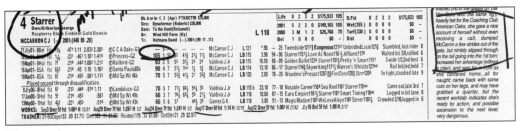

Diagram A

American Oaks, Starrer lost her jockey, Chris McCarron, at the start yet proceeded to weave through horses, hug on to a tight rail and won going away. You may see the specific comment line as also reported by the analysis handicapping in the Gazelle Handicap (which is also included in Diagram A). The importance, and/or humor in regard to Starrer was that if there had been a jockey on Starrer's back when it won, it probably would have been regarded as one of the best rides of all time. The reality is the horse did this all on its own because the horse has been trained to do that, to run through holes and to run along the rail. Obviously, not having McCarron's 121 pounds in the saddle probably also effected Starrer's ability to be successful. I would note that my bet on Starrer in the Gazelle Handicap was for naught, and that it appeared that the horse was not prepared for that particular race and may have injured itself when it ran solo. The purpose for including this example is to show that sometimes the ability of a jockey is over-rated, and that it is the horse that counts.

More often than jockeys providing spectacular star-studded rides (like the invisible Casper on Starrer), it is the case where jockeys provide incredible inept rides and lose winnable races. The phrase, "You're a bum" or "What a clown" rings heavily in a number of track grandstands and OTB rooms following incompetent rides by jockeys.

> "You are walking down a country road. It is a quiet afternoon. You look up and far, far down the road you see someone walking toward you. You are surprised to have noticed someone so far away. But you keep walking, expecting nothing more than a friendly nod as you pass. He gets closer. You see he has bright orange hair. He is closer—a white satin suit spotted with colored dots. Closer—a painted white face and red lips. You are fifty yards apart. You and a full-fledged clown holding a bicycle horn are twenty yards apart. You approach on the lonely country road. You nod. He honks and passes."
>
> — Steve Martin, Comedian, *Cruel Shoes*

Do not expect that a jockey's skills will enable him or her to produce a winning effort from a horse unlikely to produce one. However, be fully cognizant of jockeys who are clownish and very unlikely to provide a ride that will meet the needs of the animal, and get both into the winner's circle. Jockeys with extremely low percentage wins should be avoided, unless they are on an animal that it is an absolute standout. Even good jockeys can provide extraordinarily bad rides (example, Frankie Dettori riding Swain in the Breeders Cup Classic, which was probably the worst ride in a major race in the history of horse racing). Nevertheless, poor novices or lower level jockeys tend to provide poor rides on a routine basis. In the major Grade I, Grade II, Allowance, and Stakes races, top jockeys win a disproportionate number of the races. One of the principal reasons for this is that trainers will switch jockeys to a more prominent, well-known rider. Basically, it is a business for the trainers and the owners, and trainers will often switch to an upper tier jockey for major races. Horseplayers should be extremely aware of a significant jockey change from a lower tier, lower percentage rider to a higher percentage jockey, particularly in major races.

Here are two examples of jockey switches that I believe are extremely important (and relatively well known among handicappers on the West Coast). Each individual handicapper should look and try to identify specific patterns, which may be similar to this at his or her own track.

If a horse is a significant closer (i.e., runs toward the back or rear of the pack and closes strongly in the last quarter-mile), and if a jockey switch occurs to Eddie Delahoussaye, regardless of odds, this horse should be played. While Delahoussaye retired in early 2003, I hope he UN-retires as Gary Stevens has and we will get to see this late run again.

If a horse has not run on turf previously, or has been only moderately successful on the turf, and jockey Kent Desormeaux takes the mount, this horse should be considered for play. However, a review of the racing form should take place to see if Desormeaux has ever ridden this horse previously. If Kent Desormeaux has not previously ridden the animal, he should be considered a strong play.

In summary, I do not believe it is necessary for the individual horseplayer to be familiar with the specific riding skills of each individual jockey. Watching an extensive number of races, certain characteristics will jump out (such as the above two characterizations regarding Desormeaux and Delahoussaye). However, specific knowledge in this area is not required. More important is the statistical percentage winning ability of the individual jockeys at whichever track you choose to play. Better jockeys will win more races, partly because they are better, and partly because they will get better horses. Even more importantly, the top tier of ten to twenty jockeys will win most of the Classic, Grade I, Grade II, and Breeders Cup races. There will be exceptions but they will be relatively rare.

One note here on foreign jockeys, who come here to ride in the United States, such as the (infamous) previously mentioned Frankie Dettori. Set out below is a notable generalization, which I believe will help individuals handicapping in races where you observe a jockey on a foreign horse of which you are not familiar. Jockeys in Europe predominately ride on turf courses, courses that are significantly deeper than most turf courses in the United States. If a foreign jockey is riding in the United States in a turf race, that jockey should probably be handicapped much as any other higher tier jockey within the United States. Conversely, if that jockey is riding on a dirt course (or a significantly hard turf course), that jockey should probably be relegated to the equivalent of lower tiered jockeys in the United States.

> **"Be swift as the wind...majestic as the forest...**
> **firm as the mountains, as unfathomable as the clouds,**
> **move like a thunder bolt."**
> — Sun Tzu, *The Art of War*

OWNERS

I used that quote above not because owners of racehorses are generally any of those things, except perhaps unfathomable. Generally in horse racing there are two types of owners: those who are clueless, and those who are rich and clueless. The majority of horse racing owners are what could only be characterized as the idle rich. Significant family fortunes have been spent on racehorses successfully (Phipps, Paulsen, etc.) and unsuccessfully (names too numerous to mention). Generally, the owners of the racehorse know very little regarding the training and specific needs of the racehorse. There are a few notable exceptions, including the ownership group of Golden Eagle Farms.

My advice to anyone interested in going into horse ownership is the following. Find a very, very, very, very good trainer. Tell him you are patient, expect to spend large sums of money, race infrequently, and with only periodic success.

As a handicapper, I have found zero correlation between ownership of horses and success on the racetrack. I have found a strong correlation between the amount of money available to the owner, and the number of horses which they will own. For example, someone like Satish Sannan, Bob and Beverly Lewis, Frank Stronach, or other similar owners own a disproportionately large number of higher quality racehorses and therefore will win disproportionately large numbers of major races. However, I have never seen a weighty *percentage differential* regarding ownership victory, with the possible exception of Golden Eagle Farms.

Therefore, my advice regarding "handicapping" owners is the following: Completely disregard any ownership interest in the horse, and look directly to the jockey, horse's ability, and trainer.

"He was as near living flame as horses ever get."
— Joe Palmer on Man o' War

TRAINERS

One of the greatest sources for information concerning training and breeding of horses is in *The Blood Horse Magazine,*® of which I am an avid and faithful reader. Frequent articles concerning equine health, reproductive capabilities, training methods, medication, and various other training techniques are frequent in the magazine. I will admit with great honesty that before my subscription to *The Blood Horse Magazine,*® my knowledge of particular training and equine health techniques was minimal, and limited to my experience with event riders. *The Blood Horse Magazine*® contains articles about how trainers train horses, and the new techniques that they are using. It is an invaluable resource to allow the handicapper to become knowledgeable about specific techniques that are being tried and experimented with.

Regardless of which magazines or articles are read regarding horse training, one thing is clear: A horse rushed into training, or treated with impatience in training, will likely be very unsuccessful. Most trainers are in the training business for the money, and therefore need to get the horses to the racetrack as quickly as possible. This is not the ideal circumstance for a two-year-old whose bones have not fully formed, and soft tissue not fully set. However, this is the nature of horse racing. The ongoing argument as to why horses are no longer as sound as they were twenty to thirty years ago is a moot point to the horse handicapper. Handicappers will still see two year old races, they will still see three year old horses break down, and they will still see horses with great potential retired at four to five years old due to stud fees and infirmities. It is my opinion that there is nothing the individual horseplayer can do, other than to cry when a horse breaks down, and insure periodic donations to funds for racehorses no longer able to race. There are extraordinary foundations around the country that deal with retired racehorses. As I sit and write this book, I look at my retired racing greyhound sleeping on his mat. I guarantee that if you have the resources to care for a retired athlete (racehorse or greyhound), it will make you and your family extremely happy.

Studies of horses have determined that they are less intelligent than dogs, apes, and other animals, and that they learn differently than other animals. Traditionally horses are pack animals, and have an extreme sense of leadership. Additionally, negative experiences which horses undergo at human hands can send negative thought patterns into the horse's brain, which the horse will remember forever. Horses may not be particularly intelligent, but they seem to never forget a bad experience. Anyone who has ever trained horses, could tell you of experiences where a horse spooks on the track, (maybe merely seeing something as simple as a shadow in the stands), and was always thereafter afraid to run by that same section of the track. Additionally, imparting pain to the racehorse through the "breaking" technique can periodically ruin an animal permanently for use on the track.

The breaking process, where the horses are acclimated to having a saddle and rider placed on their back, is an extremely traumatic process. Contrary to the ideal that many people formulate that the horse was born to be ridden, the fact is the horse was born to run on its own, eat grass, and walk around pastures. It is not the natural instinct for the horse to be broken, nor is it for it to be ridden in circles or jumped over fences. Accordingly, a process must be set by the trainer to insure that the yearlings are broken, hopefully without undue trauma to the animal. My softer side wishes there could be "horse whisperers" for each of these animals, though the cost and proceedings for that would be unfeasible.

It is a universal axiom in training circles that the horse's first experiences on the track, out of the gate, running with other horses, etc., will set the standards the horse will act on for the remainder of its time at the track. Bad habits can be broken, whether they be acting up in the paddock, slow breaking from the gate, etc., but this is a time consuming and difficult process for the trainer. Horse handicappers are full of stories about the horse that will not win—the horse that has all the ability, all the best speed, all the best stamina but refuses to pass horses down the stretch, and always settles for second or third. Often, the reason for this behavior was poor training initially or bad experiences on the track.

Trainers themselves can be put into two groups, much the same as jockeys. There are the extremely elite trainers around the country, such as Bob Baffert, Bobby Frankel, Bruce Headley, Allen Jerkens, Richard Mandella, Neil Drysdale, and others. Then there is a second tier of trainers who win a much smaller portion of races nationwide. Perhaps a third category of trainers should be noted, and that is the trainer who virtually never wins. This trainer will show statistics of one win from fifty races, one third from twenty races, etc. It is my opinion that trainers who never seem to win, will in fact rarely win and their horses can almost always be tossed out from your picks. It is not that these trainers will never win with a horse, but it is likely that they are unskilled in their training methods and have very poor stock. The few wins that they may have can probably be off-set by the numerous times where you will be able to automatically exclude these trainers from your handicapping. The most successful trainers win with around eighteen percent or more of the horses they train. If you see trainer percentages similar to that at your particular track, you should consider those trainers in your handicapping.

One of the most successful means of handicapping is finding horses that have been claimed by a successful trainer from a lower tier trainer. When this occurs, part of the poor form of the previous races of the animal should be discarded. The obvious reason for this is that the better trainer will get more out of the animal through better training techniques. What these specific training techniques are will be particular to the individual trainer. It may not matter to the handicapper what these specific techniques are (new blinkers, training with tongue tie, etc.), but the key is that this trainer has some techniques that appear to make the horse run better. Often horses like this will present a significant wagering opportunity and present much higher odds because they have been under performing. It is important to note here that the key is that the horse went to a better trainer. It does not matter that the horse may be going at the same distance or running on the same surface as previously; merely the change to a different trainer should be indicative of a possible better run.

The astute handicapper will go beyond merely individual training percentages, and be able to determine that various trainers at their track do better on particular surfaces (turf as opposed to dirt) or distances (sprint as opposed to route), and will make specific notations in their handicapping regarding this. While this particular attempt at statistical record keeping may seem time consuming, it is probably one of the most successful means of determining whether or not horses will win.

Set out below is a brief list of factors that should be considered about each particular trainer and their individual records. It would be this writer's suggestion that this only be done for the major trainers at any individual track. In other words, identify the primary successful trainers at any track, and then make a determination by keeping records of races, and how trainers do concerning certain specific identified areas. This record may disclose that particular trainers are exceedingly successful in one area or another, and this may provide an excellent betting opportunity because these horses are sometimes under bet.

Factors to consider are as follows (this list is not all-inclusive and should be added to by each individual handicapper):

- Record with horses returning off of a layoff (seven weeks or more)
- Record with horses returning off of an extensive layoff (six months or longer)
- Record with horses moving from turf to dirt
- Record with horses moving from dirt to turf
- Record with horses moving from sprint to route
- Record with horses moving from route to sprint
- Record with horses increasing or decreasing in distance work patterns (a three-furlong work, subsequently a five-furlong work, a mile work, etc. Note: It is this handicapper's opinion that horses that are generally worked at one mile and then provided a three-furlong work are being set up for a positive race)
- Record with un-raced maidens (first time starters)
- Record with horses moving up the claiming ladder
- Record with horses moving down the claiming ladder
- Record when moving horses from one track to another
- Record and preferences for a particular jockey

The final area I would like to discuss in this chapter is the concept of jockey and trainer combinations. Trainers have the ability to ride different jockeys if their stable is sizable. All handicappers are aware of particular jockey and trainer combinations, which seem to win with disproportionate percentages. Any time that such a ratio is seen by an individual handicapper of jockeys riding with a particular trainer and winning, this should be noted with a ★ (star) on the program for that particular race.

I will identify three examples of trainers who use particular jockeys to advantage. I provide these only as examples, so you will be able to determine your own individual scenarios where you see trainers and jockeys linking to provide frequent winning (or horses in the money). It should also be noted that for particular distances or surfaces, the trainer and jockey combination might be more pertinent. One of the combinations I set out below is the rider David Flores with Bob Baffert as a trainer. I have found that with this combination it seems to be more pertinent for horses who will be sent to the lead.

Three examples of significant jockey/trainer combinations:

Trainer			Jockey
Bob Baffert	◁	▷	David Flores
Bill Mott	◁	▷	Jerry Bailey
Jerry Hollendorfer	◁	▷	Russell Baze

At your individual track, look for winning jockey/trainer combinations: It can be a lucrative opportunity.

The Blood Horse Magazine®
Or online at *http://www.bloodhorse.com*

NOTES:

4
Speed Figures and Pace

"How can the average horse bettor make a small
fortune with minimal preparation? Start with a large
fortune!"
— Frederic Donner

The advent of the wide spread use of speed figures, which were popularized and explained to the average horseplayer by Andrew Beyer, changed the very manner in which handicapping took place. Beyer himself did not originate speed figures, but he codified them in such a way that now they are in every DRF at every track in the United States. Previously, horseplayers, including myself, had sought to derive their own speed figures by trying to develop specific usable numbers, but with only minimal success. Every successful handicapper had compared the final times of races, believing that faster times meant a better horse. The problem was not the knowledge of whether the tracks ran fast or slow on a particular day, but *how* fast or *how* slow. Unless you are able to physically be at the track and monitor all times at all distances, it was almost impossible to find the track variant. The horseplayer would have to be at the track and personally time the various races, knowing that at separate distances the variant might be different due to wind, track conditions on various sections of the track, etc. This was an extremely daunting task for even the most ardent handicapper.

However, it was clear even with the rudimentary speed figures I personally was attempting to develop at my home track (Long Acres in Seattle, Washington), that speed type relationships were essential to the success of a wager. One of the particular difficulties at Long Acres was the frequent changing of the track surface due to the rains (which are virtually constant in Seattle), and which seriously altered the track variant from day to day. Accordingly, the final times at various race distances could mean virtually nothing compared to how "fast" the horse had actually run. My personal experience at Long Acres was that a rough track variant could be determined, but my margin of error was extremely high. All I was able to do was to determine which horses ran particularly slow, or particularly fast, on specific racing dates. Interestingly however, during this time period when I frequented Long Acres in the late 1970s and early 1980s, this was a radical type idea that speed could be more determinate than class. Even with my rudimentary methods, I was able to secure some wins at Long Acres with this technique.

The difficulty in determining one's own speed figures, and again I speak of that term crudely because all I had done was take the final times, was essentially solved for the vast majority of horseplayers in 1992 when the DRF began to include Beyer's Speed Figures in its past performance line. Beyer Speed Figures, in concept, are designed to utilize final race times to allow the horseplayer to compare all horses regardless of class, track, and (to a lesser extent) distance. A speed figure takes into account the final time of the race, and how fast or slow the track was. Mr. Beyer's Speed Figures also (correctly) take into account that two-fifths of a second is more important in a six-furlong race than in a one-mile race. In other words, a chart is set up to convert times at different distances to give speed figures equal weight at all distances, and also variances for the day are determined for different distances. There are also other factors that Beyer's Speed Figures take into account. For a full and very complete discussion on how his figures can be determined I refer you to his books *Picking Winners, The Winning Horseplayer,* and *Beyer on Speed.*

While I do not find Beyer's Speed Figures to be absolutely uniformly accurate across tracks, quality of surfaces (wet, heavy, sloppy, etc.), or even across all distances, I do believe they are more accurate than any speed figures even the most ardent handicappers could produce on their own. Beyer's Speed Figures are produced by a team of spotters and analysts at tracks around the country who have a desire to be accurate. Reputations are on the line, and Mr. Beyer adequately explains issue resolution when out-of-line speed figures are identified. Instead of producing one's own speed figures, I advocate that the Beyer Speed Figures should always be used, but in conjunction with the individual handicapper's experience regarding the accuracy of speed figures. Subsequently, I will identify a number of factors that I have identified which should alter the interpretation of a Beyer figure. The most important of these factors is the pace of the particular race involved. Therefore, my overall advice is to look at the Beyer figure and give it great weight, but betting solely on this number will not necessarily pick you winners; even lazy and stupid gamblers can identify the highest speed figures, because they are printed in the DRF.

> **"A racehorse is an animal that can take several thousand people for a ride"**
> *— 14,000 Quips and Quotes*

Before I discuss factors which must be considered in interpreting Beyer Speed Figures, I will (with deference to Andrew Beyer, who I consider the premiere authority on horse racing, possibly because he dislikes jockeys as much as I do) identify some situations where Beyer Speed Figures should be disregarded entirely, or at least their use minimized in relation to the other handicapping techniques available to the horseplayer. I list these here so that when you see these situations you will know not to rely on the figures:

1. Speed figures earned on good, slow, heavy, and muddy tracks (and particularly heavy tracks) are not equatable to figures earned on either fast or sloppy tracks. Disregard figures earned under these track conditions when handicapping a subsequent race on a track

that is sloppy or fast. However, if the track comes up with a similar condition, use the Beyer with even greater weight. If a horse previously ran a big Beyer on a heavy track and the track is now again heavy, the horse will likely run extremely well again, regardless of more recent Beyer's earned on different track conditions. I cannot over emphasize these points. Beyers may equate from fast to fast and slop to slop and slop to fast and fast to slop, but the other conditions (good, slow, heavy and muddy) equate only with each other (i.e., good-good; slow-slow; heavy-heavy; and muddy-muddy).

2. Speed figures earned in extremely long or extremely short races are to be disregarded entirely. Two-year-olds sometimes run two-furlong races, and some tracks periodically card one and three quarter or two-mile races. Beyers received in these races are completely irrelevant to races in the more traditional distances of five-furlongs to one and one-half-miles. The most obvious reason for this is that horses in two-furlong races are basically running as fast as they can from the very beginning of the race. Yet, at more traditional distances horses do not run in this manner, and figures earned at extremely short distances have minimal predictive reliability for other distances. As a corollary, a race run at extremely long distances are not in essence really races in the normal sense. When you observe most "marathon races," basically the horses are cantering around the track for a mile and one-half and are being urged to run for the last few furlongs. Therefore, a final time speed figure will have very little correlation to the effort that the horses actually put forth. A horse, similar to a human being, can run at a certain speed for extremely long distances without taxing the "energy reserves," and marathon races tend to be races within a race.

3. Turf Beyer figures have little relationship to dirt Beyer figures (and vice versa). Horses switching surfaces should be assessed more on breeding, fitness, and other factors as opposed to Beyers. I only use turf Beyers in a horse switching to dirt (and vice versa) to show overall fitness and improving (or declining) form. This is not to say the Beyers cannot be indicative of a horse's ability, just that the actual absolute figure appears to have little relationship to figures earned on the other surface.

4. Generally, (and correctly) horses at the major tracks (Churchill Downs, Belmont, Santa Anita, Hollywood, Saratoga, etc.) will receive higher Beyers than horses at second tier tracks (Turf

Paradise, Ellis Park, Emerald Downs, Hawthorne, Philadelphia Park, etc.). This is generally as it should be—better and faster horses run at the major venues. Still, if a horse ran a standout race at a second tier track, and you observed the race, and still the horse subsequently receives a "poor" Beyer, take that Beyer with a grain of salt. My experience is that many of these type of horses outrun their Beyers if they next run at a major track or in a more important race at the second tier tracks. I will sometimes disregard the low speed figures when handicapping these "step-up" horses. I caution the reader however that you must have actually observed this "stand-out race" to know that the horse was underrated in the Beyer given. This situation happens rarely, but it occurs because the people rating the time adjust the figure downward, not believing a second tier track horse can run such a large figure so they reexamine the variant set and downgrade the entire card. Often they are correct (almost always in fact), but unique mistakes when Beyers are set at a second tier track (or even a lower tier track) can be a huge betting opportunity if these horses move up to the "big show" major tracks.

The above four circumstances are the only situations where I disregard speed figures. The much more common situations are discussed below, where Beyer Speed Figures must be emphasized to a greater or lesser degree, taking into consideration all other handicapping factors.

"I once bet on a horse so slow, I bet it to live."
— Henny Youngman

Once Beyer figures began to be printed regularly in the past performance section of the DRF, it did not take long before betting the highest figure (obtained in the most recent previous race) became a losing proposition, primarily because of low odds. Probably more important however, to identify the best horses, the figures given must be used in the context of numerous other racing factors, probably the most important of which is pace of the race. There are a number of outstanding books on speed figure handicapping that go into extensive detail on how to relate speed figures to other handicapping techniques, and I encourage you to read them if you find that you want to delve into speed. Here, however, I will only highlight situations that affect how you should view speed figures. These are my opinions that I have seen demonstrated at the tracks I have handicapped (predominantly the major tracks). I offer these considerations here so that as you conduct your own handicapping at your own tracks, you will be alert to watch for these speed figure discrepancies. In addition, you should identify particular situations at your own racing oval, where a Beyer Speed Figure idiosyncrasy may be happening. I emphasize here again that it is the situation at your own tracks that will offer you the greatest betting opportunities, and if you are able to determine specific situations where Beyers are inaccurate, you will secure significant betting opportunities on these animals later on.

Set out below are a series of considerations that you should look for when attempting to determine if a Beyer Speed Figure discrepancy exists. If you observe these discrepancies to be occurring, do not disregard the speed figures, but attempt to adjust them in a manner which is consistent with what you have viewed at your individual venues.

1. Speed figures are a great clue regarding comparisons from one track to another (i.e., a horse going from Churchill to Santa Anita) and a great way to identify a good betting opportunity. Still, a horse's figure at one track is more indicative/predictive of what he should run at that track in his next race, than if he is running at another track. Some horses like (or dislike) certain track surfaces, and when a horse transfers from one track to another, the horse's speed figure may not be consistent with what the horse ran at the previous track. As an example let us say that a horse runs at Churchill Downs in the mid-90 Beyers and subsequently goes to California and runs in the mid-80 Beyers. If the horse continues to run in the mid-80 Beyers at the California track, it could be a sign that the horse is no longer fit. However, it could be simply that the horse does not like the West Coast track. If this horse were to subsequently return to Churchill Downs, this horse might be under bet, expecting that its Beyer at Churchill will be in the mid-80s. Yet, there is a distinct possibility that the horse's Beyers might return to the mid-90s, making him very competitive in certain Churchill races. Obviously, the converse is also true: If the horse returns to Churchill and begins to run in the 90s again and subsequently returns to Hollywood Park, it would be ludicrous to

expect that this horse will now continue to run in the mid-90s. This is so because he has already shown that at his current fitness level, his Beyers at Hollywood Park will be in the mid-80s and he may be an immediate throw-out.

2. Speed figures are more consistently predictive of success/failure at the sprint distances than in longer races. This is directly due to "pace" issues where a horse gets the opportunity to go slow and control the pace in a long race and coast home in a slow time; the low Beyer may not tell what the horse might have been able to do. In many route races, more tactics are employed, and therefore the speed figures may not be as predictive because the final time can be extremely slow due to the slow early fractions set. Obviously pace and other factors should be a component when considering longer races. Most often in sprint-type distances, there will be some horses that will push forward the pace, and it will be easier to determine whether the speed figures earned were legitimate. This is not to say that speed figures are not useful at longer distances, only that they are more predictive at shorter distances.

3. A horse's speed figure must be considered in conjunction with the trip that the horse has received. If the horse was "three wide," or "shut off at the head of a stretch," the Beyer the horse received may not be any indication of the effort of which the horse was capable. Conversely, many troubled comment lines are to me, relatively unimportant. For example, a horse breaking a step slow in a one-mile race should have virtually no predictive ability as to whether the horse will run well. In my mind, more important than a troubled racing line is an incredibly stupid ride by a given jockey (which occurs in almost every race you view). For instance if a horse is a stone cold closer, and the jockey (with his ego directly disproportionate to his brain size) takes the horse out to the front, the horse fades and runs a terrible Beyer, this is absolutely zero indication of what the horse was capable of. I hope that the trainer (or the angered owner) will complete a jockey switch, and tell the next jockey to hold off the pace somewhat. Again, this may present an opportunity because the speed figure earned may be low compared to the horse's ability, and therefore the trip the horse receives and the stupidity of the individual jockeys involved must be considered in regard to the Beyer obtained. Specifically, in regard to jockey stupidity, I would even go so far as to say that there are certain jockeys

that when they get on a horse will actually increase the Beyer speed figure of this horse because they are better than the previous individuals who rode the horse. Therefore, Beyers should be considered as adjustable upward or downward, depending on who is riding the animal.

4. If a horse is consistently a distance animal (one mile or longer), and receives at such races a Beyer in the mid-70s range, and then runs in a sprint (let's say six furlongs) and runs a Beyer in the 50s, this Beyer has no predictive reliability of what the horse will run at later races at the longer distances. Often trainers run horses in events to induce additional speed, and shorter sprint horses are run in longer races to get more "bottom" into the horse through more stamina. Therefore, prep races, or races that a horse runs at a distance which the horse seldom runs, are not predictive of success at different distances. Accordingly, when you see a racing past performance line where a horse has run ten races at one mile or above and his last race was at six furlongs (even if there was not a layoff involved), the speed figure earned at this sprint may be disregarded, and instead the previous Beyers at the distance races should be considered.

5. If a track has an *extreme* bias (speed, closer, rail, three path, etc.), the figure the horses received should be considered irrelevant if it is out of line with other figures. While the Beyer folks are great at dealing with biases, extreme biases throw wrinkles in, and Beyers that are given that are out of line with a horse's past races are probably better disregarded. Obviously, this is a judgment call, but everyone has seen a track with an extreme bias occurring, and while it may present a great betting opportunity, Beyers received on these racing dates (both good and bad) are probably better disregarded for subsequent races. This is one of the reasons I believe it is essential to watch for bias when watching the early races on a particular race date.

6. Horses which are two and three years old improve steadily with age as long as they remain sound, and these animals generally (as humans do) improve in spurts. A horse may receive a 70 Beyer in one race, and stay at that level for two more races and then go 90+. You can think of it as a growth spurt in a seven-year-old child if you want, but basically expect horses (sound ones) to gradually increase their speed figures an average of one to two points per

month from two years old until toward the end of their three year old career. A 60 Beyer horse at two and half years should be a 70 to 80 horse a year later at three and a half. This would be more useful if they progressed evenly, but the "spurt factor" occurs. My approach with younger horses is to closely consider Beyers (particularly Beyer improvement) but to also closely assess their physical changes from race to race, and whether the trainer is training the horse for the particular race. Bottom line: Young horses improve inconsistently and make handicapping their races double tough. Take a look at how the horse looks in the paddock and post parade —you will find some high priced winners. Alternatively, spend more time on other older horseraces, and go deep in the younger horse events. Steady Beyer improvement in younger horses may be much more important (and predictive of success) than periodic "spike" Beyers that are out of line with the horse's previous races. One final note on the age of younger horses, is that not all horses are born on the same day; however, all two year olds are considered two year olds, regardless of when they were foaled. Accordingly, older two-year-olds and older three-year-olds will often be more mature and will run better than their younger counterparts.

7. Horses "bounce" or appear to bounce from a handicapping standpoint. In other words, if a horse runs an exceptionally high Beyer which is out of line with their previous Beyers, often this horse will not perform at that level (or even at their previous levels) in the next race. This is especially true if the high Beyer occurred off a racing layoff of more than three months. My personal opinion is this often occurs because a horse was used hard and is not quite ready to do it again. One way to avoid this bounce effect is a longer than normal gap between these two races, accompanied by continuous workouts between races. If a horse generally races every three weeks, ran an exceptional Beyer, but waited five weeks before his next outing with consistent training in between, the likelihood of a Beyer bounce is minimized. In regard to speed figures, great note taking is helpful. We must specifically write down notations about a race where we feel a horse was used hard. Conversely, we must note when a great Beyer is received but the horse ran easily. Keep track. The bottom line is that bounces happen, and a huge jump in figures will usually be followed by a figure decrease.

8. A horse's most recent speed figure is the most important. It means more than a figure earned multiple races back, unless the most recent figure is due to an off track, strange pace considerations, horrible jockey activities (very common), etc. As a corollary to the above statement, what I consider even more important than the most recent speed figure is a series of increasing Beyer figures. Two races of increasing Beyers are great, three races are better, and more than three races are huge. I find that this is one of the most predictive indicators that shows a horse is improving in form, regardless of class, surface, etc. Increasing Beyers, particularly ones that are increasing consistently are very predictive of a positive next race. Obviously, the greater question is where do these Beyers plateau out, but my experience is that bettors should use increasing Beyer speed figures with great weight, taking the chance that the horse has not peaked. While eventually the horse will peak, or plateau (or even decline), it is virtually impossible to identify when via the number of increased Beyers, their ratios, etc. Instead, the smart handicapper will use the increasing Beyer technique to continue to play the horse until a peak is actually demonstrated. Horses are like any other creatures, generally they are getting better, or getting worse, and they do not stay at the same peak level for long periods. Conversely, a series of decreases in Beyer figures obviously shows the horse is off form or injured. Decreasing Beyers are always a source of caution, and even if the last speed figure received is better than many in the next race, it is likely that the horse may recede even more, and therefore this Beyer may not be predictive of a positive effort in the next race.

9. One of the factors I consider to be the most important in Beyer Speed Figures is to determine when a difference is important and when it is not important. Some people will point to a one or two point difference, and indicate that one horse is better by one or two points than another. I find this an extremely erroneous application of speed figures, and one that is not determinative of success. In my experiences, the differences between the speed figures

of two horses are only relevant if it is three to five points different. In *Beyer on Speed,* Andrew Beyer states that in sprint races, three Beyer points is equivalent to a length difference or more (*Beyer on Speed,* p. 33). I have found one of the most frequently missed plays by many handicappers is to automatically try to find the winner without considering that there may be multiple possible situations where different horses can win the race. It is obviously a bad decision to base a major win play on a Beyer difference of just two to three points.

10. Horses run in patterns. Just as increasing Beyers are likely to lead to another increasing Beyer, decreasing Beyers will likely lead to another decreasing Beyer. Further, if a horse is very consistent and runs similar Beyers, it will likely do this again. Increasing Beyers should be given weight in the belief that the horse will continue to improve. Decreasing Beyers should also be given weight believing that the horse will continue to decrease in form. However, one of the greatest betting opportunities is a horse that remains consistent—a horse that runs his race every time. Often these horses are overlooked in the wagering because they may tend to run second, third, fourth, consistently. This does not mean that these horses cannot win the next race, but only that they were in fields where their consistent Beyer was not able to be victorious. My experience is often that horses with these type of Beyers will go off as the fourth and fifth choices in a field, because other horses from different fields won in their previous starts (though they may have received similar or even lower Beyer Speed Figures). Horses that run their race every time often will continue to do this throughout their careers, and can be good betting opportunities on the win end periodically. I would caution here that sometimes horses don't "want to win," and therefore run in the middle of the pack regardless of jockey urging, etc. This does not mean that these horses cannot be used, but that these horses should be used with caution only in the win scenario. This is a difficult distinction to make between horses that are a racing opportunity where their consistent Beyers will win, or the horse that has higher Beyers but will always lose because it does not have the heart to win. This again, is yet another opportunity where it is essential that the horseplayer be familiar with the individual animals upon which he/she wagers. If a horse always goes to the wire but never seems to get up, it may mean that the

horse does not have the heart to pass other horses, or conversely, a horse that once passed simply gives up. The astute horseplayer will be familiar with these animals and be able to judge their Beyer in that context.

PACE

I consider pace to be the most mitigating and modifying factor concerning speed figures. Set out below is a relative general discussion of how pace can effect a race, and how it can affect speed figures.

> "Two roads diverged in a yellow wood,
> And sorry I could not travel both
> And be one traveler, long I stood
> And looked down one as far as I could
> To where it bent in the undergrowth;
>
> Then took the other, as just as fair,
> And having perhaps the better claim,
> Because it was grassy and wanted wear;
> Though as for that, the passing there
> Had worn them really about the same,
>
> And both that morning equally lay
> In leaves no step had trodden black.
> Oh, I kept the first for another day!
> Yet knowing how way leads on to way,
> I doubted if I should ever come back.
>
> I shall be telling this with a sigh
> Somewhere ages and ages hence:
> Two roads diverged in a wood, and I—
> I took the one less traveled by,
> And that has made all the difference."
>
> — Robert Frost, *The Road Not Taken*

I use the above quote by Robert Frost (in addition to the fact that I love the poem), because I believe the successful handicapper has the option to utilize "the road less frequently taken" by utilizing pace figures in conjunction with the road more frequently taken (i.e., speed figures). Unlike Mr. Robert Frost, the handicapper can use both roads and use them frequently on a road to success. I specifically start out this section on pace with the acknowledgement that I have never been a particularly good pace handicapper. I have to work hard to determine how the race went, and how the pace may have had an impact on how the speed figures were calculated. At this point, I would like to acknowledge the assistance that I was able to obtain from a book called *The Race is Pace* by Huey Mahl. Some of the charts shown in later sections of this chapter were reprinted with permission. I would suggest that if you want to be a better pace handicapper, you should review this well-written and logical book. My experience with pace handicapping is that individuals who were successful in statistics will be the best pace handicappers, because they will be most comfortable with the charts and numbers involved. I admit that one of my truly poor grades in college was in statistics, and that may be the reason I struggle with pace handicapping. However, while I struggle with it, I still attempt to do it because I believe that the pace of the race is what can distort and skew Beyer Speed Figures most often. All the previous factors discussed may be irrelevant compared to the pace of the race and the amount of impact it has on Beyers.

As an initial example on how pace works I give the following example. We will assume in the following example that there were no particular track biases on the day in question, and that the times were accurate, and that the horses in question were on the lead at the time of each fractional pace call:

	Fractional Times		Final Times
Horse 1	22	44^5	110^5
Horse 2	23	46	110^5

Which horse is better? The answer is obvious if we assume this occurred on the same track and that there were no biases: Horse 1 is much the better animal. Horse 1 ran faster early, faster in the middle, and had the same final time. Horse 2 ran slower, slow in the middle, and had the same final time. Obviously Horse 1 is a better play in the next race. Concerning speed figures, these horses would have received the exact same Beyer figure. In the next race, with the assumptions that I made, Horse 1 is going to receive much greater backing by me as a bettor than Horse 2. The reason is that if we assume Horse 1 and Horse 2 attempt to go to the lead, Horse 1 can go through significantly faster fractions than Horse 2 and will most likely put away Horse 2 quite early in the race.

Using that as an example, it is important to note how races are timed for the numbers provided in the DRF. These races are timed by a series of spotters that provide information to one of their assistants calling out the various lengths that horses are behind at certain fractional times in each race. The spotter is going to tell his assistant that Horse 1 is three lengths back at the one-quarter mile pole. Then with the common deduction that one length equals one fifth of a second, three fifths of a second would be deducted from the fractional time of Horse 1 at the quarter pole. Whatever the time of the lead horse at the one-quarter pole, three fifths of a second would be deducted from that time, arriving at the fractional time for the horse. At this point I provide two important caution statements regarding this:

1. One fifth of a second, while closely approximating one length, is not exactly the same for six furlong races and races that are longer. Many well written pace handicapping books go into extreme detail on how to average out fractional times at different distances. However, I find that just the innate knowledge in the horseplayer's head should be able to determine that a length is more important in a shorter race than in a longer race and should be given somewhat more proportionate weight.

2. The spotters who are identifying the horses and how far they are back at the fractional post do a good job (I could never do it), but they are not universally accurate. I have found that horses racing in the mid-pack, say four to five lengths behind the leader, may be miscalculated in lengths by as much as two to three lengths. This factor is even more pronounced with deep closing horses where their lengths may be off by as much as four to five lengths. It is important to note that these lengths may be shown as closer in the past performances than they actually were or farther back than they were.

My personal method is that because of the inaccuracies of the spotters and the concept of one length not always equaling one fifth of a second, I only believe that the formula is accurate for horses within three lengths of the lead at each fractional call. Again, this is a general standard that I have seen: When horses are within three lengths of the lead horse, the lengths behind given by the spotters tend to be quite accurate. With horses I observe to be running within the mid-pack, I disregard the fractional lengths behind and instead, refer to these horses in my notes as rate/closers. Horses at the back of the pack are referred to as deep closers only, again disregarding the amount of lengths behind. While this is a generalization, I believe it is more accurate than to believe that a horse is exactly eight lengths behind when it is in mid-pack when in fact he may be ten lengths (or six lengths) behind. Here I would note that in the book *Handicapping Speed* by Charles Carroll there is an outstanding chapter (Chapter 5) called "The Mechanics of Time," that goes into great detail (but is still understandably written) concerning how races are timed. It is an interesting section if you are interested in the inaccuracies of timing in particular races.

The most important factor in regard to pace is knowing how your own track functions. Track biases, as well as wind, etc., will affect pace calls as much or possibly more than they would affect speed figures. Pure fractional times can also be affected by biases.

In the example given previously concerning Horse 1 and Horse 2, Horse 1 is the superior animal. Another example may also be demonstrative of when a betting opportunity occurs. Check the fractional times of the following two horses:

	Fractional Times		Final Times
Horse 1	23	46	110
Horse 2	22	44	110

The times for Horse 2 would obviously be significantly superior. However, now let's assume that these are the fractional times for the lead horse in that race, and that Horse 2 was in fact back two lengths behind at the first fractional call, three lengths back at the second fractional call and was third, three lengths back at the finish. Accordingly, using the "one fifth of a second equals one length," Horse 2 has adjusted fractional times as follows:

	Fractional Times		Final Time
Horse 2	$22^{2/5}$	$44^{3/5}$	$110^{3/5}$

Perhaps the Beyer Speed Figure would take into account the difference in the final times, but here it is also clear that Horse 2 is the superior animal. Therefore, it is important to note that a horse that ran in second or third or even a further back position may well be the "speed in the race" in a subsequent race.

Set out below is the basic concept of how pace works, but again I suggest that if you are extremely interested in pace, you review *The Race is Pace,* by Huey Mall, or even some other books that are more complicated (for those of you with a more statistical bent).

A horse can run at approximately 32 miles per hour for two to three miles with very little reserve being drained; even at this pace, the horse would be able to significantly accelerate if the jockey so requested. Conversely, the virtual maximum speed of a thoroughbred is 43 miles per hour (according to Huey Mall). Accordingly, all pace differentials occur between the thirty-two miles per hour and the forty-three mile per hour range. At this point I would like to make a note that all handicappers must consider: speed and fractional times are more important in sprints because they are more indicative of how the horse is exerting itself. In longer races the ability (or more commonly the lack of ability) of the jockeys is much more important. Horses are saved, and energy in them is saved, by appropriate jockey rides. In longer events, a jockey conserves the energy of the horse and does not waste it. Well, that's what good jockeys do; bad jockeys use the energy of the horse inappropriately, and find that the animal has nothing left for the stretch run. As with all other handicapping techniques it is important to understand that the ability of the jockey may affect how the horse responds to pace more than anything else.

To show an example in general terms on how pace works, I have received authorization to use a series of charts from the book *The Race is Pace.* Diagram A shows a six-furlong race where the horse received fractions of 22, 23, and 24 seconds respectively for each quarter mile, for a three-quarter mile total 1:09 effort. The chart represents the relationship between mile per hour versus the time broken down by the quarter poles listed at the top, and smaller sub-sections $1/16$, $1/8$, $3/16$, etc. The chart is a step down chart, and unmistakably the horse did not run

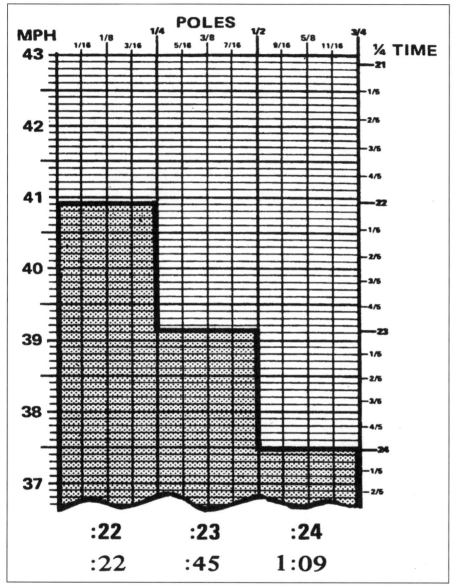

Diagram A

exactly forty-one miles per hour and then immediately shift gears into thirty-nine miles per hour. Accordingly, this is more appropriately shown as the characterization on Diagram B that demonstrates the actual pace of the animal in a more collinear format. This curve is indicative of a front running horse, an animal fast early and then slowing down significantly toward the end of the race. Diagram C shows a stretch running horse that receives fractions of 23, 22⅗, and 23⅖ for a similar 1:09 total. The chart shows that the horse never got up to the

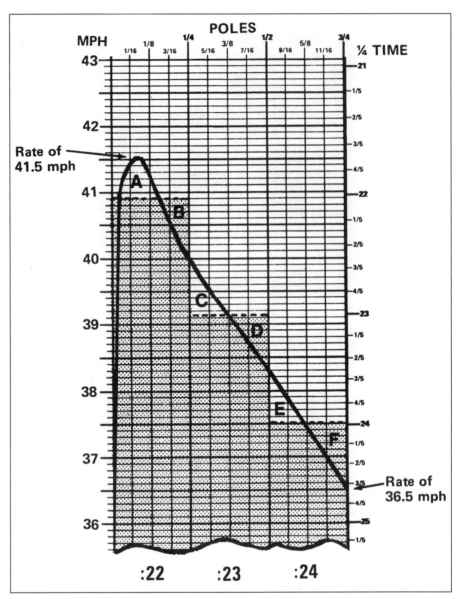

Diagram B

exact same pace of the front running horse. However this horse was running significantly faster at the end of the race (approximately one and half miles per hour faster).

If the efforts and charts of the two horses (front runner and closer) are superimposed over one another (see Diagram D), it would reveal that the closer is traveling at approximately one and half miles per hour faster in the end, and at that the front runner was traveling at a faster pace early in the race.

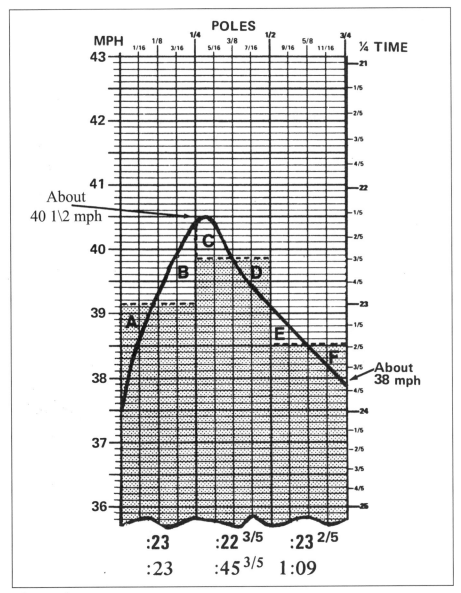

Diagram C

Pace handicapping basically would explain that if the areas under each of these curves were taken as a representation of the energy expended by each animal (if we disregard racing mishaps, which always occur), the horse with the largest area beneath its curve would be the victorious animal. As an example, in the representation under Diagram D, if area X were greater than area Y, the front runner would win. Conversely, if area Y was greater than area X, the closer would win. In that this race was set up with equal final times it would

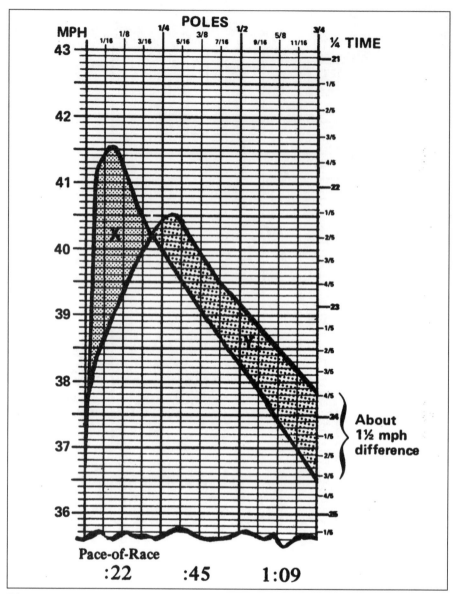

Diagram D

approximate a dead heat. Only areas X and Y need to be compared because the area below that on the chart was equal for both horses and may be disregarded.

If the above diagramed horses were watched in visual format, it would show that Horse 1 (front runner) went out to a significant lead, and then Horse 2 (closer) would catch him down the stretch, ending in a dead heat (under ideal conditions) at the wire.

The individual horseplayer does not necessarily have to make graphic representation for each particular horse in a given race. However, the concept of what was described explains much about how front runners can win on an early loose lead, and how closers can win in races where the early pace is contested. If you extrapolate slightly on the diagrams given and allow the front runner to go slightly slower during the earlier stages, leaving more for the front runner in the stretch. You can easily see that the areas in the diagrams would enable the front runner to be victorious. Antithetically, an additional forced early pace (i.e., another rabbit put out to force the pace) would increase the area for the front runner earlier, but might hamper the animal's ability to finish with any pace at all, leading the areas under the chart to be larger for the closer, leading to that horse's victory.

If a handicapper has a strong mathematical inclination, charts like this could be developed for every horse in any race. The areas under these regions can be determined through mathematical analysis, and used to identify particular horses that may be victorious (or complete posers/phonies) that would not otherwise be identified via pure speed figure analysis. I encourage those of you who have this inclination, and particularly those with computer knowledge, to develop computer programs that will allow you to do this. I guarantee that if you look at the pace aspects as explained here, you will often identify horses that have an advantage in upcoming races.

I would like to identify some specific things that will affect pace, and can make your pace analysis less predictive of the final outcomes. As with speed figure analysis, it is essential to consider other factors in the race to make a determination of how pace analysis should be utilized and how it should be weighted:

1. You must know the track bias and idiosyncrasy of your various home tracks. There are tracks around the United States, particularly in the Northeast, that have strong wind forces that affect pace. Horses do not enjoy running into the wind any more than human beings do. It is much more difficult, and it will slow down speed figures as well as pace fractional times. Wind is much more of a factor in pace fractional times than it may be in a total Beyer Speed Figure time. Obviously, in a one-mile race, run on a one-mile oval, all factors being considered, the wind should not affect the final time because while running into a head wind at one point, you will

experience a tail wind at the other. However, if we assume that the wind is in the face of the horses initially, this will greatly affect the first pace fractional time, so it would be essential to consider that a slow first fractional time (and conversely, a fast final fractional time) may not be valid for pace analytical purposes.

2. As will be discussed in the final sections of this book dealing with Zen, horses have their own type of "Zen". It is impossible to make a closer a front runner, and vice versa. Every horseplayer has the horror story of being on a stone cold closer with a large wager and subsequently watching him on the front end knowing that you have already lost before the horse makes the one quarter pole. Some horses are versatile, and can run on the pace or off the pace, but this characteristic is relatively uncommon. As with speed figures, pace fractional times for a front runner who is far back, or a closer who is close to the pace, should likely be disregarded.

3. As with speed figures, pace consideration must be taken into account when looking at the entire race regarding trips and problems. If a horse is a front runner, and experiences problems out of the gate, and finds itself far back, and has to be hustled to the front, consequently fades more than normal through the stretch—an asterisk should be placed next to this horse's pace figures (and probably the speed figures as well). Because, while it was on the pace call at the early fractional times, significant additional energy was expended for the horse to do so. The converse is true for a horse that is a closer who experiences problems being blocked down the lane or towards the end of the race. Pace figures must be adjusted for particular race occurrences.

4. When I handicap pace figures I use the lengths-off-the-lead only for horses within three lengths of the lead horse. The purpose for this is that I do not believe that horses that are farther back of the pack or toward the rear of the pack have accurate lengths behind identified by the spotters. The exception to this is at the finish line, where photographic evidence of each horse does show the specific lengths behind. I adjust for this by utilizing specific charts showing the energy type expended for horses within three lengths of the lead which shows me the energy they need to expend during the race based on the pace. Front running horses are affected by the early pace of the race, and the initial fractional times will have the most effect on them in terms of them being exhausted at the end

of the race. Raters and closers do not have to expend as much energy unless they are inappropriately kept closer to the pace by a bad jockey. Therefore, while I chart specifically the lengths back and the energy expended for horses within three lengths of the pace, I treat raters and closers differently. For each track I come up with a concept of what a chart looks like for a rate horse who rates four to five lengths off the lead, and plot it as a comparison for each race. I make the assumption that a rate horse that runs four to five lengths off the pace calls will perform in a certain specific area based on my charts of what horses like this have done before. I disregard whether the horse was four, six or seven lengths back and treat all these horses similarly. I also come up with a profile for a deep closer, have a chart produced, and super impose that on the races for the front runners within three lengths of the pace call. I generally do not make up specific charts to do this, but instead estimate it via typical fractional times. My suggestion is that if you are a computer wizard, develop statistical charts to show what rate closers and deep closers do, and come up with an average example of how this is handled at your track in regard to early, middle and final fractional times as related to the front runners.

I believe pace figures are the most important modifier to Beyer Speed Figures, and with effort and analysis, even those who are not math geniuses can use them to their advantage. These factors must be modified by the caveats that I identified through this chapter. As a final quote, I provide you with the following:

> **"To foresee a victory which the ordinary man can foresee is not the acme of skill."**
> — Sun Tzu, *The Art of War*

If you use Beyer Speed Figures in conjunction with pace figures, I believe that you will have great success and be able to identify animals that not everyone can see.

Beyer on Speed
By Andrew Beyer
The Race is Pace
By Huey Mall

NOTES:

5

Breeding Issues (Specifically Mud, Turf and Distance Breeding)

"Breed the best to the best and hope for the best"
— Anonymous

reeding issues can sometimes seem, to the average horseplay-er, to be one of the great mysteries of the horse racing game. In actuality, issues of breeding are generally secondary to the actual quality and fitness of the individual animals involved. However, breeding can have a critical impact on how horses run, particularly on specific types of surfaces, such as mud and turf. Anyone who has done a significant analysis of breeding will agree that the high pur-chase prices for horses sold at sales at Keeneland, Saratoga, Del Mar, etc., have minimal relation to how they will actually run on the track. Some horses purchased for astronomical prices have been extremely successful; a recent example of this is Fusaoichi Pegasus. This horse was purchased for an extremely high figure and was well regarded as a great three-year-old; he won the Kentucky Derby as the odds on favorite, and is currently syndicated for expensive breeding rights.

However, for every Fusaoichi Pegasus there are horses that are purchased at the various breeders' sale for large sums that do not have notable careers as racehorses.

Extremely serious horseplayers have won and lost one hundred dollar bills in bunches on bets. Still, this pales in comparison to the dollar figures bantered back and forth at a major horse sale like Keeneland, Del Mar, or Saratoga. If you ever feel down after a bad day at the OTB, pick up the next day's racing form, and look at the original purchase prices for horses running in minor claiming races at a track like Churchill Downs. Your losses will look like chicken feed.

Contrary to popular opinion, all thoroughbreds could be considered to have regal breeding. The reason for this is that all thoroughbred racehorses trace their ancestry back to a very select few original sires such as Eclipse. So generally, even the most lowly of claiming horses on any track probably have Eclipse blood in them. Eclipse, who was foaled approximately two hundred and fifty years ago, has lineage to virtually every significant racehorse that has won stakes races in the United States in the last century. I raise this point here to emphasize my opinion that it is only the most recent sires and dam-sires that strongly influence the ability of the animal which you are accessing. Back lineage charts that go back five or six generations do not seem to have significant pertinence to the racehorse you are accessing. It is best to go back only one or two generations on either the dam or sire side to access potential. Additionally, every generation of racehorses has a Cinderella horse, or a Cinderfella horse, which did not have great breeding, but scales the heights of the sport. Examples of such horses include Real Quiet, Seabiscuit, Canonero II, Seattle Slew, Smarty Jones and most famously, the gelding John Henry.

Accordingly, while breeding may help you in your handicapping, it is my opinion that other factors such as conditioning, and most recent race activity, are more important than breeding. Breeding may determine the horse's potential, but luck, training, ability, and the actual heart of the animal will actually determine its success.

Breeding can periodically offer the handicapper a significant opportunity to identify an animal that is being overlooked in the betting. I believe that these opportunities can be grouped into three basic areas. First, maiden races for first time starters, or horses that have run only a very few races. Secondly, horses that are running on the turf or dirt for the first time. And thirdly, horses that are going a route of distance for the first time, or are significantly increasing in distance. Toward the end of this chapter, I will discuss a few very specific recommendations that I have regarding horses and breeding, including horses to look for in the above situations based specifically on their breeding. However, in the next few paragraphs I will provide you with some background information on breeding in general, and various handicapping theories, which use breeding as a central concept.

Your greatest resource for turf breeding, and other types of breeding issues, are the breeding based magazines. Two predominant racehorse magazines I find useful concerning breeding are *American Turf Monthly* and *The Blood Horse Magazine.*® Specifically, *American Turf Monthly* has in-depth articles that talk about various betting strategies and turf issues. One article in this magazine was "Sire Lines and Brood Mare Sire Lines can point out likely winners in major stakes races." This article discussed sire lines as they related to Triple Crown, Breeders Cup, and other Stakes races in regard to the well-known brood mare and sire line begun with the famous foal Phalaris. While I have found this magazine is a useful resource for breeding issues, it sometimes goes back too far in the breeding line for the average handicapper to appreciate the usefulness of the information. Yet, different handicappers find different resources useful, and I suggest you purchase a copy of this magazine or similar magazines to see if you find them pertinent for your individual handicapping purposes.

I find that the most useful resource concerning breeding is *The Blood Horse Magazine,*® which provides in-depth articles about breeding and stud news. *The Blood Horse Magazine*® is an outstanding resource because it provides specific charts covering each issue of sires: dam sires, turf sires, first crop sires, second crop sires, etc. Additionally, it has a website that updates the sire lists frequently, and it also has sire issues broken down by states and other factors. That website is http://breeding.bloodhorse.com/sirelists.asp.

Set out on the following pages, and reprinted with the permission of *The Blood Horse Magazine,*® are the 2004 Leading Sires. Also included are the Cumulative Broodmare Sires, the 2004 Leading First Crop Sires, 2004 Leading Sires of 2-Year-Olds, and the Sires by North American Earnings.

Any serious handicapper should obtain a subscription to *The Blood Horse Magazine,*® if for no other reason than to maintain these charts for the comparison of breeding sire and dam sires of horses racing in maiden, first turf races, etc.

> **"The blood runs hot in a thoroughbred
> and the courage runs deep. In the best of them,
> pride is limitless. This is their heritage and they
> carry it like a banner. What they have they use."**
> — C. W. Anderson

At this point, I would like to provide a brief note on dams that a particular horse has. Dams are generally not given as much weight as sires or dam sires, but can have a significant influence on an individual offspring. Dams have fewer offspring than studs/sires do, but a diligent handicapper can produce charts regarding an individual dam and the number of winners they have produced in their breeding career. If a handicapper does not want to take the time to chart the dams, my advice is to recall particular fillies and mares that were exceptional turf or mud runners, and then specifically wait for any of their offspring to go to the track and run on those surfaces. You will see only one or two of those offspring every few years, yet it may present a good betting opportunity.

To assist you and your ability to recall good turf breeding, Bill Heller provides a significant tip in his book, *Turf Overlays.* He advises that for each race, before looking at a horse's turf record, look at its breeding, and make a predication on whether or not the horse has had any success on the turf. Heller advises that when done routinely, it will increase the handicapper's knowledge of what turf breeding is pertinent. I find this an outstanding suggestion, and one that with only a minimal amount of time, will increase the handicapper's ability to make an assessment of turf breeding. This approach can be applied to mud horses, as well. On an off track or muddy track, look at the horse's breeding, and make a determination on whether or not you think the horse would be successful on a muddy track, and then look at the off track line. However, as we will discuss later, be aware that not all off tracks are the same, and this off track number in the DRF will have more inconsistencies than the turf running line.

2004 Leading Sires

Many Sire Lists now updated daily on-line.
Go to http://breeding.bloodhorse.com/sirelists.asp
State Sire Lists updated weekly.

For stallions that stand, will stand, or stood (deceased) in North America (stallions exported prior to the 2000 breeding season are excluded), and have runners in North America. As supplied to The Blood-Horse *by* The Jockey Club Information Systems, Inc.*, this includes monies earned in NA (through Nov 14 2004); Eng and Ire (Nov 11); Fr (Nov 12); Ger (Nov 7); Italy (July 31), and the UAE (Oct 28). *Foal counts include Southern Hemisphere. Cumulative stakes winners includes all countries; some additional foreign foals may be included in the foal count. Market Value "M" is given for those stallions whose stud fee is listed as private.* **Categorical leaders are in bold.**

Rank	Previous Week's Rank	Stallion (Foreign foaled), Year, Sire, Where Stands	2005 Stud Fee	Rnrs/ Wnrs	Stakes Wnrs/Wns	GrSW/ Gr1SW	(Chief Earner, Earnings)	2004 Earnings	Cumulative Foals	Cumulative Stks Wnrs	Cumulative A-E Index	Cumulative Comp Index
1	1	**ELUSIVE QUALITY** (93, Gone West), Gainsborough Farm, KY	$100,000	134/74	5/11	2/1	(Smarty Jones, $7,563,535)	**$10,518,722**	194	16	3.38	1.82
2	2	**EL PRADO (Ire)** (89, Sadler's Wells), Adena Springs Kentucky	$100,000	195/96	16/**28**	7/2	(Kitten's Joy, $1,625,796)	$9,107,492	*562	53	2.24	1.78
3	3	**A.P. INDY** (89, Seattle Slew), Lane's End Farm, KY	$300,000	170/88	**21**/27	10/3	(Friends Lake, $611,800)	$7,889,715	628	74	3.33	**4.39**
4	4	**STORM CAT** (83, Storm Bird), Overbrook Farm, KY	$500,000	128/70	18/24	**11**/3	(Storm Flag Flying, $963,248)	$7,233,313	*933	**128**	**3.67**	3.67
5	5	**PLEASANT COLONY** (78, His Majesty)	Died, 2002	54/27	4/7	4/2	(Pleasantly Perfect, $4,840,000)	$6,457,292	620	77	3.54	2.38
6	6	**SMART STRIKE** (92, Mr. Prospector), Lane's End Farm, KY	$35,000	129/77	12/20	4/1	(Soaring Free, $1,113,862)	$6,283,707	276	29	2.69	2.23
7	7	**SAINT BALLADO** (89, Halo)	Died, 2002	154/75	3/8	2/1	(Ashado, $2,259,640)	$6,099,736	*626	49	1.96	2.08
8	8	**AWESOME AGAIN** (94, Deputy Minister), Adena Springs Kentucky	$125,000	103/54	5/9	4/2	(Ghostzapper, $2,590,000)	$6,083,070	209	9	3.04	2.41
9	10	**TALE OF THE CAT** (94, Storm Cat), Ashford Stud, KY	$65,000	180/98	8/11	4/1	(Lion Heart, $1,080,000)	$5,736,056	*385	19	2.02	2.23
10	9	**ALPHABET SOUP** (91, Cozzene), Adena Springs Kentucky	$20,000	176/101	11/15	3/1	(Our New Recruit, $1,263,795)	$5,678,838	*313	21	1.91	1.48
11	11	**DYNAFORMER** (85, Roberto), Three Chimneys Farm, KY	$75,000	155/68	10/11	5/2	(Perfect Drift, $891,795)	$5,517,274	*670	63	2.08	1.72
12	12	**GRAND SLAM** (95, Gone West), Ashford Stud, KY	$85,000	162/85	12/17	5/1	(Alke, $482,800)	$5,433,933	302	17	2.13	2.01
13	13	**CARSON CITY** (87, Mr. Prospector), Overbrook Farm, KY	$35,000	174/94	9/16	4/0	(Pollard's Vision, $1,022,020)	$5,338,087	*765	71	2.05	2.02
14	14	**UNBRIDLED'S SONG** (93, Unbridled), Taylor Made Farm, KY	$125,000	155/70	10/15	6/0	(Domestic Dispute, $413,428)	$5,195,452	*536	36	2.06	2.80
15	16	**KINGMAMBO** (90, Mr. Prospector), Lane's End Farm, KY	$300,000	153/70	14/22	6/**4**	(Rule of Law, $1,233,320)	$5,068,270	529	53	2.78	3.25
16	15	**DEVIL HIS DUE** (89, Devil's Bag), Margaux Farm, KY	$10,000	189/98	10/14	2/2	(Roses in May, $1,723,277)	$5,049,077	451	25	1.44	1.23
17	17	**NOT FOR LOVE** (90, Mr. Prospector), Northview Stallion Station, MD	$25,000	171/95	10/18	4/0	(Love of Money, $491,500)	$5,026,713	334	29	2.01	1.43
18	18	**LANGFUHR** (92, Danzig), Lane's End Farm, KY	$30,000	182/93	10/17	4/0	(Imperialism, $482,000)	$5,009,925	*497	21	1.76	1.64
19	19	**WILD RUSH** (94, Wild Again)	NA	120/66	7/11	5/2	(Stellar Jayne, $992,169)	$4,539,636	222	12	2.01	1.81
20	20	**DISTORTED HUMOR** (93, Forty Niner), WinStar Farm, KY	$60,000	119/65	12/16	1/1	(Funny Cide, $1,075,100)	$4,489,193	*283	21	2.67	1.58
21	22	**SMOKE GLACKEN** (94, Two Punch), Gainesway, KY	$30,000	146/92	8/10	3/0	(Smok'n Frolic, $258,220)	$4,392,936	226	16	2.01	1.43
22	21	**KRIS S.** (77, Roberto)	Died, 2002	105/47	10/13	4/1	(Kicken Kris, $727,000)	$4,333,808	*833	86	2.53	2.05
23	23	**BELONG TO ME** (89, Danzig), Lane's End Farm, KY	$25,000	142/77	8/15	3/0	(Ocean Drive, $505,900)	$4,129,734	*676	35	1.70	2.02
24	24	**ROAR** (93, Forty Niner), Rancho San Miguel, CA	$15,000	146/90	9/13	3/0	(Little Jim, $393,510)	$4,108,800	*479	34	1.93	1.62
25	25	**GULCH** (84, Mr. Prospector), Lane's End Farm, KY	$50,000	140/69	5/6	2/1	(The Cliff's Edge, $1,010,000)	$4,035,875	*717	54	2.14	2.51
26	26	**SKY CLASSIC** (87, Nijinsky II), Pin Oak Stud, KY	$12,500	152/70	6/11	5/**4**	(Nothing to Lose, $643,200)	$3,933,663	*521	40	1.66	2.07
27	27	**GONE WEST** (84, Mr. Prospector), Mill Ridge Farm, KY	$150,000	141/56	5/11	3/1	(Speightstown, $1,045,556)	$3,914,061	819	76	2.22	2.50
28	28	**ROYAL ACADEMY** (87, Nijinsky II), Ashford Stud, KY	$17,500	191/79	8/14	4/1	(Royal Millennium, $212,970)	$3,836,866	***1370**	102	1.69	1.93
29	29	**SILVER DEPUTY** (85, Deputy Minister), Brookdale Farm, KY	$40,000	155/84	6/14	2/0	(Bare Necessities, $328,970)	$3,832,267	657	58	2.12	1.91
30	33	**QUIET AMERICAN** (86, Fappiano), Gainsborough Farm, KY	$20,000	156/82	4/5	1/0	(Josh's Madelyn, $245,172)	$3,734,534	*469	34	1.83	1.88
31	31	**GOLD FEVER** (93, Forty Niner), Metropolitan Stud, NY	$5,000	136/77	1/4	0/0	(A Bit O'Gold, $1,029,200)	$3,718,446	*309	6	1.39	1.45
32	30	**PULPIT** (94, A.P. Indy), Claiborne Farm, KY	$60,000	95/49	7/8	5/2	(Purge, $560,400)	$3,665,472	202	13	2.30	3.38
33	32	**HENNESSY** (93, Storm Cat), Ashford Stud, KY	$35,000	147/71	7/10	4/1	(Madcap Escapade, $536,400)	$3,659,230	*708	39	1.94	2.16
34	34	**UNBRIDLED** (87, Fappiano)	Died, 2001	103/41	3/4	2/0	(Niigon, $864,610)	$3,635,638	566	40	2.92	3.10
35	35	**JULES** (94, Forty Niner)	Died, 2003	109/57	5/11	1/1	(Peace Rules, $1,024,288)	$3,614,815	*359	25	1.84	1.48
36	36	**CHEROKEE RUN** (90, Runaway Groom), Darley at Jonabell, KY	$40,000	168/91	5/6	3/0	(During, $305,280)	$3,589,838	355	19	1.67	1.73
37	37	**PETIONVILLE** (92, Seeking the Gold), Crestwood Farm, KY	$15,000	117/61	6/10	2/1	(Island Fashion, $585,000)	$3,428,002	207	15	1.76	1.33
38	38	**FOREST WILDCAT** (91, Storm Cat), Brookdale Farm, KY	$35,000	166/83	8/9	1/1	(Var, $209,038)	$3,369,513	331	25	1.61	1.93
39	39	**VALID EXPECTATIONS** (93, Valid Appeal), Lane's End Texas	$17,500	128/80	7/12	1/0	(Leaving On My Mind, $283,373)	$3,333,410	229	15	1.88	1.44
40	40	**GRINDSTONE** (93, Unbridled), Overbrook Farm, KY	$7,500	96/46	5/7	2/1	(Birdstone, $1,236,600)	$3,257,820	*245	10	1.61	2.02
41	41	**RUNAWAY GROOM** (79, Blushing Groom), Vinery, KY	$12,500	169/98	7/8	3/2	(The Lady's Groom, $262,520)	$3,249,860	*930	66	1.65	1.38
42	43	**STORM BOOT** (89, Storm Cat), Crestwood Farm, KY	$15,000	170/88	8/10	1/0	(Very Vegas, $165,498)	$3,234,962	*391	34	1.30	1.43
43	42	**AMERICAN CHANCE** (89, Cure the Blues)	Died, 2004	115/56	6/9	2/0	(Bending Strings, $415,150)	$3,225,627	*255	22	1.60	1.35
44	44	**HALO'S IMAGE** (91, Halo), Bridlewood Farm, FL	$10,000	103/55	2/4	1/1	(Southern Image, $1,612,150)	$3,211,111	*206	4	1.65	1.38
45	45	**TABASCO CAT** (91, Storm Cat)	Died, 2004	105/52	6/9	4/1	(Freefourinternet, $527,693)	$3,192,570	315	22	1.80	2.42
46	46	**THEATRICAL (Ire)** (82, Nureyev), Hill 'n' Dale Farms, KY	$50,000	136/54	10/10	5/0	(Laura's Lucky Boy, $236,730)	$3,172,586	*768	69	2.59	2.71
47	48	**SKIP AWAY** (93, Skip Trial), Hopewell Farm, KY	$15,000	120/76	8/9	2/0	(Sister Swank, $213,079)	$3,117,751	230	11	1.32	1.67
48	49	**CRAFTY PROSPECTOR** (79, Mr. Prospector), Brookdale Farm, KY	$10,000	135/81	5/6	2/0	(Pies Prospect, $413,865)	$3,100,046	*920	87	2.14	1.72
49	47	**INDIAN CHARLIE** (95, In Excess), Airdrie Stud, KY	$15,000	95/65	8/11	2/0	(Bwana Charlie, $349,690)	$3,100,019	*180	10	1.82	1.41
50	53	**IN EXCESS (Ire)** (87, Siberian Express), Vessels Stallion Farm, CA	$25,000	102/56	6/8	1/1	(Musical Chimes, $438,300)	$3,062,323	465	37	2.12	1.59
51	50	**GLITTERMAN** (85, Dewan), Wafare Farm, KY	$15,000	138/72	6/8	2/0	(Champali, $634,398)	$3,049,286	529	25	1.62	1.38
52	51	**ALLEN'S PROSPECT** (82, Mr. Prospector)	Died, 2003	187/97	4/6	0/0	(Crossing Point, $121,990)	$3,044,592	912	60	1.39	1.40
53	54	**DIXIELAND BAND** (80, Northern Dancer), Lane's End Farm, KY	$50,000	150/53	5/5	1/1	(Bowman's Band, $419,334)	$2,967,008	*1020	99	2.22	2.38
54	52	**GENERAL MEETING** (88, Seattle Slew), Golden Eagle Farm, CA	$10,000	91/48	6/10	1/0	(Yearly Report, $787,500)	$2,952,105	*376	26	2.27	1.75
55	57	**GILDED TIME** (90, Timeless Moment), Vinery, KY	$17,500	146/73	4/5	0/0	(Clock Stopper, $259,725)	$2,943,965	*676	39	1.58	2.02
56	55	**POLISH NUMBERS** (87, Danzig)	Died, 2002	134/67	7/7	1/0	(Chrusciki, $163,770)	$2,939,562	483	46	1.60	1.74
57	58	**BOSTON HARBOR** (94, Capote), JBBA Shizunai Stallion Station, Japan	NA	125/72	5/6	1/0	(Swingforthefences, $385,745)	$2,930,483	254	14	1.58	2.37
58	63	**WITH APPROVAL** (86, Caro), Brookdale Farm, KY	$5,000	156/81	3/6	1/0	(Destiny Calls, $228,570)	$2,928,796	600	39	1.51	1.82
59	56	**JADE HUNTER** (84, Mr. Prospector), Hill 'n' Dale Farms, KY	$10,000	115/61	4/7	2/1	(Azeri, $1,035,000)	$2,926,233	*732	40	1.59	1.85
60	61	**CANDY STRIPES** (82, Blushing Groom)	NA	70/34	4/6	3/0	(Lundy's Liability, $1,542,500)	$2,911,393	*945	52	1.59	1.47
61	60	**LIT DE JUSTICE** (90, El Gran Senor), Magali Farms, CA	$6,000	118/64	3/3	1/0	(Hour of Justice, $243,953)	$2,875,220	242	11	1.48	1.31
62	69	**WEST BY WEST** (89, Gone West), Jockey Club Stud of Turkey	$5,000	150/79	3/4	2/0	(Sonic West, $367,813)	$2,864,508	*505	21	1.16	1.39
63	65	**CRYPTOCLEARANCE** (84, Fappiano), Margaux Farm, KY	$12,500	**222/102**	3/4	1/0	(Cryptograph, $239,000)	$2,863,757	*853	38	1.33	1.86
64	62	**MR. GREELEY** (92, Gone West), Spendthrift Farm, KY	$50,000	162/80	3/3	0/0	(Nonsuch Bay, $119,100)	$2,861,543	*450	22	1.53	1.71
65	64	**SOUVENIR COPY** (95, Mr. Prospector), Golden Eagle Farm, CA	$10,000	123/66	2/4	1/0	(Souvenir Gift, $211,760)	$2,857,134	240	4	1.31	1.47
66	59	**REGAL CLASSIC** (85, Vice Regent), McMahon of Saratoga, NY	$10,000	140/69	3/4	2/0	(Inish Glora, $433,730)	$2,853,789	*798	45	1.58	1.72
67	66	**NUMEROUS** (91, Mr. Prospector), Haras du Quesnay, Fr	NA	124/52	4/6	2/1	(Kela, $704,212)	$2,819,228	*615	35	1.63	1.66
68	67	**HONOR GRADES** (88, Danzig)	Died, 2002	134/62	2/4	1/1	(Adoration, $607,304)	$2,809,848	*678	27	1.56	1.25
69	—	**ARCH** (95, Kris S.), Claiborne Farm, KY	$10,000	81/50	7/11	3/0	(Prince Arch, $405,946)	$2,750,948	149	8	1.70	2.17
70	68	**DISTANT VIEW** (91, Mr. Prospector), Juddmonte Farms, KY	$15,000	124/53	5/9	2/1	(Sightseek, $1,011,350)	$2,745,827	*341	14	1.76	1.92

AVERAGE-EARNINGS INDEX and COMPARABLE INDEX: Lifetime AVERAGE-EARNINGS INDEX indicates how much purse money the progeny of one sire has earned in relation to the average earnings of all runners in the same years; average earnings of all runners in any year is represented by an index of 1.00; COMPARABLE INDEX indicates the average earnings of progeny produced from mares bred to one sire, when these same mares were bred to other sires. Only 32% of all sires have a lifetime AVERAGE-EARNINGS INDEX higher than their mares' COMPARABLE INDEX.

Cumulative Broodmare Sires

For stallions whose daughters are represented by at least one runner in 2004, regardless of the stallion's origin or the country in which he stands or stood. As supplied to The Blood-Horse by The Jockey Club Information Systems, Inc., this includes monies earned in North America (through Nov 14, 2004), England and Ireland (Nov 11); France (Nov 12); Germany (Nov 17); Italy (July 31), and the United Arab Emirates (Oct 28). Some foreign stakes winners and foals may appear in statistics. **No Southern Hemisphere information is reflected.** Categorical leaders are in bold.

	Broodmare Sire	Dams	Foals	Runners	Winners	2yo Winners	Stakes Winners	*Avg-Erngs Index	*Comp Index
1.	**BUCKPASSER**, 1963-78, by Tom Fool	148	1339	989-74%	674-50%	199-15%	141-**11%**	**3.17**	1.79
2.	**HOIST THE FLAG**, 1968-80, by Tom Rolfe	102	886	661-75%	489-55%	119-13%	82-9%	3.00	1.81
3.	KAHYASI, 1985, by Ile de Bourbon	66	167	116-69%	62-37%	15-9%	10-6%	2.66	1.58
4.	DARSHAAN (GB), 1981-01, by Shirley Heights	233	918	638-69%	397-43%	138-15%	72-8%	2.32	1.56
5.	**DR. FAGER**, 1964-76, by Rough'n Tumble	117	894	719-**80%**	564-**63%**	146-16%	98-**11%**	2.27	1.80
	MARI'S BOOK, 1978-94, by Northern Dancer	110	330	209-63%	150-45%	41-12%	18-5%	2.27	1.51
7.	HAIL TO REASON, 1958-76, by Turn-to	153	1245	989-79%	747-60%	213-17%	113-9%	2.24	1.74
8.	ROUND TABLE, 1954-87, by Princequillo	177	1493	1152-77%	833-56%	273-**18%**	125-8%	2.23	1.78
	NORTHERN DANCER, 1961-90, by Nearctic	293	2487	1767-71%	1273-51%	342-14%	239-10%	2.23	1.66
	GRAUSTARK, 1963-88, by Ribot	260	1858	1395-75%	992-53%	249-13%	143-8%	2.23	1.69
11.	TROY (GB), 1976-83, by Petingo	66	447	335-75%	198-44%	48-11%	32-7%	2.19	1.56
12.	NIJINSKY II, 1967-92, by Northern Dancer	378	2759	1858-67%	1304-47%	339-12%	240-9%	2.16	1.67
	EL GRAN SENOR, 1981-Pnsd, by Northern Dancer	140	486	326-67%	212-44%	72-15%	38-8%	2.16	1.70
14.	NORTHFIELDS, 1968-93, by Northern Dancer	347	1328	953-72%	621-47%	197-15%	105-8%	2.15	1.43
15.	**MR. PROSPECTOR**, 1970-99, by Raise a Native	**469**	**2845**	**1959**-69%	**1440**-51%	**453**-16%	**272**-10%	2.13	1.66
	NUREYEV, 1977-01, by Northern Dancer	315	1523	969-64%	664-44%	187-12%	130-9%	2.13	1.72
17.	SEEKING THE GOLD, 1985, by Mr. Prospector	162	424	245-58%	171-40%	58-14%	29-7%	2.10	**1.94**
18.	PRINCE JOHN, 1953-79, by Princequillo	260	2203	1657-75%	1213-55%	328-15%	170-8%	2.09	1.58
	BLUSHING GROOM (Fr), 1974-92, by Red God	238	1565	1093-70%	775-50%	211-13%	142-9%	2.09	1.66
20.	SMILE, 1982-97, by In Reality	78	248	168-68%	114-46%	28-11%	6-2%	2.08	1.35
21.	KEY TO THE MINT, 1969-96, by Graustark	275	1643	1177-72%	835-51%	225-14%	112-7%	2.05	1.63
	RAHY, 1985, by Blushing Groom	173	436	295-68%	190-44%	78-**18%**	23-5%	2.05	1.77
23.	NEVER BEND, 1960-77, by Nasrullah	154	1215	938-77%	723-60%	213-**18%**	113-9%	2.03	1.71
	VICE REGENT, 1967-95, by Northern Dancer	306	1831	1343-73%	1001-55%	262-14%	108-6%	2.03	1.58
	LORD AT WAR (Arg), 1980-98, by General	118	346	228-66%	146-42%	37-11%	12-3%	2.03	1.77
	SILVER DEPUTY, 1985, by Deputy Minister	126	273	176-64%	116-42%	48-**18%**	21-8%	2.03	1.77
27.	SEATTLE SLEW, 1974-02, by Bold Reasoning	375	1772	1130-64%	811-46%	244-14%	126-7%	2.02	1.72
28.	ALYSHEBA, 1984, by Alydar	120	451	330-73%	225-50%	71-16%	33-7%	2.00	1.77
	SEATTLE SONG, 1981-96, by Seattle Slew	132	439	323-74%	193-44%	48-11%	27-6%	2.00	1.60
30.	HIGH LINE (GB), 1966, by High Hat	140	748	538-72%	312-42%	87-12%	47-6%	1.98	1.49
31.	MISWAKI, 1978-Pnsd, by Mr. Prospector	364	1401	975-70%	675-48%	203-14%	104-7%	1.97	1.55
	DEPUTY MINISTER, 1979-04, by Vice Regent	303	1102	754-68%	554-50%	180-16%	96-9%	1.97	1.70
33.	ROBERTO, 1969-88, by Hail to Reason	232	1682	1219-72%	874-52%	237-14%	141-8%	1.96	1.64
34.	ALYDAR, 1975-90, by Raise a Native	302	1799	1181-66%	865-48%	231-13%	127-7%	1.95	1.73
	STRAWBERRY ROAD (Aust), 1979-95, by Whiskey Road	152	440	295-67%	212-48%	56-13%	33-8%	1.95	1.71
36.	DANCING BRAVE, 1983-99, by Lyphard	147	537	299-56%	209-39%	57-11%	36-7%	1.94	1.64
	IN REALITY, 1964-89, by Intentionally	264	1736	1306-75%	1008-58%	306-**18%**	142-8%	1.94	1.63
38.	DANZIG, 1977-Pnsd, by Northern Dancer	350	1801	966-54%	663-37%	188-10%	121-7%	1.93	1.68
39.	TENTAM, 1969-81, by Intentionally	98	725	553-76%	423-58%	129-**18%**	53-7%	1.92	1.62
	TURKOMAN, 1982, by Alydar	139	378	263-70%	176-47%	48-13%	24-6%	1.92	1.66
41.	PROMINER, 1962-85, by Beau Sabreur	39	200	113-56%	52-26%	11-6%	11-6%	1.89	1.25
	SNOW SPORTING, 1966-84, by Snow Cat	61	282	172-61%	120-43%	28-10%	7-2%	1.89	1.26
43.	RURITANIA, 1969-78, by Graustark	52	318	236-74%	161-51%	48-15%	21-7%	1.88	1.65
44.	RIVERMAN, 1969-99, by Never Bend	398	2275	1621-71%	1036-46%	296-13%	164-7%	1.87	1.55
	RAINBOW QUEST, 1981, by Blushing Groom	234	789	548-69%	313-40%	115-15%	59-7%	1.87	1.60
	KING'S BISHOP, 1969-87, by Round Table	81	543	417-77%	336-62%	76-14%	50-9%	1.87	1.69
47.	RIBOT, 1952-72, by Tenerani	206	1316	831-63%	583-44%	161-12%	102-8%	1.86	1.69
	LE FABULEUX, 1961-84, by Wild Risk	196	1421	1083-76%	724-51%	187-13%	100-7%	1.86	1.57
49.	STAGE DOOR JOHNNY, 1965-96, by Prince John	250	1511	1066-71%	720-48%	183-12%	106-7%	1.85	1.63
	TUNERUP, 1976-02, by The Pruner	101	363	253-70%	172-47%	52-14%	15-4%	1.85	1.46
51.	VICEREGAL, 1966-84, by Northern Dancer	174	1095	558-51%	408-37%	115-11%	57-5%	1.84	1.48
	GENEROUS (Ire), 1988, by Caerleon	90	213	144-68%	76-36%	28-13%	9-4%	1.84	1.78
53.	ASSERT (Ire), 1979-95, by Be My Guest	152	605	406-67%	244-40%	53-9%	35-6%	1.82	1.64
54.	GULCH, 1984, by Mr. Prospector	160	469	268-57%	184-39%	64-14%	23-5%	1.81	1.77
	TOM ROLFE, 1962-89, by Ribot	273	1838	1354-74%	977-53%	209-11%	113-6%	1.81	1.57
56.	AFFIRMED, 1975-01, by Exclusive Native	301	1412	1001-71%	705-50%	196-14%	92-7%	1.80	1.63
57.	ALLEGED, 1974-00, by Hoist the Flag	398	1807	1281-71%	865-48%	225-12%	126-7%	1.79	1.62
	PLEASANT COLONY, 1978-02, by His Majesty	212	834	598-72%	417-50%	92-11%	49-6%	1.79	1.70
59.	TOP VILLE, 1976, by High Top	177	937	687-73%	410-44%	104-11%	65-7%	1.78	1.50
	FIRST LANDING, 1956-87, by Turn-to	188	1246	969-78%	746-60%	229-**18%**	100-8%	1.78	1.60
61.	SMARTEN, 1976, by Cyane	222	913	653-72%	473-52%	134-15%	53-6%	1.77	1.58
	FAPPIANO, 1977-90, by Mr. Prospector	204	1153	753-65%	556-48%	152-13%	90-8%	1.77	1.70
	BADGER LAND, 1983-00, by Codex	69	153	104-68%	73-48%	27-**18%**	15-10%	1.77	1.38
	DESERT WINE, 1980, by Damascus	112	423	299-71%	200-47%	72-17%	25-6%	1.77	1.56
	REVIEWER, 1966-77, by Bold Ruler	79	605	461-76%	350-58%	84-14%	43-7%	1.77	1.77
66.	WAVERING MONARCH, 1979-04, by Majestic Light	152	521	352-68%	230-44%	72-14%	27-5%	1.76	1.58
67.	STORM CAT, 1983, by Storm Bird	242	730	448-61%	319-44%	114-16%	38-5%	1.75	1.79
	LYPHARD, 1969-Pnsd, by Northern Dancer	418	2578	1774-69%	1191-46%	321-12%	193-7%	1.75	1.60
	SECRETARIAT, 1970-89, by Bold Ruler	337	2699	1956-72%	1347-50%	364-13%	157-6%	1.75	1.65

*AVERAGE EARNINGS INDEX and COMPARABLE INDEX: The cumulative broodmare sire Average-Earnings Index indicates how much money the progeny out of each broodmare sire's daughters has earned, on the average, in relation to the average earnings of all runners in the same years; average earnings of all runners in any year is represented by an index of 1.00. The Comparable Index is the combined Average-Earnings Index for all stallions bred to a broodmare sire's daughters, reflecting the general quality of these stallions, and indicating whether the produce of a broodmare sire's daughters does better or worse than that of all mares bred to the same stallions.

Sires by North American Earnings

The leaders are arranged by North American progeny earnings through November 14, 2004 as supplied to The Blood-Horse. Market Value "M" is given for those stallions whose stud fee is listed as private. **Categorical leaders are in bold.**

Rank, Stallion (Foreign foaled), Year, Sire, Where Stands	2005 Stud Fee	Runners Dom/All	Winners Dom/All	Stakes Winners Dom/All	2004 Dom Earnings	% of All 2004 Earnings
1 **ELUSIVE QUALITY** (93, Gone West), Gainsborough Farm, KY	$100,000	130/134	72/74	5/5	$10,482,260	100%
2 **A.P. INDY** (89, Seattle Slew), Lane's End Farm, KY	$300,000	153/170	83/88	**21/21**	$7,796,597	99%
3 **EL PRADO (Ire)** (89, Sadler's Wells), Adena Springs Kentucky	$100,000	172/195	91/96	16/16	$7,769,363	85%
4 **SMART STRIKE** (92, Mr. Prospector), Lane's End Farm, KY	$35,000	126/129	75/77	11/12	$6,212,921	99%
5 **STORM CAT** (83, Storm Bird), Overbrook Farm, KY	$500,000	93/128	54/70	13/18	$6,192,222	86%
6 **SAINT BALLADO** (89, Halo)	Died, 2002	149/154	73/75	3/3	$6,007,809	98%
7 **AWESOME AGAIN** (94, Deputy Minister), Adena Springs Kentucky	$125,000	98/103	54/54	5/5	$5,968,065	98%
8 **TALE OF THE CAT** (94, Storm Cat), Ashford Stud, KY	$65,000	167/180	94/98	8/10	$5,568,730	97%
9 **CARSON CITY** (87, Mr. Prospector), Overbrook Farm, KY	$35,000	167/174	92/94	9/9	$5,201,049	97%
10 **DYNAFORMER** (85, Roberto), Three Chimneys Farm, KY	$75,000	137/155	58/68	8/10	$5,123,272	93%
11 **DEVIL HIS DUE** (89, Devil's Bag), Margaux Farm, KY	$10,000	185/189	97/98	9/10	$5,028,464	100%
12 **UNBRIDLED'S SONG** (93, Unbridled), Taylor Made Farm, KY	$125,000	148/155	69/70	10/10	$5,027,806	97%
13 **NOT FOR LOVE** (90, Mr. Prospector), Northview Stallion Station, MD	$25,000	170/171	95/95	10/10	$5,024,426	100%
14 **LANGFUHR** (92, Danzig), Lane's End Farm, KY	$30,000	178/182	93/93	9/10	$4,997,527	100%
15 **GRAND SLAM** (95, Gone West), Ashford Stud, KY	$85,000	150/162	81/85	11/12	$4,579,958	84%
16 **WILD RUSH** (94, Wild Again)	NA	119/120	66/66	6/7	$4,536,465	100%
17 **DISTORTED HUMOR** (93, Forty Niner), WinStar Farm, KY	$60,000	116/119	64/65	12/13	$4,479,981	100%
18 **ALPHABET SOUP** (91, Cozzene), Adena Springs Kentucky	$20,000	174/176	**99/101**	10/11	$4,436,793	78%
19 **SMOKE GLACKEN** (94, Two Punch), Gainesway, KY	$30,000	144/146	90/92	8/8	$4,289,948	98%
20 **KRIS S.** (77, Roberto)	Died, 2002	83/105	38/47	9/10	$3,921,745	90%
21 **SKY CLASSIC** (87, Nijinsky II), Pin Oak Stud, KY	$12,500	141/152	65/70	4/7	$3,809,948	97%
22 **SILVER DEPUTY** (85, Deputy Minister), Brookdale Farm, KY	$40,000	152/155	82/84	5/6	$3,808,048	99%
23 **BELONG TO ME** (89, Danzig), Lane's End Farm, KY	$25,000	132/142	72/77	7/9	$3,743,264	91%
24 **ROAR** (93, Forty Niner), Rancho San Miguel, CA	$15,000	145/146	89/90	7/12	$3,731,300	91%
25 **GOLD FEVER** (93, Forty Niner), Metropolitan Stud, NY	$5,000	132/136	75/77	1/1	$3,687,022	99%
26 **GULCH** (84, Mr. Prospector), Lane's End Farm, KY	$50,000	100/140	57/69	5/5	$3,653,712	91%
27 **PULPIT** (94, A.P. Indy), Claiborne Farm, KY	$60,000	93/95	48/49	6/7	$3,649,030	100%
28 **UNBRIDLED** (87, Fappiano)	Died, 2001	99/103	41/41	3/3	$3,632,274	100%
29 **JULES** (94, Forty Niner)	Died, 2003	107/109	57/57	5/7	$3,612,719	100%
30 **HENNESSY** (93, Storm Cat), Ashford Stud, KY	$35,000	138/147	70/71	7/11	$3,589,655	98%
31 **QUIET AMERICAN** (86, Fappiano), Gainsborough Farm, KY	$20,000	142/156	77/82	4/4	$3,560,970	95%
32 **CHEROKEE RUN** (90, Runaway Groom), Darley at Jonabell, KY	$40,000	164/168	89/91	5/5	$3,513,236	98%
33 **PETIONVILLE** (92, Seeking the Gold), Crestwood Farm, KY	$15,000	116/117	61/61	6/6	$3,419,787	100%
34 **VALID EXPECTATIONS** (93, Valid Appeal), Lane's End Texas	$17,500	128/128	80/80	7/7	$3,333,410	100%
35 **GRINDSTONE** (93, Unbridled), Overbrook Farm, KY	$7,500	93/96	45/46	4/5	$3,240,144	99%
36 **STORM BOOT** (89, Storm Cat), Crestwood Farm, KY	$15,000	170/170	88/88	7/8	$3,234,962	100%
37 **RUNAWAY GROOM** (79, Blushing Groom), Vinery, KY	$12,500	164/169	97/98	7/7	$3,227,597	99%
38 **AMERICAN CHANCE** (89, Cure the Blues)	Died, 2004	113/115	56/56	6/6	$3,225,627	100%
39 **HALO'S IMAGE** (91, Halo), Bridlewood Farm, FL	$10,000	103/103	55/55	2/2	$3,211,111	100%
40 **TABASCO CAT** (91, Storm Cat)	Died, 2004	101/105	52/52	5/6	$3,174,186	99%
41 **SKIP AWAY** (93, Skip Trial), Hopewell Farm, KY	$15,000	120/120	76/76	8/8	$3,117,751	100%
42 **INDIAN CHARLIE** (95, In Excess), Airdrie Stud, KY	$15,000	94/95	65/65	7/8	$3,094,769	100%
43 **GLITTERMAN** (85, Dewan), Wafare Farm, KY	$15,000	138/138	72/72	5/6	$3,049,286	100%
44 **ALLEN'S PROSPECT** (82, Mr. Prospector)	Died, 2003	186/187	97/97	4/4	$3,042,495	100%
45 **GONE WEST** (84, Mr. Prospector), Mill Ridge Farm, KY	$150,000	85/141	41/56	4/5	$3,040,147	78%
46 **FOREST WILDCAT** (91, Storm Cat), Brookdale Farm, KY	$35,000	163/166	81/83	6/8	$3,034,514	90%
47 **CRAFTY PROSPECTOR** (79, Mr. Prospector), Brookdale Farm, KY	$10,000	128/135	77/81	5/5	$3,033,269	98%
48 **IN EXCESS (Ire)** (87, Siberian Express), Vessels Stallion Farm, CA	$25,000	102/102	56/56	6/6	$2,962,323	99%
49 **GENERAL MEETING** (88, Seattle Slew), Golden Eagle Farm, CA	$10,000	91/91	48/48	6/6	$2,952,105	100%
50 **BOSTON HARBOR** (94, Capote), JBBA Shizunai Stallion Station, Japan	NA	125/125	72/72	5/5	$2,930,483	100%
51 **POLISH NUMBERS** (87, Danzig)	Died, 2002	131/134	66/67	7/7	$2,892,259	98%
52 **WITH APPROVAL** (86, Caro), Brookdale Farm, KY	$5,000	147/156	77/81	3/3	$2,872,536	98%
53 **ROYAL ACADEMY** (87, Nijinsky II), Ashford Stud, KY	$17,500	111/191	55/79	3/13	$2,869,507	75%
54 **JADE HUNTER** (84, Mr. Prospector), Hill 'n' Dale Farms, KY	$10,000	108/115	57/61	4/4	$2,868,508	98%
55 **WEST BY WEST** (89, Gone West), Jockey Club Stud of Turkey	$5,000	148/150	79/79	2/3	$2,862,842	100%
56 **REGAL CLASSIC** (85, Vice Regent), McMahon of Saratoga, NY	$10,000	139/140	69/69	3/4	$2,853,789	100%
57 **SOUVENIR COPY** (95, Mr. Prospector), Golden Eagle Farm, CA	$10,000	121/123	65/66	2/2	$2,836,171	99%
58 **CRYPTOCLEARANCE** (84, Fappiano), Margaux Farm, KY	$12,500	**216/222**	**99/102**	3/3	$2,826,232	99%
59 **HONOR GRADES** (88, Danzig)	Died, 2002	133/134	62/62	2/2	$2,809,848	100%
60 **LIT DE JUSTICE** (90, El Gran Senor), Magali Farms, CA	$6,000	110/118	62/64	2/3	$2,767,487	96%
61 **NUMEROUS** (91, Mr. Prospector), Haras du Quesnay, Fr	$5,000	119/124	49/52	3/4	$2,762,165	98%
62 **GILDED TIME** (90, Timeless Moment), Vinery, KY	$17,500	139/146	71/73	4/5	$2,748,063	93%
63 **STORMY ATLANTIC** (94, Storm Cat), Hill 'n' Dale Farms, KY	$15,000	121/122	66/67	5/5	$2,726,546	99%
64 **WILD AGAIN** (80, Icecapade)	Pnsd	107/110	53/54	5/5	$2,714,363	100%
65 **PEAKS AND VALLEYS** (92, Mt. Livermore), Pin Oak Stud, KY	$10,000	162/163	91/91	5/6	$2,693,465	100%
66 **HONOUR AND GLORY** (93, Relaunch), Ashford Stud, KY	$15,000	158/164	81/83	5/5	$2,690,017	99%
67 **PLEASANT COLONY** (78, His Majesty)	Died, 2002	46/54	23/27	3/4	$2,680,859	42%
68 **DIXIE BRASS** (89, Dixieland Band)	Died, 2002	110/110	64/64	0/0	$2,668,763	100%
69 **HOLY BULL** (91, Great Above), Darley at Jonabell, KY	$15,000	135/139	68/68	2/2	$2,668,719	98%
70 **MR. GREELEY** (92, Gone West), Spendthrift Farm, KY	$50,000	157/162	76/80	2/3	$2,625,145	92%
71 **FRENCH DEPUTY** (92, Deputy Minister), Arrowfield Stud, Aust	NA	91/95	55/57	5/6	$2,613,782	98%
72 **TOUCH GOLD** (94, Deputy Minister), Adena Springs Kentucky	$50,000	121/125	51/52	4/4	$2,608,959	99%
73 **GOLD CASE** (94, Forty Niner), Adena Springs Kentucky	$7,500	126/127	76/76	5/5	$2,599,165	100%
74 **BOLD EXECUTIVE** (84, Bold Ruckus), Gardiner Farms Ltd., ON	$10,000	85/85	41/41	4/4	$2,594,784	100%
75 **TWO PUNCH** (83, Mr. Prospector), Northview Stallion Station, MD	$25,000	129/133	66/66	5/5	$2,591,910	100%

2004 Leading First-Crop Sires

For stallions that stand, will stand, or stood (deceased) in North America (stallions exported prior to the 2000 breeding season are excluded), and have runners in North America. As supplied to The Blood-Horse by The Jockey Club Information Systems, this includes monies earned in NA (through Nov 14, 2004), Eng and Ire (Nov 11), Fr (Nov 12), Ger (Nov 7), Italy (July 31), and the UAE (Oct 28). **No Southern Hemisphere information is reflected.** Cumulative stakes winners includes all countries; some additional foreign foals may be included in the foal count. **Categorical leaders are in bold.**

Current Rank	Previous Week's Rank	Stallion (Foreign foaled), Year, Sire, Where Stands	2005 Stud Fee	Rnrs 2yos (% foals)	Wnrs 2yos (% foals)	SW/ SH	Yearling Average	(Chief Earner, Earnings)	Earnings
1	1	YES IT'S TRUE (96, Is It True), Three Chimneys Farm, KY	$25,000	64 ...39 (61%)	13 (20%)	4/5	$75,676	(Proud Accolade, $355,200)	**$1,292,306**
2	2	SUCCESSFUL APPEAL (96, Valid Appeal), Walmac Farm, KY	$25,000	35 ...21 (60%)	15 (43%)	4/7	$42,067	(Lunarpal, $284,677)	$1,176,456
3	3	GIANT'S CAUSEWAY (97, Storm Cat), Ashford Stud, KY	$135,000	**138** ...**61** (44%)	**17** (12%)	4/5	**$291,921**	(Shamardal, $359,680)	$1,084,042
4	4	FUSAICHI PEGASUS (97, Mr. Prospector), Ashford Stud, KY	$100,000	81 ...27 (33%)	13 (16%)	4/6	$290,008	(Roman Ruler, $330,800)	$1,055,341
5	6	CAPE CANAVERAL (96, Mr. Prospector), Overbrook Farm, KY	$15,000	56 ...33 (59%)	13 (23%)	3/8	$32,032	(Galaxy, $106,384)	$789,195
6	5	MORE THAN READY (97, Southern Halo), Vinery, KY	$20,000	59 ...32 (54%)	15 (25%)	3/4	$77,994	(Ready's Gal, $155,200)	$771,557
7	7	DIXIE UNION (97, Dixieland Band), Lane's End Farm, KY	$30,000	51 ...23 (45%)	12 (24%)	1/4	$108,623	(Im a Dixie Girl, $145,200)	$641,655
8	8	PRECISE END (97, End Sweep), Lakland North, NY	$6,000	45 ...25 (56%)	10 (22%)	2/5	$28,973	(Accurate, $115,688)	$594,109
9	9	BERNSTEIN (97, Storm Cat), Castleton Lyons, KY	$15,000	35 ...16 (46%)	10 (29%)	2/5	$22,482	(Sweet Solairo, $133,683)	$469,002
10	10	RUNNING STAG (94, Cozzene), Adena Springs South, FL	$7,500	78 ...31 (40%)	9 (12%)	1/1	$11,981	(Running Bobcats, $95,680)	$448,439
11	20	DANCE MASTER (97, Gone West), Padua Stables, FL	$3,500	17 ...9 (53%)	4 (24%)	1/1	$13,928	(Flamenco, $303,085)	$372,573
12	11	WAR CHANT (97, Danzig), Three Chimneys Farm, KY	$60,000	48 ...16 (33%)	11 (23%)	2/2	$206,107	(Up Like Thunder, $99,020)	$360,837
13	12	SWEETSOUTHERNSAINT (95, Saint Ballado), Ocala Stud Farm, FL	$2,500	51 ...24 (47%)	11 (22%)	0/2	$12,318	(Alexandersrun, $72,708)	$333,383
14	16	STRAIGHT MAN (96, Saint Ballado), Signature Stallions, FL	$6,000	68 ...28 (41%)	10 (15%)	0/2	$35,434	(Inrightclasstime, $42,920)	$329,495
15	13	CATIENUS (94, Storm Cat), Highcliff Farm, NY	$3,500	44 ...28 (64%)	11 (25%)	1/2	$10,451	(Kathern's Cat, $71,390)	$327,610
16	15	TIGER RIDGE (95, Storm Cat), Hartley/De Renzo, Walmac South, FL	$7,500	58 ...20 (34%)	8 (14%)	1/2	$33,750	(Anthony J., $103,630)	$325,294
17	14	WESTERN EXPRESSION (96, Gone West), Highcliff Farm, NY	$10,000	44 ...20 (44%)	6 (13%)	0/2	$4,800	(Winning Expression, $78,138)	$319,032
18	18	OLD TOPPER (95, Gilded Time), Tommy Town Thoroughbreds, CA	$5,000	34 ...16 (47%)	9 (26%)	1/3	$7,280	(Top Money, $94,560)	$312,473
19	17	LEMON DROP KID (96, Kingmambo), Lane's End Farm, KY	$50,000	55 ...21 (38%)	8 (15%)	0/2	$146,980	(Peppermint Lilly, $53,970)	$311,068
20	19	YANKEE VICTOR (96, Saint Ballado), Airdrie Stud, KY	$15,000	70 ...26 (37%)	11 (16%)	0/0	$61,829	(Real Dandy, $51,385)	$307,488
21	22	LION HEARTED (96, Storm Cat), Northview Stallion Station, MD	$5,000	46 ...10 (22%)	8 (17%)	2/3	$34,913	(Chocolate Brown, $76,206)	$285,152
22	21	GOLDEN MISSILE (95, A.P. Indy), Adena Springs Kentucky	$25,000	63 ...20 (32%)	4 (6%)	1/2	$102,331	(Inspiring, $115,800)	$280,309
23	23	ANEES (97, Unbridled)	Died, 2003	38 ...14 (37%)	5 (13%)	1/2	$54,722	(Swither, $128,654)	$261,565
24	24	STEPHEN GOT EVEN (96, A.P. Indy), Lane's End Farm, KY	$12,500	54 ...22 (41%)	9 (9%)	0/1	$45,489	(Didycheatamandhowe, $76,330)	$242,422
25	29	HIGH YIELD (97, Storm Cat), Ashford Stud, KY	$15,000	75 ...20 (27%)	6 (8%)	0/2	$83,611	(Stormy Jim, $62,290)	$237,712
26	25	MAGIC CAT (95, Storm Cat), Valor Farm, TX	$3,500	46 ...25 (54%)	10 (22%)	1/1	$9,067	(Major League, $67,100)	$220,519
27	30	UNTUTTABLE (96, Unbridled), Stonehedge Farm South, FL	$5,000	21 ...13 (62%)	4 (19%)	1/1	$32,620	(Favalora, $52,390)	$217,577
28	27	CHESTER HOUSE (95, Mr. Prospector)	Died, 2003	56 ...26 (46%)	6 (11%)	0/0	$59,444	(Exceptional Ride, $61,465)	$215,672
29	26	CHIEF SEATTLE (97, Seattle Slew), Spendthrift Farm, KY	$10,000	57 ...23 (40%)	5 (9%)	0/1	$47,735	(Bold Outlook, $68,400)	$215,534
30	28	RICHTER SCALE (94, Habitony), Wafare Farm, KY	$10,000	37 ...13 (35%)	4 (11%)	1/1	$68,399	(Quite a Ruckus, $110,653)	$195,033

2004 Leading Sires of 2-Year-Olds

For stallions that stand, will stand, or stood (deceased) in North America (stallions exported prior to the 2000 breeding season are excluded), and have runners in North America. As supplied to The Blood-Horse by The Jockey Club Information Systems, Inc., this includes monies earned in North America through Nov 14 2004; Eng and Ire (Nov 11); Fr (Nov 12); Ger (Nov 7); Italy (July 31); and the UAE (Oct 28). Cumulative stakes winners includes all countries; some additional foreign foals may be included in the foal count. Market Value "M" is given for those stallions whose stud fee is listed as private. (¶ indicates a sire represented by his first crop to race) **Categorical leaders are in bold.**

Current Rank	Previous Week's Rank	Stallion (Foreign foaled), Year, Sire, Where Stands	2005 Stud Fee	2004 2yos	Rnrs/ Wnrs	SWs/ SHs	(Chief Earner, Earnings)	2004 Earnings	Cumulative 2yoWnrs (%Foals)	2yoSWs (%Foals)
1	1	STORM CAT (83, Storm Bird), Overbrook Farm, KY	$500,000	65	29/16	4/6	(Sweet Catomine, $799,800)	**$1,872,334**	931...197 (21%)	49 (5%)
2	2	¶ YES IT'S TRUE (96, Is It True), Three Chimneys Farm, KY	$25,000	64	39/13	4/5	(Proud Accolade, $355,200)	$1,292,306	64...13 (20%)	4 (6%)
3	3	¶ SUCCESSFUL APPEAL (96, Valid Appeal), Walmac Farm, KY	$25,000	35	21/15	4/7	(Lunarpal, $284,677)	$1,176,456	35...15 (43%)	4 (11%)
4	6	AWESOME AGAIN (94, Deputy Minister), Adena Springs Kentucky	$125,000	61	21/7	2/2	(Wilko, $880,494)	$1,092,503	209...23 (11%)	5 (2%)
5	4	¶ GIANT'S CAUSEWAY (97, Storm Cat), Ashford Stud, KY	$135,000	**138**	**61**/17	4/5	(Shamardal, $359,680)	$1,084,042	138...17 (12%)	4 (3%)
6	5	¶ FUSAICHI PEGASUS (97, Storm Cat), Ashford Stud, KY	$100,000	81	27/13	4/6	(Roman Ruler, $330,800)	$1,055,341	81...13 (16%)	4 (5%)
7	7	¶ VALID EXPECTATIONS (93, Valid Appeal), Lane's End Texas	$17,500	75	31/18	3/7	(Leaving On My Mind, $283,373)	$974,034	231...74 (32%)	10 (4%)
8	12	¶ CAPE CANAVERAL (96, Mr. Prospector), Overbrook Farm, KY	$15,000	56	33/13	3/8	(Galaxy, $106,384)	$789,195	56...13 (23%)	3 (5%)
9	8	NORTHERN AFLEET (93, Afleet), Taylor Made Farm, KY	NA	37	13/7	1/1	(Afleet Alex, $680,800)	$788,590	209...41 (20%)	6 (3%)
10	9	PETIONVILLE (92, Seeking the Gold), Crestwood Farm, KY	$15,000	44	25/8	2/3	(Runway Model, $447,050)	$787,140	209...41 (20%)	6 (3%)
11	10	¶ MORE THAN READY (97, Southern Halo), Vinery, KY	$20,000	59	32/15	3/4	(Ready's Gal, $155,200)	$771,557	59...15 (25%)	3 (5%)
12	11	KINGMAMBO (90, Mr. Prospector), Lane's End Farm, KY	$300,000	65	25/8	2/4	(Divine Proportions, $481,006)	$751,790	529...68 (13%)	15 (3%)
13	14	CARSON CITY (87, Mr. Prospector), Overbrook Farm, KY	$35,000	73	30/14	2/5	(Classic Elegance, $204,006)	$713,273	759...189 (25%)	31 (4%)
14	13	THUNDER GULCH (92, Gulch), Ashford Stud, KY	$40,000	124	47/10	2/2	(Sense of Style, $369,000)	$704,671	531...50 (9%)	7 (1%)
15	19	WILD EVENT (93, Wild Again), Bridlewood Farm, FL	$7,500	33	16/9	1/1	(Aclassysassylassy, $488,800)	$674,955	80...21 (26%)	1 (1%)
16	15	¶ DIXIE UNION (97, Dixieland Band), Lane's End Farm, KY	$30,000	51	23/12	1/4	(Im a Dixie Girl, $145,200)	$641,655	51...12 (24%)	1 (2%)
17	16	FOXTRAIL (90, Heading Back Home)	NA	68	19/6	2/4	(Wholelottabourbon, $286,230)	$613,200	133...17 (13%)	4 (3%)
18	20	A. P. JET (89, Fappiano), Sugar Maple Farm, NY	$5,000	93	40/13	2/3	(Karakorum Splendor, $121,650)	$604,803	298...34 (11%)	7 (2%)
19	21	SMART STRIKE (92, Mr. Prospector), Lane's End Farm, KY	$35,000	48	23/10	3/6	(Pelham Bay, $118,702)	$604,423	276...46 (17%)	8 (3%)
20	18	¶ PRECISE END (97, End Sweep), Lakland North, NY	$6,000	45	25/10	2/5	(Accurate, $115,688)	$594,109	45...10 (22%)	2 (4%)
21	17	WHISKEY WISDOM (93, Wild Again), Windfields Farm, ON	$5,000	36	10/6	2/4	(Moonshine Justice, $283,914)	$591,731	167...16 (10%)	4 (2%)
22	22	PEAKS AND VALLEYS (92, Mt. Livermore), Pin Oak Stud, KY	$10,000	63	23/12	3/3	(Higher World, $213,210)	$563,610	325...47 (14%)	6 (2%)
23	26	AFTERNOON DEELITES (92, Private Terms), Clear Creek Stud, LA	$4,000	67	27/13	2/4	(Three Hour Nap, $158,400)	$557,912	286...56 (20%)	8 (3%)
24	24	A.P. INDY (89, Seattle Slew), Lane's End Farm, KY	$300,000	81	22/7	1/3	(Dance With Ravens, $223,820)	$549,502	628...92 (15%)	16 (3%)
25	28	TALE OF THE CAT (94, Storm Cat), Ashford Stud, KY	$65,000	65	30/13	0/1	(Canadian Gem, $98,205)	$528,414	296...64 (22%)	9 (3%)
26	23	SWISS YODELER (94, Eastern Echo), Pepper Oaks Farm, CA	$5,000	81	28/13	0/2	(Mr. Fondue, $82,528)	$522,273	181...43 (24%)	5 (3%)
27	29	DOUBLE HONOR (95, Gone West), Farnsworth Farms, FL	$3,500	62	35/9	2/4	(Cut the Mustard, $70,400)	$519,479	192...66 (34%)	3 (2%)
28	27	WHEATON (90, Alydar), Pin Oak Lane Farm, PA	$3,500	88	35/19	2/4	(Departing Now, $71,106)	$515,776	239...58 (24%)	4 (2%)
29	25	DANZIG (77, Northern Dancer)	Pnsd	37	15/9	1/3	(Ad Valorem, $258,357)	$511,489	994...230 (23%)	52 (5%)
30	35	STORMY ATLANTIC (94, Storm Cat), Hill 'n' Dale Farms, KY	$15,000	82	40/16	1/3	(Frosty Royalty, $74,060)	$497,542	209...40 (19%)	4 (2%)
31	31	VICTORY GALLOP (95, Cryptoclearance), WinStar Farm, KY	$30,000	55	24/6	2/3	(Victorious Ami, $188,600)	$490,009	138...17 (12%)	4 (3%)

When you observe first time starters, or lightly raced maidens, or horses making an initial switch to turf, dirt or mud, use the charts from *The Blood Horse Magazine®* as follows. The charts from *The Blood Horse Magazine®* will show whether the sires or dam sires have produced significant turf winners; this should be considered in first time or early turf experiences for the horse. Sires and dam sires that produce a high percentage of winners (which would be demonstrated by the sire or dam sire's placement on the first crop or second crop lists) should be considered in maiden races. These charts can be a valuable resource when races are extremely complicated and hard to decipher due to large field turf races, maiden special weight, and maiden claiming races. There are additional resources through various services that will provide detailed information regarding first time starters as opposed to second time starters for various sires and dam sires. However, I consider this information not as pertinent as the overall success of the sire in producing winners as shown by the charts. In other words, while it may be significant that a horse produced by sire A tends to win more in his second start than in his first, I believe that this is outweighed by the fact the sire produces winners. The horse should probably be bet in his first, second and third race to determine whether he has the ability, which should have been passed down through his breeding.

One of the original or highly taught concepts in breeding is what is known as the "dosage index." The dosage concept was that horses from certain breeding lines were assigned points. These points were passed through down to their progeny. Horses from each generation were designated as the leaders of their generation, and accordingly, passed higher points down to their decendants. The points were totaled for an individual horse, and the horse received a number, which was known as the dosage number. The primary rational behind the theory was that it would predict winners of distance races, particular at Classic distances. Classic distances are greater than one and three-sixteenth miles, as represented by the three Classic races of The Kentucky Derby, The Preakness, and The Belmont Stakes. The primary time when the dosage index was discussed was around the Kentucky Derby, where no horse with a dosage greater than four had ever won the Derby. However, because the dosage index had been tinkered with endlessly by changing the particular horses that made up the best of the generation, the dosage theory became less reliable.

Therefore, while the dosage theory can provide help, it is not an absolute concerning distance. The dosage index you see can be useful as to the likelihood that a horse will run well at distance. One of the great inadequacies to my mind of the dosage index, even in regard to the Kentucky Derby, was that while horses "without dosage" had not won the Kentucky Derby they had often ran second and third (sometimes in extremely close races with the victorious animal). Therefore, in regard to distance breeding, I believe that instead of using dosage (other than as a general guideline), it is more appropriate to create charts that show that certain horses produce progeny that do better at certain distances. Conversely, certain horses are more likely to produce sprint contenders when their offspring run on the track.

Another common handicapping index that people utilize for turf and mud breeding are the Tomlinson Ratings, which can be found for most horses in the DRF. The general concept is that if the mud rating is higher than 320 points, it is a horse that merits consideration on a wet track. If the turf rating is more than 280 points, it merits consideration in a grass race. Reprinted with the permission of the DRF is its explanation of Tomlinson Ratings. While Tomlinson Ratings oversimplify the ability of the horse based on breeding, they can be a useful handicapping tool if the handicapper is not aware of the value of the sire and dam sire breeding (based on the individual charts already discussed).

TOMLINSON RATINGS

Every horse whose sire and maternal grandsire have had a meaningful sample of offspring is assigned two Tomlinson Ratings – one that assesses his likely aptitude for grass and one for muddy or sloppy dirt tracks. These ratings, updated twice each year, are derived from tens of thousands of race results. The ratings, which appear next to the "Turf" and "Wet" headings in each horse's career box, can range from 0 (totally unsuccessful) to 480 (spectacularly successful.) A dash (–) means that the horse's sire has had an insufficient number of runners to create a rating. An asterisk (*) means that the sire has had a limited number, or fewer than 80 starters, on a particular surface.

Tomlinson Ratings, in career box

Life	25	5	4	6	$186,397	100	D.Fst	19	3	4	4	$117,670 96
2000	5	0	1	1	$14,440	96	Wet (400)	3	2	0	1	$54,777 100
1999	12	3	1	3	$135,540	100	Turf (320)	3	0	0	1	$13,950 89
Bel	3	1	0	1	$44,700	96	Dist	7	3	1	0	$55,384 91

Tomlinson Ratings are most useful when a horse has no or few starts on grass or wet dirt and become less useful once a horse has clearly established his ability on these surfaces. They also may suggest whether a horse beginning his career on the dirt should be given less consideration now than when he tries the grass in a subsequent start.

MUDDERS AND TURFERS

Mud Rating of 320 +
Merits further consideration as a horse who could run particularly well over a wet track.

Turf Rating of 280 +
Merits further consideration as a horse who could run particularly well over the grass.

"A horse gallops with his lungs, perseveres with his heart; and wins with his character."
— Frederico Tesio, *Breeding the Racehorse*

An additional factor that should be mentioned in regard to breeding is the selection of the jockey to ride a horse on a surface switch (i.e., a horse running for the first time in a turf race). This may provide an indication of the trainer's intent regarding the horse. If your turf breeding analysis indicates that a horse may do well on the turf, and the trainer selects a good quality turf jockey, this is usually a strong indication that the horse will run well on the turf. This would be an example of one of the areas where I would emphasize breeding extensively in my handicapping. If I observe that a horse has outstanding turf breeding based on his lineage, and then I see a turf work and a good turf jockey aboard, I will usually play the animal. This is regardless of the animal's prior form on the dirt. These same factors are applicable to a switch back to dirt, a distance change, or a move to an off or muddy track.

All individual handicappers have a particular "mud line" (mud breeding) that they consider important. The description of the track is essential here because a track surface considered being "off" does not necessarily describe the exact condition of the surface for handicapping purposes. Each handicapper should attempt to keep track of sires and dam sires that appear to produce notable winners on off tracks. Below I will provide you with two particular sires which if observed in the sire lines of a horse are an indication the horse may run well in the mud or slop. As a general rule (this is a broad based rule), many handicappers feel that horses with turf breeding will run better at off tracks than they do on fast dirt. Therefore, if at an absolute loss on how to handicap a race when the track is off consider looking at the sires that produce successful turf offspring as shown in the *Blood Horse* charts. I caution that this is not a strong handicapping angle, and is useful only in a race you feel you must include multiple pick 3 or pick 4 type wagers. I offer two sires I consider to be two of the predominate (and relatively common) sires that you will see in the lineage in various racehorses, and that do well on off tracks:

— Halo
— Relaunch

> **"I love… to see the domestic animals reassert their native rights, any evidence that they have not wholly lost their original wild habits and vigor… the seeds of instinct are preserved under the… Hides of … horses, like seeds in the bowels of the earth, an indefinite period."**
> **— Henry David Thoreaux, from the essay *Walking***

If you do not consider yourself an outstanding handicapper regarding the breeding angle, you are in good company. Many of the people who breed these horses are virtually stunned at the success that some of the animals achieve, and conversely amazed at the lack of success that certain well-bred horses have. One universal-breeding angle that should be mentioned is the actual breeders themselves. *The Blood Horse Magazine*® describes notable breeding operations around the country that have had successes, and runs articles on others in the horse industry that may be pertinent to the handicapper. The reason for these breeders' success is indicative of their knowledge that certain combinations produce racehorses that are likely to do well. While at a national level these successful breeders can be identified when their horses run, my suggestion is more specific. I advocate that in the particular region for which you are handicapping, you identify two or three breeders, much as you would do for jockeys or trainers. When you have identified two or three breeders who do well and have a significant number of horses that run well in your particular jurisdiction, always look for the horses from these farms. Look to the first time starter and maiden races, and consider playing on this basis alone (unless they appear to be clearly outmatched).

I offer two general observations I feel are pertinent to turf horses.

1. Horses coming from Europe (and particularly horses bred in Ireland) will generally do well on tracks in the United States, which are more yielding. Generally, horses in Europe run on tracks that are more yielding and the breeding is more conducive to animals that will have success on those tracks. Most United States West Coast turf courses tend to be hard, and European turf horses often do poorly there, but may perform well on yielding tracks found on our East Coast.

2. First time starters also running in a first time turf race generally do not win on the West Coast of the United States. In other words, when a horse makes the first start of its career in a turf race these horses do not usually emerge victorious. This does not mean that they will not win in a second or third start, only that they do not usually win the initial outing. This is not to say that a horse that makes his initial start on dirt and then switches to turf for its second or third outing will not be successful. This is a broad generalization, but in large fields, it may be beneficial to disregard first

time starters that are also first time turf. This does not appear to hold as true for East Coast tracks, yet it has some validity.

Successful players will primarily use the resources of the charts they develop about mud sires, turf sires, and distance sires to pick their selections. The more you feel comfortable with the breeding of horses, the more you will periodically see an opportunity to utilize breeding as a handicapping angle that many others will not see. The novice handicapper will not have any concept on how breeding can effect a horse, particularly on a surface switch or a distance move. Since a horse's form does not necessarily transfer well between dirt and turf and vice versa, breeding knowledge may provide the insight for the handicapper to pick a winner that many others would not normally see.

Turf Overlay's
By Bill Heller

NOTES:

6
Trip Handicapping

"A trainer can always find an excuse for a defeat, whether it's a mistake in judgement by the jockey or the conditions of the track, or a bit of poor racing luck."
— Billy Reed

The nature of trip handicapping lends itself enormously to the observant handicapper. As we will see later in the Zen sections, "Zen" is closely linked to keen observational skills, and so it is essential that the horseplayer know how trip handicapping works. Often in the books I suggest to the reader, I have advocated older books like the original Bible of horse handicapping, *Ainslie's Complete Guide to Thoroughbred Racing*. The reason why I suggest older books is that the more recently published books on speed, pace, Tomlinson Ratings, etc., are often so mathematically complicated as to be virtually indecipherable.

It is foolish to think that a horserace with so many variables, both human and animal, can be solved by affixing various numbers to speed, pace, breeding, weight, etc. Instead it is more important to understand the value of pace figures, speed figures, or breeding ratios, and how they are applicable in the overall concept of how a race was run, or is *likely* to be run. Ideally, the concept of trip handi-capping should put all the pieces together and allow handicapping science to meet handicapping art.

The idea of trip handicapping is to look at how a previous race was run, and to determine how a particular horse finished, viewed in the context of the horse's trip. Did he benefit from a speed bias, a path bias, a slow pace, no other speed horses, other horses having trouble, etc.? It is looking at the overall concept of how the horse ran in a previous race, and then predicting how the next race will be run. If you review the two following examples, you will immediately see the relevance.

Horse A's last race: he goes directly to the front on a speed favor-ing track, runs in the one path all the way, misses some bumping which occurred on the first turn involving the only two other speed horses, goes through sluggish fractions and wins without being urged or challenged. (Obviously, Horse A got a dream run.)

The concept of Horse A's next race (the one you are now handicap-ping): It is at the same track and distance, although the speed bias has disappeared and the track favors neither speed nor closers. Horse A is in a seven horse race in the six-post position, and is one of four hors-es that wants the early lead; there are three strong closing horses. (It is clear from this race hypothesis, a prediction of factors which could effect how the race goes—that this race might pan out very different-ly for Horse A, he might still win, but he will not win easily and the odds will be low even if he does—it is likely that I would go with oth-ers that offer better potential returns.)

The example above is a clear example of how the trip concept should affect your analysis of a horse and a horserace. As a corollary, let's assume that Horse A gets burned in a speed duel and a closer wins going away, and Horse A fades to last by fifteen lengths and is not urged down the stretch. Now, the same Horse A will likely get under-bet in his next start. I am hopeful it is a race with a speed bias, an inside post, filled with closers and no speed; then I will be all over Horse A.

Trip handicapping does not easily lend itself to a number. For example, if Horse A's Beyer Speed Figures were 85, then 65, and final-ly 90 in the hoped for third race scenario, what is the legitimate speed figure? No, you do not average them! The answer is that it does not matter: The astute handicapper must assess the figures *in the context* of how the last races *were* run and how the subsequent races are *likely* to be run. With these concepts in hand, a 65 Beyer Speed Figure horse now has the potential (with the right scenario) to pop a 90+ figure. What a wagering opportunity.

> **"The point of warriorship is to work personally with**
> **our situation now, as it is."**
> **Chogyam Trungpa, Shambhala,** *The Sacred Path of the Warrior*

So how do you trip handicap? Most authors who discuss trip handicapping give credit to harness racing. Sulky drivers with the ability to get the best position are often victorious. While I agree with the concept that most horseplayers may relate trip handicapping to harness racing, I see a much better example in Greyhound dog racing. After you have read this chapter, go watch a few dog races and buy a puppy program; after you watch a few races, you will come back forever understanding the concept of trip handicapping. Dogs that go to the front win a disproportionate amount of races, sometimes because of speed bias, but more often because they do not get in bumping incidents with other dogs, nor are they forced to go wide (though some dogs prefer to run wide which always costs time). I make a statement here that I guarantee will help you understands trips: Go to the dogs.

OK, I know you are saying that dogs do not have jockeys, and therefore jockeys will ensure good trips and limit mishaps for your horses. My retired racing Greyhound "Van" is smart, and while his head is somewhat narrow, limiting his brain size, realize that jockeys have a disproportionately smaller head than you do also. Hmmm. In addition, the greyhound does not have deceit in his heart. In plain English, the dog wants to run, and he will not be strangling himself on the backstretch to stall his momentum, the way a deceitful jockey will to a horse. Now you know a little about puppy racing (a bonus in a horse handicapping book), and how it can show you trip concepts clearly.

What affects the analysis of a trip? The answer is everything. The key to trip handicapping is to be ultra-vigilant, you must watch replays, and you must scour for all the horses you are considering. Videotape replays are the ammo of a trip handicapper's arsenal, because often the comment line in the racing form can be misleading. The DRF tends to overemphasize bumping and blocking at the expense of the path the horse ran in, and very rarely denotes speed and pace bias at a track, and even more infrequently identifies brutally inept rides by those jockeys with greyhound size brains. The good handicapper must watch the race, and the replays, to see how an animal's finish must be considered in the context of the trip which it received. Then a cogent analysis can be made of the upcoming race to see what trip the horse might now receive. You can make a lot of money on a horse like Horse A discussed earlier, that wins only one of four or five starts. Trip handicapping will show you when to pound Horse A and when to shun him like the plague (in his case maybe the chestnut plague as opposed to the black plague).

> **"Let your own discretion be your tutor. Suit the action to the word, the word to the action."**
> **— William Shakespeare**

So now you have the videos of previous races (or access to them), you know what a bad/good puppy trip looks like (remember you saw a race or two), you have your other handicapping techniques about speed, pace, breeding, etc. So what do you look for in your video fantasy? (No, not that kind of video.) Set out in the following paragraphs are factors you should be on the lookout for in an effort to determine how a trip transpired.

PROBLEMS

The things a trip handicapper observes first are problems a horse had in a race. Broke slow, hit the gate, hopped at the start, blocked in mid stretch, floated wide, premature move, etc. The list is endless. A bit later on I will discuss specific difficulties I consider being extremely noteworthy, but here regarding problems I emphasize three generally important factors:

1. Some problems are not pertinent. The classic example is a stone cold closer that gets a poor break; because he probably is going to be taken back anyway, this should likely be disregarded. Bumps may not be severe (they may not change a horse's motion for

instance), and bad breaks may not be too big a deal. When you trip handicap, you must also consider whether or how a problem influenced a race.

2. When assessing problems you must look for the converse—a dream trip. An absence of problems is just as noteworthy about a horse's trip as when he has trouble.

3. Just because a horse encounters problems does not mean he will do well the next time. He might not have been a factor regardless. Do not overstate the effect of a problem; simply note it and how it might have affected the animal's performance.

I believe the following problems can have a strong influence on the outcome of a horse's performance in a race. This list is not all-inclusive and you should add to it other problems you observe in your own handicapping that you find influential.

- A bad break from the gate of any type by horses that want to be in the lead. This is particularly true in sprint races.

- Horses that are floated wide on the final turn. This is especially harmful for strong closer types.

- Horses forced to, or that choose to, run wide around any turn, not necessarily the final one. A horse loses about one length for every path he is wide on a turn. A length is the difference between winning and losing in a large number of races.

- If a horse's momentum is altered (i.e., he is checked, shut off, yanked, pulled, blocked, strangled, ad infinitum). Specifically, this is relevant if it occurs at the point in the race where the horse usually makes his move. Clearly, if a closer is blocked on the backstretch, it may not matter too much. However, if he is shut off down the home stretch, this may be key. Similarly, if a speed horse is shut off early, he has possibly been negatively affected. Furthermore, horses that are allowed to run after the finish line should be monitored. Sometimes a horse will be held up, and then show flashes of speed even after the finish line. This speed after the finish is a great omen.

- Any problem that occurs during the final stretch run should be considered. This is where good jockeys get good, bad jockeys get bad, and incompetent jockeys get like Frankie Dettori on Swain in the Breeders Cup Classic.

"Horse sense is the thing that a horse has which keeps him from betting on people."
— W. C. Fields

FACTORS OTHER THAN PROBLEMS

In addition to problems, there are important factors the trip handicapper notes as things that affect how a horse travels:

1. "Track biases"—There are all types of track biases and they will all affect how a horse runs (the most obvious is a speed horse on a speed favoring track). The astute handicapper notes whether a bias existed when the horse ran, and then how the particular horse ran his race. Here are some biases you should watch for:
   - Speed favoring (common)
   - Closer favoring (uncommon—and a hell of a betting opportunity)
   - Path biases (dead rail, deep three path, speed rail, etc.)
   - Distance biases (The most common distance biases are tracks that seem to allow "short" horses to carry their speed for longer distances, or conversely tracks that seem to tire horses and insure that sprinters stretching out always lose. As a specific track example, Turf Paradise in Phoenix, Arizona, often has a distance bias, which favors horses that should tire but allows them to hold up longer).

2. "Pace"—Trip handicappers should familiarize themselves with how pace can hurt or harm (see Chapter 4). If a horse was hurt or helped by a pace scenario, this is instrumental in assessing the horse's performance, and even more important in predicting how the pace will occur in today's race.

3. "Middle Moves"—The trip handicapper's Holy Grail. When a horse makes a so-called middle move, he is showing a short burst of acceleration in the midst of a race, neither at the beginning nor the end. I have always felt that when I see a middle move, the horse is a must to use in the next race. Middle moves generally show fitness, but also what I might term latent or dormant capabilities. If this move is used correctly the next time, that middle move may lead to a trip to the winner's circle. The handicapper can easily identify a middle move by observing when a horse rapidly passes a series of

horses (or gains significant lengths on them) during some part of the race.

4. "Jockeys can be seen as trips"—Some jockeys are good front runners (David Flores) while others are good closers (Eddie Delahoussey); others are good on turf (Jerry Bailey) or dirt distance races (Pat Day). The point is that if you see a jockey change (good or bad), this will affect how the horse runs.

5. "How hard was the horse used in the race"—If a horse is hard ridden to the wire, many handicappers see this as a negative for a subsequent race, but I tend to disagree. A hundred-pound jockey can only do so much to affect the momentum of a thousand plus pound animal, so stretch urging does not mean as much as it may sometimes appear. A horse that wins easily (and without urging) probably would not win by too much more if urged and whipped decisively. Still, how a horse is urged and ridden does factor strongly into a trip handicapper's arsenal in two situations:

    ❧ Very few horses (even the greatest in the world) are what are called "push button" horses. Push button horses are so resilient and flexible that at multiple times during a race a jockey can ask for speed (i.e., "push the button"). Most horses are more one dimensional, and only have one burst of speed (or perhaps no burst, if a horse is what is called one paced). If a handicapper sees a jockey ask for this burst of speed too soon (or too late), it is a heads up that the horse may get his button pushed more effectively the next time. Sometimes this will be interpreted as a middle move, but it is slightly different. If you see push button ability or a middle burst, and even if ridden incompetently to a losing finish, the good trip handicapper will know to use the horse in his next outing.

    ❧ If a horse is eased or pulled up down the home stretch, the horse's placement may not be indicative of his overall ability. The horse may seem on paper unbelievably awful, losing by fifteen lengths, when if he had been ridden diligently to the finish, the margin may have been seven or less. Many jockeys (particularly the cheaters, and the dishonest ones) ease the horses when they know they will not finish in the money, realizing that this will increase the odds on the horse in his next outing.

6. "Cheating as related to trips"—All horseplayers like to relate tales (or tails in the case of buzzers), where blatant cheating was observable to all (particularly the trip handicapper). Detecting the cheating is the key, because only the worst cheaters put a carotid neck choke on a winning animal, which is observable by everyone. These types of cheaters do not last long as jockeys, but the more experienced cheaters are more adept. They run a horse wide (often via excessive left-hand whipping), withhold the horse on the backstretch, or intentionally get the horse blocked. Sometimes this is due to gross incompetence, sometimes due to cheating; either way, the trip handicapper must look at chicanery as an angle, and it is even more important than a troubled trip because it shows specific intent. Obviously, if a horse is purposefully stiffed in its last few starts it provides a great possibility for an overlay later. Do not allow a cheating jockey and trainer to profit alone—use your eyes to see something amiss and win for yourself.

> **"Some people have more money than brains—**
> **but not for long"**
> — *14,000 Quips and Quotes*

HOW MUCH WEIGHT DO YOU GIVE THE PROBLEM TRIP AND THE OTHER FACTORS?

Now you know what to look for! How much weight do you give to the problems and the other factors? A length, two lengths, or did it absolutely end any chance the horse had? I do not believe the answer is in the number of lengths or points added to a pace or speed figure, but instead, the individual player must use experience to interpret how much effect the trip issues had in relation to all the other factors. The more races you watch, the more you will be able to assess how the horserace was affected. A final note: If you observe cheating, follow that horse and play it; if you think you observe cheating in its next race, play it even harder until it wins (it will, at a good price).

Trip handicapping is conceptual (unlike figure and number oriented areas), and so it is difficult for "techno-wiz kid" number types. It is for this very reason that it is probably the most useful of the handicapping techniques (along with how the horse looks on the track [see

Chapter 8]). It allows you to interpret various visual *and* numerical data to find winners. Moreover, as you will see in later sections that are related to Zen philosophy, success in trip handicapping can be greatly assisted by a Zen-type methodology of seeing through to what is there.

The Winning Horseplayer
By Andrew Beyer

NOTES:

7
Workouts and Conditioning

**"With money in your pocket, you are wise,
and you are handsome and sing well too."**
— Jewish Proverb

The purpose of this chapter is to discuss the types of workouts and conditioning that you will see noted in the *Daily Racing Form,* and actually observe at the track if you go and view the workouts in the morning. Obviously, a fit and in-shape horse will almost universally defeat a non-fit, poorly conditioned animal. Commentary in the DRF speaks endlessly (and needlessly) about the speed and type of workouts that are shown at the bottom of the past performance section. It is my strongly held opinion that there is very little in the workout section of the DRF that will show you anything of value concerning your handicapping. I have long held the opinion that the workout times as shown are skewed so completely out of scale to be unusable by handicappers. I had never observed a written verification of my opinion in this regard until I read a book called

Handicapping Speed by Charles Carroll. In Mr. Carroll's book there is a section called "The Works" beginning on page 100. I had purchased the book to become more acquainted with the nature of how speed handicapping applies to horseracing, but I was pleasantly surprised to read that the author felt the same way I do regarding workouts.

In magic and parlor tricks, we have all seen a rabbit pulled out of a hat. The hat is always displayed as empty, and then with the wave of a magic wand, poof, out comes Peter Cottontail. In truth, does the hat have anything to do with the appearance of the rabbit? No, it is the magician's slight-of-hand which leads to the carrot muncher's arrival.

The horse's workout times are much like the empty hat. The times you see are merely an illusion, it is the skill of the trainer (and countless other factors) that lead to the "poof", and 'Hooves Your Daddy' in the winner's circle.

One of the most commonly held misconceptions about workouts is that the actual time (which is shown at the bottom of the racing form) is valuable. My experience has shown that the actual time is unrelated to the nature of the fitness of the animal. The reason for this is that the individual times that are shown can be greatly skewed by the nature of how the trainer trains the horse, the clocker times the workout, etc. Likewise, beyond what can only be termed as larceny, a trainer sometimes moves a horse more slowly in an effort to show a slow workout to get higher race time odds. More commonly the inaccuracies in the workouts occur due to decreased visibility at the morning time of first light, as well as the actual distance being worked not being the exact distance which is being timed. In other words, when the racing form shows that a horse worked three furlongs handily, perhaps the exact workout distance was slightly less or slightly more than three furlongs. This difference could be disproportionate to the actual time the clocker observes. Moreover, a horse can be worked fast through hard riding to get a "bullet" workout (the fastest workout for the day at that distance), which is worthless to the handicapper because the horse was used so hard to get the bullet.

It is my experience that the clockers' rating system of describing the workout as breezing, driving, handily, etc., is open to interpretation by the individual clocker. The difference between being able to determine whether the horse was hard used is essential, and unless you personally view the workout to determine whether the horse was being urged, the categories of breezing, etc. are meaningless. As is well stated in Mr. Carroll's book, at some tracks you will never see the times of horses breezed and ridden handily being identical. Clockers determine the final time of the workout, and if it is fast for the day, they will categorize it as handily "H," and if it is slower, they will categorize it as breezing "B." This provides no useful information to the handicapper whatsoever.

The characterization that all workout times, etc., should be disregarded by the handicapper is a radical departure from many people's concept of handicapping, but I believe one of the most accurate and useful ideas that I can impart to you is when to disregard useless information.

> **"I wish your horses swift and sure of foot."**
> **— William Shakespeare**

I believe the only time there is any possibility of accuracy concerning the workouts, is when horses are worked from the gate. These times tend to be more accurate because the actual distance is fixed, and while this can be manipulated due to the actual effort the jockey/training rider puts on the horse, the times tend to be more consistent and more useful. Still, I do not use from the gate workouts as having any great value for their time, but more for informational purposes. Often horses will have difficulty in loading into the gate in actual races, and/or will have difficulty breaking from the gate. If such a horse shows a gate workout following a difficult break or loading incident in it's previous race, I consider this a significant handicapping key, because the trainer is probably "schooling" the horse on how to operate from the starting line. This is one of the few areas where I believe looking at the workout section can be of value.

Under the workout section, there are a number of abbreviations that are used which the horseplayer should be familiar with. The purpose is not that they are useful to your handicapping, but that you will appear better versed in training techniques if you know the particular verbiage involved. Commonly used abbreviations are:

1. "b"—The clocker considered this workout "breezing" (or particularly easily done by the jockey).

2. "h"—The clocker considered this workout to be done "handily" (meaning the horse was urged though not whipped to get the time).
3. "d"—The clocker observed that the horse was "driven" to the finish (meaning whipped or used hard).
4. "dogs"—The training was done around cones or pylons to keep the inner part of the track protected. Again, this is completely irrelevant.
5. "g"—The workout was from the gate (we know there may be a little information of value here).
6. "ⓣ" —The horse worked on a turf course.
7. "tr. t"—The training was conducted on the training track (i.e., if the characterization was CD tr. t, this means the training was at the Churchill Down's training track).

As was indicated previously, the times concerning the training are not important. However, there are two or three characterizations about the notes of the training that may be significant for various handicappers. One of these discussed previously was when the horse was worked from the gate. I consider this to a somewhat valuable clue if the horse has had previous problems in its last start, or is a maiden first-time starter that needs some gate work or experience leaving from the gate. Another designation that is pertinent and valuable is that the horse worked on the turf track. If a horse is going to be a first-time starter on the turf and shows a workout on the turf track, sometimes this is a significant event. The trainer is making the determination on how the horse will handle the turf. If the horse worked on the turf, I consider it a positive sign if he then continues to make his first start on the turf. I do not consider it pertinent whether or not the workout was on the training track or on the main surface of a particular track.

All major tracks generally have a rule that following a significant layoff, a horse must have one workout (or possibly two) on the track before he will be allowed to be entered into a race. The stated purpose for this is to ensure that the horse is fit enough so that he will be competitive in a particular race. One of the situations that I have seen (particularly among unscrupulous trainers) is that if a horse has had a significant layoff (six months or more), the trainer will ensure that the workouts are exceedingly slooooowwwww. The purpose for this is that many handicappers will completely disregard a horse that has had an extended layoff and that has extremely slow training times. I am not saying that you should play layoff horses with slow times, but I am suggesting that you should not throw them out on that basis alone. Later in this chapter I will identify one of the few areas where I believe training/conditioning is important, and it is with layoff horses, but again the actual workout time is meaningless.

> **"What is defeat? Nothing but education, nothing but the first step toward something better."**
> — **Wendell Phillips**

As stated previously, my experience with workouts is that they have little value. However, it is possible to observe certain patterns that can be of value to the handicapper. I will start out with the value of workouts that I see that appear to be "above board." I will then go forward to show an entire series of considerations that the astute handicapper should make concerning workouts that appear to be thievery options, and deceitful on the part of various trainers.

LEGITIMATE CONDITIONING AND TRAINING CONSIDERATIONS

While disregarding almost all aspects of training and conditioning of the horse, there are a series of considerations I look for. These generally are indicative of a horse's overall fitness, and may be helpful in your overall handicapping. I would add that I do not particularly stress these items in my handicapping, although I do mark them in my notes.

1. In extremely high level events (i.e., Grade I key races such as the Travers, Florida Derby, Santa Anita Derby, The Arlington Million, all of the Classic Races, and all of the Breeder Cup Races), all the workouts and training times will probably be accurate because of the number of press and media watching the workouts. The articles, which you will see regarding these times in the DRF, tend to be accurate and probably can be utilized as legitimate handicapping keys as to the fitness of the horses. These workout articles are the only occasions I will concern myself with the times and the nature of whether the horse worked handily, breezing, driving, etc.

2. While it is not important that the horse worked at a training track at a particular track, I find it a significant negative if a horse is training

at a different track than the one where it is scheduled to run. If a horse were training at Fairplex (a fair circuit oval in Southern California) and was subsequently going to run at Santa Anita or Hollywood Park, I would consider this a negative.

3. If you are diligent enough to go to the track and watch the workouts and you see a horse that appears to have gone the correct distance by your view of the mile poles, and appears to have been ridden "softly" by the jockey (in essence actually breezing) and you are able to get a time on this horse (by your own stopwatch), note this. Be sure to review the racing form to see if in fact the clockers have provided an incorrect time or more likely characterized this effort as handily, indicating that the horse was urged. If you see the horse runs easily and the racing form shows that the horse was urged, this may be a good opportunity because the horse will be under bet.

4. For horses coming off a layoff (especially of six months or more), the times of the workout are still not important, but the consistency and the gaps between the workouts are pertinent for handicapping purposes. What I look for is a consistent pattern of workouts approximately five days to one week apart for a six week to two-month period. If the horse has that much consistency of workouts, it is likely the trainer is legitimately trying to train the horse into shape. Although the times may not be pertinent, the fact that the horse is being trained consistently is an indication that the horse may run significantly well off the layoff. Conversely, if a horse is coming off an extremely long layoff and shows only one or two workouts, this may show that the horse is not ready to run. In particular, many handicappers see a strong positive to three workouts in a space of fifteen or fewer days.

5. Workouts that are gradually increasing in distance (i.e., initial workouts are three furlongs then four furlongs, etc.) are generally indicative of trainers trying to get the horse into shape. After a series of these "giving the horse a little bottom" workouts, sometimes the horse may be worked at a shorter distance (often three furlongs) just prior to its next race. This is a positive sign that the trainer is attempting to put more speed into the horse. The fact the trainer worked the horse at three furlongs may be a positive key as to the horse's overall race time speed potential.

Finally, in my last comment regarding legitimate training and conditioning, I provide the most important key that I can contribute regarding the actual training and conditioning of horses that you see in the DRF. The training and items you see in the racing form are not pertinent compared to how the horse looks on the track on the day of its race. Chapter 8 of this book will discuss the particular ins and outs of how the horse is viewed on the track and the condition it displays. These factors show the actual physical conditioning of the horse, and the trainers are not able to mislead you as to the horse that you are viewing in the post parade and the paddock. Consider that the efforts you put forward in regard to negotiating the difficulties of the previous training times should instead be put to better use by looking at how the horse appears on the track on the day of its race.

TRAINING "LARCENY TECHNIQUES"

Most trainers are scrupulous individuals. However, a portion of trainers, as well as owners and jockeys, use questionable practices during training as well as during races. Things you should look for during training which may indicate larcenous or thievish intent by the trainer, and may provide you an advantage when the race goes, include:

1. A horse that has been running extremely slow in its training, and then runs an out of character bullet workout, probably did not deserve this time or this time was manipulated by the trainer. This was probably done to induce the owner to run in a race, or may be specifically designed to lower this horse's odds when this horse has no chance of winning. Extreme differential training times should always be disregarded.

2. The point that I am going to provide to you here is very important. Speak it quietly amongst your closest friends and confidants at the track, but do not say it too loud because someone may be listening o'er your shoulder. Certain trainers have a miraculous ability to produce a horse's victory out of thin air and poor training, and these are the box car odds that you sometime see and look back on and see no reason why this horse won. This is not training magic; it may be pure luck, or more often, pharmacological magic. The trainer or someone within the barn found a unique compound or substance

to alter the manner in which the horse runs. Watch at your venue and if you see horses (often coming off a layoff) from one individual trainer paying extremely high odds, consider that this is possible larcenous intent on the part of the individual group. Do not be fooled that you cannot be a partial winner in this conduct. Do not automatically discard these horses in your wider "stretch" tickets because of off-putting form and training. Know that "training" can involve many factors, both honest and dishonest.

3. One of the more common illegal methods used on horses at a track is to use a device called a buzzer. This device is an electrical shock device concealed on the jockey's person; during the stretch, the horse is hit with the buzzer, inducing a significant burst of speed in some animals. It should be noted that this is a relatively rare occurrence in racing, but it does happen. In addition, some horses do not respond positively to the buzzer, and hitting a horse with a buzzer that does not respond may cause a horse to stop or, in fact, even buck the jockey off (which would be a wonderful thing). Nevertheless, horses have been hit with buzzers for a long time in the United States, and the practice went as far as to have a winner of the Arkansas Derby (one of the three major Kentucky Derby preps) be disqualified when Billy Patin used a buzzer on the winner Valhol. You may be wondering why I have included this in the training conditioning section, and here I have a significant tip for you (which was provided to me by a person who is an owner of racehorses). In addition to using buzzers during the races, which is absolutely prohibited and will garner a jockey disqualification in the race and disbarment from a track, buzzers are also used in training horses. The purpose of this is to induce that same burst of speed by hitting the horse (generally in the neck) with the buzzer. Trainers (very unscrupulous ones) know that if the horse is hit with the buzzer he will show that great burst of speed. Then in the race a horse is not hit with the buzzer but is slapped on the neck in the same exact area, and since the horse is expecting that same shock, he sometimes will run with that same additional burst of speed.

You may be wondering how you can use this information? Here is my answer:

If you go to watch the workouts, the horse that is hit with a buzzer will universally shoot it's tail directly in the air when the buzzer hits them. If you see this in a workout, immediately proceed to find out when that horse is going to run next and bet it. You will find that as the horse goes down the stretch, he will either be hit with the buzzer again and his tail will go in the air, and you may win from direct larceny, or as he goes down the stretch, the jockey will hit the horse in the exact same position where he has been struck before, but not have a buzzer and the horse may respond in the exact same way. You may profit from quasi larceny.

Handicapping Speed
By Charles Carroll

NOTES:

8

How Does the Horse Look on the Track

"Round hoofed, short jointed, fetlocks shag and long,
broad breast, full eye, small head, and nostrils wide,
high crest, short ears, straight legs, and passing
strong, thin mane, thick tail, broad buttock, tender
hide: look, what a horse should have and he did not
lack, save a proud rider on his back."
— William Shakespeare

One of the most common areas in which even the best handicappers are weak is watching the horse on the racetrack and observing his attitudes and motions before his race. At every racetrack in the country, there is a paddock area where the horses can be observed before the race. Also, there is a post-parade where the horses can be viewed immediately before the race as they move along the racetrack. During this period, extremely important information and data concerning each individual horse can be obtained. Many handicappers, even serious ones, fail to closely view the horse on the track.

This is a mistake, particularly in maiden races. The look, demeanor, and conformation of the horse on the racetrack may be the principal clue as to whether the horse will be victorious, or an over bet loser with good breeding but bad conformation.

During most of my own horse-playing career, there was limited hard data as to the exact conformation details that would be desired in particular types of racehorses. It seems obvious from watching human sprinters and long distance runners that there might be significant differences between a horse who would be a short distance sprinter as opposed to a horse that would be a long turf distance specialist. The differences are there in horses, though they might not be quite as apparent as observing a 100-yard dash sprinter and an Olympic caliber marathon runner.

Generally, all the information concerning conformation and horse body type was based on analysis of breeders and trainers who observed the majority of these horses in training and on the track. However, with all of this said, there has always been the often spoken axiom that "all horses look good in the winner's circle". While conformation and body type, etc., is important to the overall success of a horse, the most important factor in any horse is his degree of effort and heart. This can only be seen during the race. As a side note, recent analysis in *The Blood Horse Magazine*® has shown that horse heart size can be analyzed in yearlings via ultra sound evaluation. This is an evolving equine science that is something for the astute handicapper to consider in years upcoming.

> **"Here is living harmony in horseflesh: an embodiment**
> **of rhythm and modulation, of point and counter point**
> **that sang to the eye and made music in the heart"**
> — John Hervey

On the following page, you will see Diagram 1, showing the basic parts and areas that involve the equine athlete. A good horseplayer will become familiar with most of the areas identified in this diagram. One of the major areas of concern is the leg. The legs are complex structures that must bear the load of a thousand pound animal running at amazing speeds. While the beauty and grace of a horse in motion cannot be denied, there are specific factors a horseplayer should consider when looking at a horse's feet, ankles, cannon, knees,

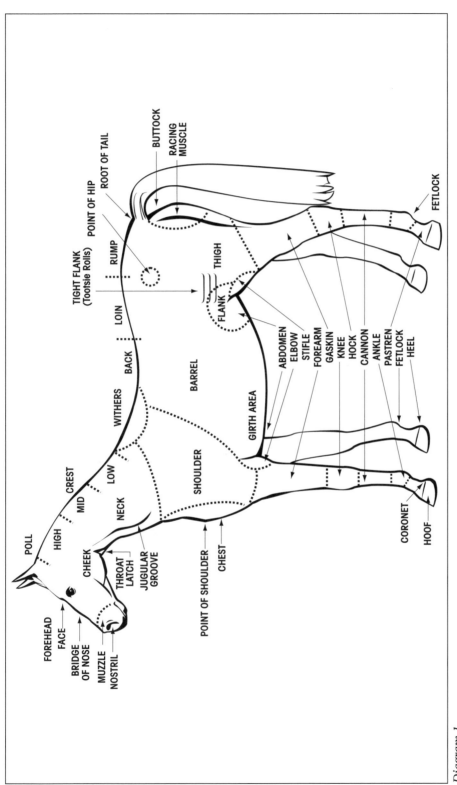

Diagram 1

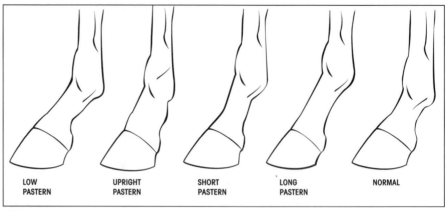

| LOW PASTERN | UPRIGHT PASTERN | SHORT PASTERN | LONG PASTERN | NORMAL |

Diagram 2

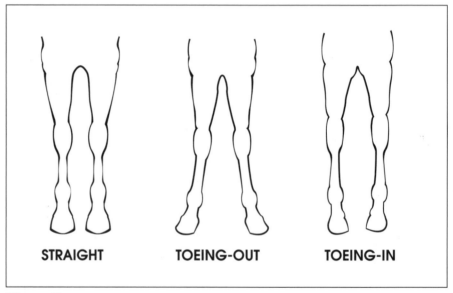

STRAIGHT   **TOEING-OUT**   **TOEING-IN**

Diagram 3

and hocks. In diagrams 2 and 3, you will see areas that are pertinent even during a casual observance of a horse. Diagram 2 discloses the different types of pastern lengths in horses. Diagram 3 shows a front view of a horse showing straight, toeing in, and toeing out. It is not impossible for horses that have toeing in or out to be successful racehorses, but if this deformity is dramatic, it is unlikely that the horse will be as quick or as agile as a horse with straighter legs.

The following handicapping tip from this section should be underlined and noted in bold face for future maiden races: *No maiden first time starters should be played if they have dramatic toeing in or toeing out.* It is not impossible for these horses to win, but being able to toss them will limit the number of horses you will be forced to bet. This is a great help in large maiden fields with minimal other data other than breeding and workouts.

Generally, the pastern is sloped at approximately an angle of 45 degrees from the fetlock to the hoof. If the fetlocks are more upright than this, too much shock is sent up to the knee and shoulder of the horse, likely causing knee and other problems; if the pastern is sloped more than this, the horse will incur significant injuries from scraping its fetlocks on the ground. This second type of deficiency causes significant soreness in horses and a decreased desire to run hard or exert themselves down the stretch. Often this condition can be seen on the track via the wraps that are used on the horse. A determination should be made to see if the wraps around this area have been damaged during the pre-race exercising by hitting the ground (even at slow speeds).

Generally, trainers and breeders prefer a horse with a slightly higher neck, proceeding downward into a relatively broad, though not overly broad, chest area. This is additionally one of the other primary indicators whether a new maiden type horse will have difficulty running. An extremely narrow chest generally will not contain enough lung power for the animal to successfully race, and will cause the horse to run incorrectly when tired. However, a horse with a wide chest not suited for its body style is also a potential negative, and can cause a horse to paddle by moving its front legs in a rotating outward motion to clear its chest. An extremely narrow or extremely broad chest can cause a bad action in the horse's motion and decrease its ability to reach the finish line.

> **"…I am not an expert in horses and do not speak with assurance. I can always tell which is the front end of a horse, but beyond that, my art is not above the ordinary."**
> — *Mark Twain, A Biography*

In addition, handicappers should be concerned during the post parade and paddock viewing with the size of the horse's hoofs, as well as the type of shoe that is placed on the horse. It is generally treated as an axiom of wide spread validity that horses with larger hoofs do extremely well in turf races, and will also have some success in sloppy dirt tracks with a hard base. Horses with smaller hoofs will do better on muddy racetracks where the base is not hard. The importance of the above suggestion cannot be overstated in that often horses will transfer from turf to dirt, and yet will have extremely small hoofs. These horses can sometimes be seen as a non-factor in these races. Additionally, a horse may have run on a sloppy racetrack with a hard base and not been successful, but subsequently, may be running on a muddy racetrack, which is deep throughout. In this case a horse with large hooves will tend to fair poorly and also may be extremely over bet having previously run well on a sloppy (not muddy) racetrack.

The types of shoes worn by a horse are extremely important. Different people have different theories on how different shoes affect different horses. The absolute answer is that the horse must be well shod, and comfortable to be successful. Beyond this, the only two absolutes I have seen in horse racing are:

1. If you see "stickers" being used on a horse in a turf race, bet the horse.
2. Never bet a horse with bar shoes.

Generally, stickers being used in a turf race is a sign that the trainer is attempting to gain additional traction for a horse and while it is relatively unusual for horses in a turf race to wear stickers, I have seen it be highly predictive of victory. Bar shoes on the other hand are usually a sign that the horse has a bad hoof or hooves, and it decreases traction. I have found that throwing out any horses with bar shoes is one of the best handicapping keys concerning equipment or horse conformation.

Diagram 4 shows the basic types of shoes that you will see at the racetrack. Mud caulks are generally the shoes worn by many horses on an off or muddy track. Generally, I will not play horses that are slick shod in muddy or off track racing.

**"A race track is a place
where the human race is secondary."**
— Anonymous

Set out below are a few additional tips that you may want to consider when you assess a horse's condition and conformation at the

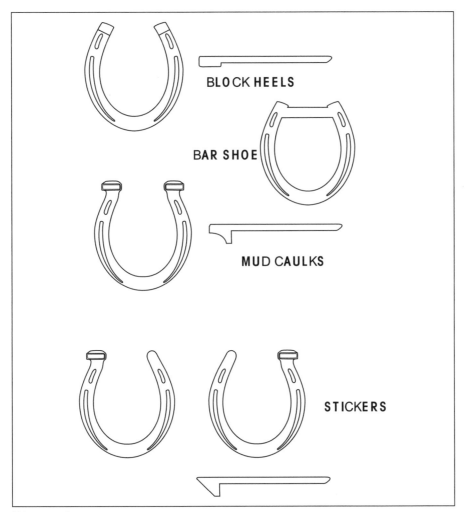

BLOCK HEELS

BAR SHOE

MUD CAULKS

STICKERS

Diagram 4

racetrack. For the information I am greatly indebted to author Trillis Parker and her book *Horses Talk It Pays to Listen (the Paddock and Post Parade)*. In my opinion without question, this is the most universally cogent and detailed book on horseracing condition and conformation available.

Here are some of the specific highlighted ideals, which Trillis Parker is looking for in the equine athlete:

1. Horses that are in the post-parade walking on their toes or appearing to dance on their own, and not at the direction of the jockey, present a strong indicator that the horse is fit and ready to run successfully.

2.   If you see a horse's ears pinned back against his head, generally this means the horse is angry or fearful, and it is likely that this horse will have already "run its race" and not do well.

3.   If you see the whites of the horse's eyes, again this is an indication that the horse is frightened and will be unlikely to run a successful race. I think of a horse's eyes as a window or mirror to the animals' heart and mind. If he is frightened, it is likely neither his mind nor heart is ready to give a competitive race. Always look at a horse's eyes in the paddock before a race.

4.   Tongue-ties, a device that ties the tongue to the lower jaw, generally are an indication that there has been some sort of breathing problem previously. This may be viewed as a positive or negative sign depending on the horse's last race.

5.   The dappled or shiny coat is a positive indication of a horse's health and ability to run. At the major tracks around the United States, most horses will have shiny coats, but dappling or natural spotting that occurs is a strong indication that the horse is fit. It is difficult to describe dappling, but if you go to a major racetrack on a large event day, ask a trained horseplayer to show you a horse that has dappling. In major Grade I or Grade II races, many of the horses will be in this condition.

6.   Much like a dog, a horse's tail can tell a great deal about its personality. A swishing, swinging tail generally shows anger or discomfort, but an "arched" tail, which extends just off the buttocks and hangs down is an extremely positive sign.

7.   Leg wraps and bandages around the horse's legs are often seen by many handicappers as a negative sign, but there are many different types of bandages and wraps, and I personally tend to disregard this information unless they are new front wraps. New front wraps are defined as wraps that are left on during the race on a horse that has previously not worn front wraps. I will commonly disregard this horse from my betting, but I will watch how he performs in this race. If he performs positively, I will assume that the trainer placed the front wraps on either for a legitimate purpose, or to dissuade wagering on him, or to decrease the likelihood of others claiming the horse.

8.   One of the primary ways that a horseplayer assesses a horse's condition is to look at the horse's flank or rear abdominal type region to

see if there is tightness and muscling in this area. A horse that is fit in this area will generally perform well, and I will tend to bet them more than other horses that do not appear to be as fit. As with humans, a horse can appear to have a relatively good backside and chest, but excess weight will show up in the belly and flank region.

9. The primary region a horseplayer looks at on the animal is the rear rump or buttock of the horse, and a horse that is extremely well conditioned and in shape will show definition and striating of muscles in this region. This is a good sign in any animal.

10. Kidney sweating—The knowledgeable player should watch for any horse that is excessively sweating when others in the post parade are not. If a horse is excessively sweating or is "washy," you may want to throw him out. If the horse is washy, but still wins, it may mean he was just much the best (or that he sweats excessively). Animals are different and like human runners, prizefighters, or tennis players, some sweat a little, some a lot. Additionally, if you see excessive sweating around the kidneys (same location human kidneys are) this is okay if in same proportion as the other horses unless the sweat is discolored. If the sweat is yellowish or darkish it is an indication the animal is sick, and will not run well.

11. The final area is the use of blinkers on horses. Blinkers are a device that does not allow the horse to see behind it or beside it. Horses have different vision than humans, and blinkers generally will prevent distractions and will allow the horse to be focused, either from the gate, or down the home stretch. Blinkers are a notable addition that good bettors look for, but blinkers are not positive for all horses; some horses like to see around them and when they wear blinkers they run "dull". Sometimes, the addition of blinkers will cause the horse to be extremely agitated because the horse cannot see his surroundings, but often the opposite is true of horses that are high-strung (i.e., high-strung horses tend to be more calm when in blinkers). My advice with blinkers is multi-fold: Always include a first time blinkers horse if you feel that the horse has any legitimate possibility of winning. However, watch the initial race that a horse has with blinkers and make an assessment whether or not it helped or hindered the horse. Finally, blinkers come in a number of different types. There are partial blinkers that only partially obscure the vision of the horse, half blinkers, and full blinkers (which obscure

all of the vision for the horse except to its immediate front). I have not found in my betting that there is any significant difference between types of blinkers. The horses will be effected by each of them differently and the assessment must be made as to each individual horse.

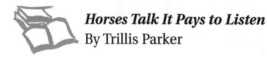

Horses Talk It Pays to Listen
By Trillis Parker

9
Other Factors

"He who is prudent and lies in wait for an enemy who
is not, will be victorious."
— Sun Tzu, *The Art of War*

The purpose of this chapter is to set out a series of miscellaneous handicapping ideas and factors that I have observed through my experience in horseracing, which could prove to be pertinent to your analysis. These concepts do not fit squarely into any individual category so I include them here as a laundry list that you should consider when you handicap. This list is not all-inclusive and individual handicappers will find various different factors that they consider important.

LAYOFFS

It is difficult to know the exact fitness of an animal that is racing after returning from a layoff. After assessing pertinent trainer statistics concerning whether or not they succeed off layoffs, I will then determine if the horse has a significant series of conditioning works before its first start. I will generally not play horses that have been involved in extremely long layoffs unless they have a trainer who is particularly adept at getting these types of horses to be victorious in their initial return starts. However, if a horse does run off a long layoff and does not run particularly well, I will assess that horse's race closely to make a determination of whether or not he will be successful in his second or third race off of the layoff. It is generally accepted that layoff horses run their best race in the third race in that current form cycle.

INCREASING OR DECREASING A HORSE'S RACING DISTANCE

If a horse increases in distance from six furlongs to a mile or decreases from a mile and a sixteenth to say seven furlongs, there are different factors for the handicapper to consider. Generally, a horse that is increasing in distance will show more speed in a longer race, if he has any speed whatsoever. Conversely, a horse decreasing in distance will tend to have more "bottom" and more stamina at the end of the decreased distance race.

SURFACE CHANGES

If a horse moves from turf to dirt he will generally have more stamina on the dirt but will be rated slower. If a horse is moving from dirt to turf I will assess the turf breeding on the horse and am not too concerned with the form on the dirt.

HORSES DROPPING OUT OF MAIDEN SPECIAL WEIGHT

Generally, one of the most obvious handicapping indications of success is a horse that has run in maiden special weight races unsuccessfully and is now dropping into the maiden claiming ranks. Maiden special weight droppers, regardless of Beyers, pace, etc., should be given extra consideration.

WEIGHT

My personal feeling is that the weight on the horse's back is of relatively minimal importance. Cross Country and SteepleChase horses routinely carry a hundred and fifty pounds or more, and run over fences at two miles and longer. My feeling is that the percentage differential between a hundred and fifteen pounds and a hundred twenty pounds is relatively minimal for the animal. In fact, in weight restricted races (i.e., stakes), generally the racing commission will assign higher weights to the horses it feels will be most successful. Therefore, a high weight in these races (though complained about constantly by trainers) may be indicative that at least the track officials feel this is the best horse.

LASIX

Most horseplayers agree that Lasix, which is a bronchial dilator, allows clearing of the horse's lungs from mucus and blood, is a positive racing addition. First time lasix horses tend to run their best race, and while many handicappers feel that the reason for this is some magical quality, it just may be that the horse needs the medication. However, it is obvious from the number of horses that are put on the medication, that it in fact increases the horse's performance, at least in the first one or two races in which the horse runs on the medication. If you see the first Lasix indication (1L), know that this is a positive addition for your horse.

ILLEGAL DRUGS

The illegal use of drugs in horses does occur. Do not fool yourself. The only advice that I have in protecting yourself against illegal drug use is to monitor smaller stable trainer statistics. If you see an extensively high percentage of in the money finishes from a trainer who previously (in other meets) did not have the same statistics, consider the possibility that this may be due to illegal manipulation and drug usage. Consider an additional plus sign (+) in your handicapping for horses from these stables. Like the buzzer and other illegal methods, there is only one comment to make, people cheat, get over it.

HORSES RUNNING FOR THE FIRST TIME IN THE UNITED STATES

Often, when horses run in the United States, they are also receiving Lasix for the first time and one of the handicapping angles that I use is the Euro-Lasix theory. Horses coming to the United States, based on their form overseas, tend to outrun their program-documented ability (particularly when they are on first time Lasix). Horses that are Euro-Lasix should usually be played regardless of their odds, and while oftentimes these horses do not win, they tend to show up in the minor placing of second, third, and fourth at extremely high mutual odds. You discount them at your peril. Conversely, horses that have run on first time Lasix, and first time in the United States, tend to exhibit an effect in their next start known as the "Euro-bounce." In other words, horses that run well in their first time start in the country on first time Lasix tend to regress in their second start in the United States, and then return back to proper form in their third, fourth, etc., starts.

POST POSITION

Each track in the DRF shows the success of postpositions at the current meet. Some post positions, ordinarily the outside ones (eleven or twelve), or the very most inner ones (one or two), will have a considerably disproportionate percentage of winners and losers. The outside post has a minimal number of winners, sometimes due to the amount of distance to the turn where it is difficult for an outside horse to "get itself into" the race. Sometimes the rail can be so dead as not to allow the horse to "escape the rail." The bottom line on post position is that the individual handicapper must assess whether at their own track certain post positions are a disadvantage, or an advantage, and this must be broken down into the type of race (sprint, distance, turf, sprint, and turf distance).

LISTEN TO OTHER PEOPLE'S ANALYSIS

No one has all the knowledge to know everything or to see every angle in every race. Astute players listen to the analysis that other individuals in the OTB or at the track present. You may find additional information that may assist you in a particular race or there may have been something that you missed. When someone starts to tout a long odds horse, listen to what he or she has to say; perhaps they may be able to provide you with information that will assist you. Do not be so arrogant as to presume that even with your handicapping ability that you have all the answers. Listen and learn.

"THIS F***ING RACE IS IMPOSSIBLE"

It happens: Races are impossible and they can be undecipherable. Do not feel that you must play every race, and if you find a race that is too difficult, be confident enough in yourself to simply not play that race. Or if you must play, utilize an "all" in the race. In some types of multiple race bets, where there are other races that you feel more confident about and can find a "single" horse, utilizing an all may provide a high odds winner.

CHANGING TRACKS

Some horses need a race over the track surface to be successful. If a horse is racing on the track for the second or third time, consider the possibility that it may improve its status based on this factor alone.

MAJOR CLASS DROP

If a horse is taking a major drop in class, and if it is meeting the cheapest field of its career, it should be given extra consideration. It could mean that this horse is up for sale, or is on its last legs, or it could also be that the owner and trainer are looking for a sure win and the ability to put more confidence back into the horse.

FIRST TIME GELDING

Ow! The truth is that first time geldings tend to run better in their first start after being gelded (castrated). I do not know why, I do not want to know why, but they do, so consider it as a factor.

ENTRIES

An entry is a race where two horses are coupled in the wagering generally under the same trainer and owner. These two horses run separately, and if either wins, your win bet would cash. Entries win many races, not because there are two horses, but because the horses may be able to set the race up for each other. In other words, if one of the horses is a consistent stretch runner, often the other entry mate will be a rabbit and go out to the front to insure an honest pace. While entries are not sure winners (and sometimes are over bet), make an assessment as to whether one horse is a speed horse and the other a closer. It is a potential positive factor for your handicapping if the rabbit/closer entry is present.

CLAIMED HORSES

Horses that have been claimed by a new trainer (i.e., purchased in their last race), were purchased/claimed because the trainer and new owner felt that they could find a way to have them become more successful. If a successful trainer claims a horse, consider that it may improve in its next start. Conversely, if a successful horse is claimed from a successful trainer by a lower tiered trainer, this may be a negative. The new trainer may not be able to get any more out of the horse than the previous trainer did, and may get even less. Even more important is the "reclaim" phenomenon. If a successful trainer loses a horse and then some races later claims the horse back, this is significant. The trainer already knows the horse and has gone out of his way to get the horse back. Expect a successful run when next out after a reclaim.

SPECIFIC RACE CONDITIONS

Sometimes the racing secretary (the individual who writes the conditions of the race) will specifically form a race to induce a particular horse to enter. This can occur in an allowance race that a specific high profile equine star can use as a prep to a Grade I or Grade II. Often a telltale sign of this is that the written race will be set three weeks prior to a major stakes at the same track. Sometimes it may be difficult for the neophyte horseplayer to determine if a race has been written to lure a specific horse to enter. This is an area where reading the DRF articles and commentary line will provide guidance. If you determine that a race was written for a specific horse and that horse enters, ALWAYS use that horse in multiple race tickets. The horse may get over bet, but he will probably win.

> "Prey passes the tiger who sometimes merely looks,
> sometimes pounces without hesitation,
> but never fails to act."
> — Deng Ming-Dao

The point of the last quote is to help you consider that it is important to know when and where you should wager, but also what factors you should use. The above list can be added to indefinitely, and I hope you will find numerous other factors you consider to be of value, separate from the primary factors discussed in this book. Likewise, I would encourage you to do extensive reading and research as to your particular track, which may have specific factors that you should consider.

Ainslie's Complete Guide to Thoroughbred Racing
By Tom Ainslie

10
Miscellaneous Issues which can Help your Handicapping (What Type of Bet to Make)

"Achieve results, But never glory in them.
Achieve results, But never boast.
Achieve results, But never be proud.
Achieve results, Because this is the natural way."
— Lao Tzu, from the *Tao Te Ching*

My goal in this particular chapter is to discuss with you miscellaneous issues which can assist you in your handicapping and which will also make you a more pleasant human being to be around (and more likely to be spoken of highly at your track or OTB). I make the claim in this chapter that I will provide you with information that I guarantee will make you happier at the track, and will also make you more well-liked, more successful, smarter (and probably even better looking as well). How many chapters in any book can make that offer? Furthermore, in the final section of this chapter, I will discuss the various types of wagers that the handicapper can choose from. Finding the right horse to bet is important, but choosing the correct wager can be just as determinative of betting success.

Set out below are a few general headings under which I will provide you with some guidance on issues, perhaps not directly related to handicapping, but issues that can affect your success and happiness just the same.

> **"Just take it day by day, like the drunks do."**
> — King of the Hill (Television)

ALCOHOL AND GAMBLING

Most horse players drink; a few do not drink at all, some drink a little, a few, drink a lot, and an even smaller percentage drink to excess. Alcohol will effect how you handicap and how you wager. Every bettor who drinks has a story about how they hit a big race early in the day, but then proceed to get smashed and throw all their winnings back in on bets that they would not have made if in a more sober frame of mind. A few drinks may just allow you to be more relaxed in your wagering and not bet with "scared" money. The point when discussing drinking and gambling is that with anything you do, you should monitor how you have played based on your consumption of a mood altering substance. If you find repeatedly that you tend to have extensive loses if you drink heavily; you should consider not drinking to excess. More importantly, I am not an advocate of handicapping under the effect of alcohol; instead, your handicapping should be done the night before with a clear mind. The specific consideration of the types of wagers you will make should be made the night before, and then on the day of the race, the fine-tuning of your selections should take place. I see no problem with consuming a few beers or drinks while doing this fine-tuning, but the majority of your handicapping should be done in a clear frame of mind.

> **"All soldiers taken must be cared for with magnanimity and sincerity so they may be used by us."**
> — Chang Yu, as quoted by Sun Tzu, in *The Art of War*

ETIQUETTE AND GAMBLING

The above quote is indicative of the concept that we should be honest with the fellow gamblers and considerate of their place and space in the wagering realm. Additionally, consideration for your fellow players will periodically manifest itself in a significant tip, which may be provided to you because you have always been courteous and forthright in your demeanor. Every horseplayer has stories about a fellow gambler who everyone at the track or OTB despised because of his or her bad attitude.

Here are a few specific things that you as a player can do to make the wagering experience better for everyone:

1. State your wager correctly to the teller (the name of the track, the race number, the dollar amount of the wager, the type of wager, and then the number(s) of the horse(s) that you intend to play). An example of this would be: in the fifth race, at Santa Anita, a $1 trifecta partial wheel, one, two; with the one, two, three, four; with all: (1,2/1,2,3,4/all). If you know how to call out your bets correctly, not only will you please the teller, you will please the people behind you in line who want to get their bets in.
2. Have your money out of your wallet (or purse) ready to pay the teller after the teller punches your ticket.
3. The teller is always right, even if the teller punches the wrong ticket. It is your responsibility as a player to check your ticket for accuracy. The corollary to this is that you never go back to the teller and complain that they gave you the wrong ticket, and that you did not check it until after the race. As a player, you want to find the teller most likely to provide you accurate and quick service, and who is likely to minimize errors on your ticket. Generally, you can think of the teller as a sub-contractor, and if you are the contractor, you will always try to choose the best sub-contractors to do your work. However, as the contractor or overseer of the entire project, it is your responsibility to review the correctness or the accuracy of the work of the sub-contractor.

DON'T BE A WHINER

Everybody who plays horses (or gambles of any sort) loses, we all get terrible beats, and we all complain. Complaining is okay, but blatant whining, moaning, tearing tickets up and throwing programs is unacceptable behavior. I have to make a significant effort to control my temper when I wager, and those around me tell me I have improved immensely. There is no reason you should ruin the time for those around you by incessantly complaining. Make the comment to those around you, be unhappy, and then turn the page. Sometime you will be on the other side of that "bad beat" (the horse you need that gets the benefit from receiving an unbelievably poor ride on the favorite). I will relate a brief story that will insure that "Thou dost protest too much" will not apply to you. At an OTB in the Phoenix area, there is an individual nicknamed "Ferret Face" and while this person is generally a nice person outside the OTB, he can be incredibly burdensome to have at your table. The most humorous incident I recall with this bettor was when he borrowed a fellow players program; he made a few marks on it, and when the race went off and Ferret's horse did not win, he tore the other player's program in half and threw it on the floor. The bottom-line: Don't be a Ferret.

ALLOW OTHER PLAYERS TO BET THEIR WAGERS

If you are going to bet a race that is not going off for ten minutes or so, be aware that there are other races scheduled to go to post almost immediately. Let other players in the line behind you make their wagers if they intend to play the races that are going off.

BE GENEROUS

I split being generous into two sections. Be generous toward your teller, as well as the people in the room. If you hit a significant race, and any time you hit a "signer" (a ticket, which exceeds the minimum Internal Revenue Service tax liability, currently $600 or more for a $1 wager); buy the room a round of drinks. It is good sportsmanship to do so after a win, and hopefully it will increase the camaraderie, as well as increase the likelihood that you will be offered the same when someone else hits a good race.

You should always tip the teller when you win. The tip should ordinarily be in proportion of the win you had. If you are a $2 win player, and the horse paid $18.60, feel free to leave at least the 60 cents, and consider periodically leaving $1.60 tip. I will relate a story here about how not to tip; I feel confident I can defend it because the teller to whom it happened is a friend of mine. In the Phoenix area, a well known, well-paid basketball coach made a wager with my teller friend.

He was victorious to the tune of $4,322.70. When the winning coach returned to collect his ticket he tipped my teller friend all of $2.70, which was insulting in itself, but made worse when the coach had the audacity to state, "Win your fortune with it." My friend, who has quite a temper, stated that he had to restrain himself from coming back through the window and greeting this coach in a one-on-one fashion. The reason you tip your tellers is that it is considered common courtesy, and that is the way the tellers make the majority of their money.

There is also a selfish reason you should tip your teller. Sometimes the tellers have weighty inside knowledge that will be useful to you in the end. Often this knowledge is that the owners or trainers have a horse that they have just bet heavily on. Some owners and trainers are heavy bettors, and will frequently make large wagers on their horses, but some are not and will only wager on their horses if they feel there is a strong likelihood the horse will win. Trainers and owners bet the same way that regular bettors do: they have to go to the window, and tellers have this particular knowledge. If you have frequently and courteously tipped your teller, I will be surprised if the teller will not provide you that information knowing that if you win, you will also provide a good gratuity. The second selfish reason for good tipping is a negative rationale. In the story above concerning the coach, my teller friend indicated that it would now be impossible for this coach to come to his window and receive good service. Tellers are human, and a teller could decidedly create the potential for you to have a bad ticket in your hand. I hope that this coach never makes a bet with my friend again, but if he does, my suggestion to him would be to check his tickets for accuracy. Tip your tellers because it is the right thing to do, and know that it may bring you positive benefits in the end.

DO NOT GLOAT

The same way good bettors do not whine excessively, they do not boast when they win. The "I won, I won" can get a little old. Cheer your horse in, have some fun, smile, and go on. The bettor screaming around the room, shoving his ticket in your face saying how he just hit a huge trifecta can get annoying very quickly. I like to remind my girlfriend that it is akin to pointing at your beautiful girlfriend, and yelling out to everyone in the room that you had sex with her last night. Everyone is probably already jealous anyway, and they already know—so why throw it in everyone's face.

"They've laid their snare damned cunningly-like a cob web. If you make any movement, if you raise your hand to fan yourself...(we) feel a little tug...We're linked together inextricably. So you can take your choice."
—Garcin, from Jean Paul Sartre's play *No Exit*

HOW THE MUTUAL POOLS OPERATE

The mutual pool is the way horse wagering, dog wagering, etc., takes place. You are betting against all the other players who are making the same type of wager. Additionally, from all the money wagered into various pools, the government and the track take a certain percentage, and that percentage taken varies from fifteen to thirty percent. Generally, with exotic wagers such as superfectas, etc., the takeout percentage is higher. Beyond takeout, it is essential that the horseplayer know how a mutual pool is distributed.

Let's assume that the trifecta pool (every wager in the race that is attempting to pick the first three horses to cross the finish line in order) has $25,000 in it. Let us assume the take out is twenty percent. Twenty-percent times $25,000 equals $5,000 and is the amount the state and track have removed from the mutual pool, leaving $20,000 that all bettors are trying to get a piece of. Here is where the concept of the mutual pool becomes important. Let us assume that in the hypothetical race that the favorites run one, two, and three. There were 1,000 winning $1 tickets. In other words, there were 1,000 trifecta winners; therefore, $20,000 divided by 1,000 will lead to a winning ticket price of $20 for each ticket. Now let us assume that instead, the horses were all long shots and that there were only two winning tickets and your winning ticket now becomes worth $10,000. From the above example, you can see the mutual pool is a fixed amount of money, and the actions of any individual gambler will effect how the mutual pool grows. If a bettor makes a wager, the pool will increase, and if he makes the correct wager, the payoff will decrease for the other winners. As a dramatic example, let's continue with the three long shots that won. Suppose that those two winning tickets are present and that an additional bettor decides to wade into the mutual pool. He makes a $3 trifecta wager, which accurately selects the horses (you are going to wish that this is your ticket) and now there are five $1 combinations each paying $4,000 ($20,000 divided by five). One gambler has $12,000 and the other two somewhat "unlucky" though still happy, bettors get $4,000 instead of $10,000.

Now that you know how the concept of mutual pools work, it is important to know and understand that mutual pools are separate. One of the greatest misconceptions of many bettors is that simply because a horse has very low win odds (i.e., is a favorite in the win pool), this will make him the favorite in other pools such as exactas, doubles, etc. Conversely, because a horse is a long shot in the win pool, this does not mean that the horse is always going to be a long shot in other pools. Most tracks today will actually show what the potential payouts are for various wagers, and there will be charts that will show you what the likely payoffs are. They are displayed on various screens around the racetrack, and if you are considering making an exacta or other wager utilizing a horse that is an extreme win pool favorite, it behooves you to look at the other payoff odds. It is not uncommon to see two win pool favorites run one-two, but have an exacta or trifecta payoff that is significant.

ODDS/MORNING LINE ODDS

Morning line odds are the odds that are set by the track odds maker. It is merely an educated guess at what the horses will go off at in the win pool odds at race time. It is important for the bettor to realize that the morning line odds are nothing more than one handicapper's guess as to the odds that the various horses will pay. Often, the actual race time odds are significantly different than the projections of the morning line odds, and this can present an opportunity for the bettor in multi-race wagers. Many bettors bet what is called "the bottom of the program" or the morning line selections. In other words, in multiple race wagers all they do is look at the "guesses" that the tracks handicapper projected as the first three favorites, and utilize them in pick threes, doubles, etc. As often happens, those morning line odds are skewed, and the projections far off. My advice here is simple: Don't be swayed by the morning line picks or odds. Do your handicapping independently, and try to find your own victorious animals.

> **"It is reported that 75% of the people are fools, and the rest of us are in great danger of contamination."**
> — *14,000 Quips and Quotes*

One final idea regarding the nature of odds: Many people gravitate toward the favorites because they believe that it is more likely that favorites will win. Favorites win approximately one in three races, and often do not provide enough of a wagering opportunity to recoup your investment. Good handicappers need to be good bettors, and one important factor in this is not to be afraid of high odds horses. If your handicapping and observational skills have led you to a horse you believe has a high percentage possibility of being victorious, yet this horse is 20 to 1, do not immediately assume that you are wrong and everyone else is right. Look again at the animal on the track, and insure that he is not washy, or otherwise showing physical signs that he may not be ready to race. If he appears to be fit and fits your handicapping style, you should be wagering on him heavily. When your selections are going off at higher odds, you should play more, not less. This is true regardless of whether or not you are going to play the animal to win, or in other types of wagers. Generally, I disregard the odds I see; both morning line and race time odds, and do not let it effect my handicapping or my choice of wagers. There is one exception to this rule that I follow, and I provide it to you as a point to consider. If I have concluded that a horse does not appear to have any chance in the race, and yet his win odds are low (he remains a favorite), I will consider including this horse on multiple race tickets. He is what I would call a "throw in horse," reasoning that perhaps there are others with greater specific knowledge. In other words, if I find a horse that I do not particularly like, but he is being bet down to favoritism, I will sometimes include this horse (making the assessment that I may have been wrong).

HANDICAPPER NOTATIONS AND SCRIBBLES

Each individual handicapper will generate his or her own notations to denote a horse's speed, fitness, breeding, etc. One book that goes into great detail about notations regarding a horse's condition is Trillis Parker's *Horses Talk it Pays to Listen*. Specific alphabetic notations are provided for various conditions such as dappling, racing muscle, etc. Andrew Beyer's books also provide descriptive information on how to make notations on speed, pace, and trip issues. I would recommend these two books as a reference for horseplayers trying to determine which notation they wish to mark to highlight certain factors. My opinion is that each individual handicapper will come up with specific notations (shorthand), which identify factors which the individual handicapper believes are important. My advice about notations is that they should be as abbreviated as possible so that they can be written down quickly and reassessed before a wager is made.

**"Our five senses are incomplete without the sixth—
a sense of humor."**
— 14,000 Quips and Quotes

WHAT TYPE OF WAGER/BET SHOULD YOU MAKE

After you have determined the likely winners or contenders, a determination must be made on what type of wager you will make. The older handicapping books concentrated excessively, and mistakenly, on win wagering. While there are undoubtedly times to make win bets, with the new more liberal, exotic wagers available, other types of wagers present greater opportunities for the bettor. For a long time, I heard from numerous bettors that exotic wagers were garbage bets, and that no one could ever come out ahead by trying to pick four horses in order in one race, or alternatively picking six horses in six consecutive races. This is factually an inaccurate analysis, and extremely wrong-headed thinking. Exotic wagers present an opportunity for the individual player to receive windfall type profits from relatively small investments. A win player would never be able to secure a $5,000 win on an individual race without wagering a very large sum of money. Someone attempting to hit the superfecta (the first four horses in order) can receive such a windfall type $5,000 victory by investing only a relatively small amount of money. Obviously, it will not be easy to pick the first four horses, but one multi-thousand-dollar victory allows for multiple $24 to $48 bets.

My general concept on wagering is that the actual type of wager that you choose should be most closely influenced not by your handicapping style, but by your type of personality. In broad terms, if you are a now, now, now person, and you want or feel the need for immediate gratification, you should restrict yourself to win, superfecta, trifecta, and exacta types of wagers. One race will provide you the gratification of having been successful in your handicapping, and you will not have to wait for several races to see whether you are successful.

Conversely, if you are a patient person and are willing to wait out longer periods of activity to determine success, you should consider bets such as doubles, and pick 3's. These multiple race wagers often tend to pay more than win tickets and single race tickets, yet they are more frustrating because a mistake in any of the races will cause you to lose. If you are methodical and very patient, you should consider making wagers such as pick 4's (picking the winner of four races), or consider bets such as place pick all's (in which you are attempting to pick the first or second finishers in each race on the card). Finally, if you are one of those individuals with the patience of Job, and can truly withstand frustration, you may want to consider multi-race carry over wagers such as twin trifectas (picking the first three that cross the finish line in two consecutive races) or pick 6 bets (picking the winner in six consecutive races).

If you are just beginning as a handicapper, you should probably start out as a small win player, and then proceed to the exotic wagers. Older handicappers can recall when the only wagers available were win, place, and show, the daily double and possibly a trifecta on the last race. Currently, due to bettor demand, most tracks have trifectas and multiple pick 3's on all races throughout their cards. Once you have observed enough races, it will become clear that the exotic wagers are the wagers that tend to return the most money. It is more difficult for an individual player to pick three or four horses (whether they are in the same race or different races) than it is to pick a single winner, and based on the mutual pool concept, a decreased number of winners will significantly increase the payout. Realistically, the highest priced winners you are ever going to see are going to return approximately $100 for a $2 win wager. Conversely, a significant pick 3 or trifecta wager can often pay in the multi-hundred dollar range and even in the multi-thousand dollar range.

One of the most significant complaints that I hear when I discuss trifecta, superfecta and multi-race wagers, is that players ask how is it possible to pick four horses in a row (either four consecutive winners or horses running one, two, three and four). My answer is that generally that is not what you do. Exotic wagers are not exotic at all. Let's look at a potential superfecta wager as an example: Say there are ten horses in a race, and you feel quite confident that you can identify the horses that will run first and second. Now let's assume that among the other eight horses you are able to identify only one that stands out slightly from the others by being somewhat above the others in ability. We'll assume the first two horses you picked, as the potential victorious horses are relatively short odds. Therefore, a win wager on both of them or an exacta box would likely make a minimal return for your handicapping efforts. Let's assume that these horses are numbers four and seven in post order, that the third horse that you selected as being somewhat above the other horses is priced at approximately 10 to 1, and that horse is post position number six.

Now what do you do? You do not do the four, seven exacta box. You might want to consider the four seven, with the four seven, with the six trifecta (4,7/4,7/6). However, you are not convinced that the six is an absolute lock for third, but you believe he will run decently in the race. This is how I would play the race. I would bet a $1 superfecta partial wheel four seven, with the four seven, with the six, with all (4,7/4,7/6/all) and then the four seven, with the four seven, with all, with six (4,7/4,7/all/6). Now the question remains, how much did that cost? Each wager cost $14, making the total of your investment $28. This is not a particularly large amount to invest. You have turned a complicated bet into finding the exacta, and then finding a contender. If you are correct in this race, I would be able to say with virtual certainty that your investment of $28 will return more in the superfecta pool than would a $14 exacta box on the four and seven. My suggestion is that before you start to make wagers such as this, you go to the track, make an assessment, and then look and see what the pay-off tells you. You will be pleasantly surprised that often your exactas, which are paying $14 for a $2 bet, are providing you the opportunity of hitting $300-400+ superfectas.

The above example shows again the concept of how an exotic wager does not require you to actually be able to identify all four animals in order. Using the above example again briefly, let us assume that you only like the four and seven and thought every other horse in the race was terrible. Then a consideration could be to play the trifecta four seven, with the four seven, with all (4,7/4,7/all). If you are deep pocketed enough, maybe a superfecta four seven, with four seven, with all, with all (4,7/4,7/all/all).

Additionally, this same concept can be used in pick 3's and pick 4's, where using an all in a race that seems to be difficult can present a lucrative betting opportunity. Here, I will provide one brief example of a pick 4 using this strategy. Let us assume that in the first race you have narrowed it down to the post positions four and seven. In the second race, which is a ten-horse field, you are not able to distinguish between any of the horses and believe that all of them have a chance. In the third race, you feel confident you have selected a single horse that will win (for our example, the post will be five). The final race you have three selections (post positions one, two and three). Your $1 pick 4 wager would be as follows: the four seven, with all, with five, with one two three (4,7/all/5/1,2,3). This wager will cost you $60 for a $1 wager. Again, with the small investment you have covered a lot of bases and made it possible to get a lucrative return, particularly if a long shot comes in where you have used the all.

A final betting strategy suggestion on multi-race wagers: handicap inclusively as opposed to exclusively. If you feel certain (or as certain as a gambler can feel) that a horse is a winner, single out the horse. However, in the next race if you believe that there are four horses that can win and it is difficult for you to differentiate, include all four of them. Do not attempt to make changes and end up losing when the one of the four that you threw out is victorious. I would explain this concept more specifically: the surer you are, the narrower you should be (fewer horses), and the more unsure you are, the broader you should be (more horses).

An interesting para-mutual fact concerning wagering strategy is that a horse you handicapped may have a value that changes throughout the racing card. This is also one of the concepts that I see even serious, good players struggle with. Value here is a relative term, and what I mean should be exemplified by the following. Let's say you have handicapped the first three races at a particular track and in the second race the horse you feel is most likely to win is the four horse. Let us say that he is noted in the morning line odds at 20 to 1. I have heard some players say that they could not believe my horse is going to be 20 to 1 (before the race even goes off). Instead, I would see this as a huge betting opportunity because the second race has not yet gone. Because many players just bet off the morning line, none of these players will like your four horse, and even serious handicappers who did find the four interesting may now discount him because they perceive that his odds will be high and his chances of victory are low. Going back to the example, I would play in the first race a double wheel all, with the four (all/4). If there was a pick 3, I might also play all, with four, with all (all/4/all). I would additionally go back and play similar doubles and pick 3 wagers with the horses that I liked in the first and third races: a $5 pick 3 the two three, with the four, with the five six, etc. (2,3/4/5,6). The reason I would include the all tickets is that I would not want to be correct with the four and miss the wagering opportunity by having my handicapping be inaccurate in the first and third races. However, I would "load-up," using the four as a key with the horses I like in the first and third races. Let's take the example a little further and say the first race goes off and a long shot wins. Now the second race is going to post and the four is not 20 to 1 but 5 to 1. Awwww, the vindication of the handicapper: The horse I have been telling my friends about and they laughed when he was 20 to 1 is now 5 to 1. However, they are unlikely to be in my potential winning double pool, all, with four (all/4) or my pick 3 pool where I played all, with four, with all (all/4/all). As I wait for race two, my horse is going off at 5 to 1. One might ask, do I need to put additional win money on him or use him more in the single race exotics (trifecta, superfecta, etc.)? Probably not, because now his odds are significantly decreased and everybody has seen him, and I am probably looking pretty "fat" for my double and pick 3 wagers.

Now let's carry the above example the other way so you can understand that a horse's value can increase by the time the race goes off. Let us say again that you have handicapped the first three races. You like the four in the second race and you note that he is the 2 to 1 morning line favorite, and selected by all the individuals in the DRF. You just now found a horse that has minimal value in multi-race exotics, unless he happens to be bracketed by long shots. You will probably want to make somewhat smaller wagers on him in these pools. While you feel it is likely he is the victor, realizing that everyone has seen this horse, you know these wagers will not return large sums of money to you. Now let's assume that the second race is going off and your horse is not 2 to 1 but in fact is 10 to 1. You should now consider making a win or trifecta key type wager on this horse because he presents a winning opportunity in that mutual pool. I offer one cautionary statement here: When you see a horse that has morning line favoritism and then goes off at extremely long odds, you should examine the horse closely. Examine the horse on the racetrack to ensure that the horse is not in poor condition or injured. In general, horses that are high morning line odds and then go off at lower mutual odds are good wagers, but horses that are morning line favorites and then go off extremely long, seem to be poorly predictive of victory.

Individual bettors will find the particular wagers that best suits their personality style and make-up. It is an experimentation process, and an evolving one.

Horses
By Leroy Neiman
(A beautiful coffee table art book by the famous Neiman—which has a wonderful "racetrack" section)

11

Let's Put Everything to Use— Let's Handicap a Race

"Look straight ahead. What is there?
If you see it as it is. You will never err."
— Bassui Tokusho, Zen Monk, *Japanese Death Poems*

Now that you have a solid grasp of most of the major handicapping techniques you will need, let's use a race example to test some of these abilities. I tried to locate a general horserace that was neither too complex nor overly simplistic for example purposes. I decided to make it a fair test in that I would identify a race that had approximately eight to ten horses at a major track. Additionally, one of the facets of many other handicapping books that I have found to be somewhat problematic is the author's way of utilizing a race from which they made tons and tons of money. Obviously, if it is a race they selected that they were extremely victorious at, whatever handicapping techniques they are espousing will fit the race to a tee. Instead, I decided to pick from a racing card, which I did not attend, and complete my handicapping, then obtain the videos and race results to see how my handicapping turned out. I chose a typical West Coast mid-week racing card from Wednesday, March 6, 2002. I had handicapped two particular races that I thought would be of interest. One of the earlier races had a series of scratches in it, which made the handicapping analysis invalid. However, the second race I selected, the fifth race from Santa Anita, stayed intact without scratches and it will be the race I am going to use as an example.

The only saddening result here is that my handicapping was correct on this race, but because I am true to my cause and did not wager on it (to maintain the authenticity of my results), I cannot claim that I secured my fortune in this race.

Set out below, reprinted with the authority of the DRF, is the fifth race at Santa Anita from Wednesday, March 6, 2002, a six and a half-furlong allowance race for non-winners of more than one race.

Now that you have the race in full format, handicap based on the techniques that you have become familiar with in the earlier chapters in this book. Once you have done that, turn to the next two pages and you will find the authoritatively pure discussion on how this race can be handicapped.

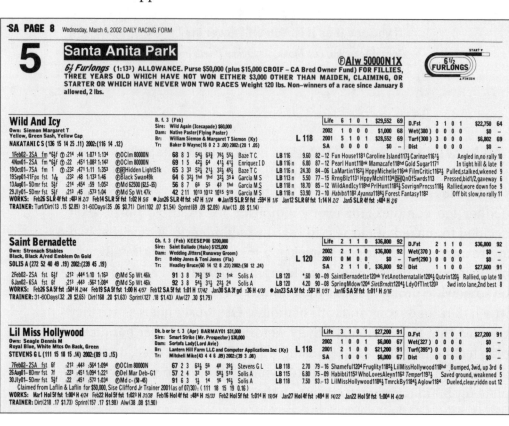

Duel

Own: Kuelbs J Michele
Turquoise, Black V-sash/hoop, Black
SMITH M E (132 21 13 13 .16) 2002:(120 20 .17)

Dk. b or br f. 3 (Mar) FTSAUG00 $80,000
Sire: Two Punch (Mr. Prospector) $20,000
Dam: Deviltante(Devil's Bag)
Br: Brushwood Stable (Pa)
Tr: Mitchell Mike(43 4 4 6 .09) 2002:(39 3 .08)

L 118

Life	1	1	0	0	$14,250	54	D.Fst	1	1	0	0	$14,250	54
2002	1	1	0	0	$14,250	54	Wet(380)	0	0	0	0	$0	–
2001	0	M	0	0	$0	–	Turf(180)	0	0	0	0	$0	–
SA	0	0	0	0	$0	–	Dist	0	0	0	0	$0	–

Previously trained by Jenkins Rodney
4Jan02-7Lrl fst 6f :224 :464 :594 1:133 ⒻMd Sp Wt 25k 54 10 3 1hd 2hd 21 1½ Rocco J L 122 11.00 71-29 Duel122½ Late Nite Fan122no Last Call For Love1173¾ 2wd,dueled,driving 11
WORKS: Mar2 Hol 5f fst 1:012 H *8/28* Feb25 Hol 4f fst :501 H *5/9* Feb19 Hol 3f fst :354 H *4/21* Feb14 Hol 4f fst :481 H *5/23* Feb9 Hol 4f fst :474 H *2/23* ●Feb4 Hol 3f fst :352 H *1/7*
TRAINER: 1stW/Trn(187 .14 $1.39) 61-180Days(17 .00 $0.00) 2ndStart(11 .27 $2.91) Dirt(218 .17 $1.73) Sprint(157 .17 $1.98) Alw(38 .08 $1.90)

Icantgoforthat

Own: Broberg A & Knapp P
Black Chartreuse K On Back
STEINER J J (33 2 2 0 .06) 2002:(35 4 .11)

B. f. 3 (Mar)
Sire: In Excess*Ire (Siberian Express)
Dam: Texinadress(Copelan)
Br: Michael E Pegram (Cal)
Tr: Knapp Steve(16 1 3 1 .06) 2002:(11 1 .09)

L 120

Life	10	3	2	1	$137,120	83	D.Fst	10	3	2	1	$137,120	83
2002	2	1	1	0	$51,480	83	Wet(385*)	0	0	0	0	$0	–
2001	8	2	1	1	$85,640	73	Turf(320)	0	0	0	0	$0	–
SA	5	2	1	0	$93,120	83	Dist	3	1	0	1	$39,000	75

16Feb02-4SA fst 6f :213 :444 :571 1:101 ⒻⓈBoo La Boo107k 83 2 4 1½ 1½ 11 2½ Steiner J J LB 119 b 6.80 86-11 Lady George122½ Icantgoforthat1192 SuperHigh1174 Inside, worn down 6
25Jan02-6SA fst 6½f :214 :45 1:103 1:173 ⒻⓈAlw 50000N1X 75 6 3 1hd 11 12 11 Steiner J J LB 120 b 6.10 85-15 Icntgoforthtl1201 ExcessivPryr120hd CusI'mTricky120½ Dueled,clear,held 8
28Dec01-4SA fst 7f :214 :443 1:102 1:24 ⒻⓈCal Br Champ150k 65 7 4 51¾ 2hd 2hd 44½ Steiner J J LB 116 b 47.40 80-16 Lady George1211½ Super High1141½ *Daddy's Gold*1141½ 5wd,3wd,weakened 10
8Dec01-4Hol fst 6½f :214 :443 1:10 1:162 ⒻⓈGoldenBallet50k 65 3 4 2hd 2hd 3nk 45½ Steiner J J LB 119 b 11.50 83-08 *BllBllBll*1192 Ddddy'sGold1173½ Mrtil'sPrincss117no Bmpd strt,lost whip1/8 7
28Nov01-1Hol fst 6f :223 :452 :574 1:111 ⒻClm c-(50-45) 72 5 1 1hd 2hd 2½ 2½ Flores D R LB 119 b *1.40 83-17 Brittonzmydy114½ Icntgoforthtl192½ ObspoKd1175 Fought back, gamely 5
Claimed from Pegram Michael E for $50,000, Baffert Bob Trainer 2001(as of 11/28): (595 127 92 87 0.21)
3Nov01-9BM fst 6f :22 :444 :572 1:103 ⒻⓈBam's Penny60k 52 4 4 31½ 33 79 713¾ Carr D LB 116 b 2.90 74-11 CinnfulBrid1153 *Bigboystoy*1172½ CourtlyColors114¾ Prssd pace outside 8
11Oct01-1SA fst 6f :22 :45 :572 1:103 ⒻClm 50000(50-45) 73 4 2 11½ 13 14 14½ Flores D R LB 116 fb *.50 86-12 Icantgoforthat1164½ SmokesTopGun1131½ *WidowBlck*116no Inside, handily 5
27Sep01-5SA fst 7f :22 :451 1:114 1:251 ⒻⓇCal Sires100k 52 6 3 11 12 1½ 46 Flores D R LB 116 b *.70 73-15 Moossa's Girl1152 MamaMama116no Shalini1144 Veered out start,wkend 6
13Sep01-10Fpx fst 6½f :213 :451 1:101 1:163 ⒻBustles&Bows50k 67 4 3 31 31½ 34½ 39 Garcia M S LB 114 b *1.40 86-09 GreenEydLdy1146 PstYou1143 Icntgoforthtl1144 Awkward strt,stdied1/4 8
20Jly01-5Dmr fst 5½f :214 :46 :592 1:062 ⒻⓈMd Sp Wt 47k 57 5 1 1hd 11½ 11½ 14½ Flores D R LB 118 b *.40 80-18 Icntgoforthtl1184½ *Toby'sBby*1181 JeweledSlew118½ Dueled,clear,driving 6
WORKS: Mar2 SA 3f fst :39 B *21/21* Feb11 SA 3f fst :344 H *2/16* Feb5 SA 6f fst 1:121 H *2/9* Jan21 SA 3f fst :362 B *9/24* Jan15 SA 6f fst 1:134 H *5/15* Jan8 SA 6f fst 1:122 H *2/18*
TRAINER: Dirt(63 .13 $2.66) Sprint(62 .13 $2.70) Alw(9 .11 $1.58)

No Turbulence

Own: Grenier & Grenier & Lewkowitz
White, Turquoise Emblem On Back, Lime
DESORMEAUX K J (252 44 42 42 .17) 2002:(225 40 .18)

B. f. 3 (Feb) WASAUG00 $35,000
Sire: Skywalker (Relaunch) $7,500
Dam: Kildare(Flying Paster)
Br: Coal Creek Farm (Wash)
Tr: Kruljac J Eric(23 0 6 3 .00) 2002:(68 12 .18)

L 118

Life	7	1	1	1	$54,960	77	D.Fst	6	1	1	1	$52,020	77
2002	2	0	0	1	$17,200	76	Wet(370)	0	0	0	0	$0	–
2001	5	1	1	0	$37,760	77	Turf(350)	1	0	0	0	$2,940	55
SA	3	0	1	1	$23,100	76	Dist	0	0	0	0	$0	–

2Feb02-8TuP fst 1 1/16 :234 :47 1:104 1:431 ⒻArizona Oaks75k 69 1 1hd 31 3nk 44 47 Martinez S B L 121 *.60 82-13 *BellaCsh*1212 ClceClunes1211½ LdyContinentl1213½ Angled out, weakened 6
6Jan02-3SA fst 1 1/16 :232 :472 1:114 1:44 ⒻSantaYsabel-G3 76 1 1½ 1hd 3½ 33 34¼ Desormeaux K J LB 116 4.20 80-14 BellaBellaBella115nk TmrckBy1164 NoTurbulence11610 Bit crowded start 4
5Dec01-1Hol fst 7f :222 :454 1:111 1:234 ⒻMd Sp Wt 36k 77 4 1 3½ 2hd 12½ 19 Desormeaux K J LB 119 2.80 80-17 NoTurbulnc1199 *StonbridgLdy*1191½ NordcWthr11910 3 wide,clear,driving 4
26Oct01-5SA fst 1 :223 :462 1:113 1:382 ⒻMd Sp Wt 40k 62 2 54½ 74¾ 66½ 46 25½ Baze T C LB 117 13.00 73-23 TmrckBy1175½ *NoTurbulence*117no ChezLFmm1171 4wd into lane,late 2nd 7
4Oct01-1SA fst 1 :224 :462 1:111 1:38 ⒻMd Sp Wt 40k 61 4 44 52¾ 53½ 45 48 Baze T C LB 117 4.40 73-16 TurquoiseBed1172 *TmrckBy*1171 ChezLFmm1175 Angled in, no late bid 6
3Sep01-5Dmr fm 1 Ⓣ:222 :471 1:121 1:37 ⒻMd Sp Wt 49k 55 3 918 99¾ 76¾ 45 49 Baze T C LB 118 3.50 71-14 Farda Amiga1182½ Puff The Magic1181½ CastingCall1185 Forced out early 9
12Aug01-4Dmr fst 5½f :214 :452 :58 1:043 ⒻMd Sp Wt 47k 60 1 8 84¾ 85¾ 76½ 45 Baze T C LB 118 16.30 84-09 *Tli'sluckybusrid*1182½ Dvlsh1181½ Shzsummrbrz1181 Swung out, mild gain 8
WORKS: Mar2 SA 3f fst :37 H *14/21* Feb23 SA 5f fst 1:02 H *45/54* Jan30 SA 3f gd :362 H *7/30* Jan23 SA 4f fst :491 H *22/38* Dec27 SA 5f fst 1:01 H *25/70* Dec19 SA 4f fst :482 H *12/53*
TRAINER: Route/Sprint(41 .29 $2.78) 31-60Days(65 .14 $1.32) Dirt(289 .19 $1.63) Sprint(206 .17 $1.52) Alw(56 .13 $0.65)

September Secret

Own: Lo Hi Stable
Black, White Lo Hi/card Emblem
VALENZUELA P A (201 13 30 22 .06) 2002:(189 14 .07)

Dk. b or br f. 3 (May) KEESEP00 $20,000
Sire: Our Emblem (Mr. Prospector) $7,500
Dam: Andrushka(Giboulee)
Br: Fletcher Gray & John McDonald (Ky)
Tr: Machowsky Michael(27 8 4 4 .30) 2002:(23 7 .30)

L 118

Life	1	1	0	0	$25,200	99	D.Fst	1	1	0	0	$25,200	99
2001	1	1	0	0	$25,200	99	Wet(307)	0	0	0	0	$0	–
2000	0	M	0	0	$0	–	Turf(252)	0	0	0	0	$0	–
SA	0	0	0	0	$0	–	Dist	0	0	0	0	$0	–

10Jun01-10Hol fst 5f :213 :443 :57 ⒻMd Sp Wt 42k 99 6 2 21½ 22½ 21 11 Puglisi I L LB 118 5.70 97-08 SeptemberSecret1181 Ayanna1189 *Tempera*1182½ Came out,led 1/16,dvng 10
WORKS: Mar2 SA 6f fst 1:133 H *10/29* Feb23 SA 5f fst :593 H *11/54* Feb16 SA 5f fst :584 H *2/67* Feb10 SA 4f fst :482 H *12/39* Jan26 SA 4f fst :484 H *26/70* Jan20 SA 4f fst :473 H *7/50*
TRAINER: +180Days(5 .20 $3.20) 2ndStart(22 .18 $0.83) Dirt(144 .19 $1.88) Sprint(132 .20 $2.64) Alw(29 .17 $2.11)

Twice As Golden

Own: Lewis Beverly J & Robert B
Green, Yellow Hoops/sleeves, Yellow
FLORES D R (136 20 19 15 .15) 2002:(118 20 .17)

Ch. f. 3 (Mar) KEEAPR01 $535,000
Sire: Gold Case (Forty Niner) $5,000
Dam: Golden Ode(Opening Verse)
Br: Robert T Manfuso (Md)
Tr: Baffert Bob(139 23 22 17 .17) 2002:(123 24 .20)

L 118

Life	3	1	0	0	$24,600	75	D.Fst	3	1	0	0	$24,600	75
2002	1	0	0	0	$0	66	Wet(340)	0	0	0	0	$0	–
2001	2	1	0	0	$24,600	75	Turf(244)	0	0	0	0	$0	–
SA	2	0	0	0	$3,000	71	Dist	2	1	0	0	$24,600	75

21Jan02-5SA fst 7f :22 :443 1:094 1:23 ⒻSanta Ynez-G2 66 5 6 68 69 66 78¾ Flores D R LB 116 16.20 81-10 Dancing116½ Respectful116½ *Lady George*1232½ Bit off rail,no rally 8
31Dec01-3SA fst 6½f :212 :442 1:091 1:16 ⒻOClm 80000N 71 2 6 54 54 46 47 Flores D R LB 120 3.50 81-13 Rich Musique120½ Candor1181½ Respectful1205 4wd into lane,no rally 8
10Nov01-3Hol fst 6½f :221 :453 1:102 1:171 ⒻMd Sp Wt 35k 75 2 2 2½ 2hd 11½ 11½ Flores D R LB 119 2.80 85-13 TwiceAsGolden1191½ BeutyContest1194½ DrmDy1199 Inside,clear,driving 4
WORKS: Feb26 Hol 5f fst 1:01 H *10/31* Feb20 Hol 4f fst :481 H *8/33* Feb14 Hol 4f fst :481 H *5/23* Jan17 SA 5f fst :593 H *3/74* Jan12 SA 5f fst :593 B *7/61* Dec26 SA 5f fst 1:001 H *6/49*
TRAINER: 31-60Days(164 .19 $1.50) Dirt(664 .22 $1.69) Sprint(498 .21 $1.53) Alw(203 .20 $1.34)

Oh, so you thought I was just going to handicap it for you in the last two pages? No, the actual concept is to teach you how to handicap and how it is based on your own individual skills. After I show you the results, I will show you the general concept on how I did handicap it. The results are as follows:

SA CHARTS 2 3/6/02 DAILY RACING FORM

FIFTH RACE

Santa Anita
MARCH 6, 2002

6½ FURLONGS. (1.13³) ALLOWANCE. Purse $50,000 (plus $15,000 CBOIF – CA Bred Owner Fund) FOR FILLIES, THREE YEARS OLD WHICH HAVE NOT WON EITHER $3,000 OTHER THAN MAIDEN, CLAIMING, OR STARTER OR WHICH HAVE NEVER WON TWO RACES Weight 120 lbs. Non-winners of a race since January 8 allowed, 2 lbs.

Value of Race: $59,000 Winner $39,000; second $10,000; third $6,000; fourth $3,000; fifth $1,000. Mutuel Pool $331,654.00 Exacta Pool $229,610.00 Quinella Pool $27,776.00 Trifecta Pool $239,427.00 Superfecta Pool $90,118.00

Last Raced	Horse	M/Eqt.	A.Wt	PP	St	¼	½	Str	Fin	Jockey	Odds $1
16Feb02 4SA2	Icantgoforthat	LBb	3 120	5	1	2¹	23½	1hd	11½	Steiner J J	5.00
2Feb02 2SA1	Saint Bernadette	LB	3 120	2	8	8	73½	3½	21½	Solis A	1.80
2Feb02 8TuP4	No Turbulence	LB	3 118	6	6	7hd	6hd	66	3½	Desormeaux K J	9.00
21Jan02 5SA7	Twice As Golden	LB	3 118	8	3	5½	4½	5½	41½	Flores D R	20.30
7Feb02 2SA3	Lil Miss Hollywood	LB	3 118	3	4	6½	51	4hd	5hd	Stevens G L	9.70
10Jun01 10Hol1	September Secret	LB	3 118	7	2	1hd	1hd	24	612	Valenzuela P A	1.70
4Jan02 7Lrl1	Duel	LB	3 118	4	7	4hd	8	8	73	Smith M E	40.20
1Feb02 3SA5	Wild And Icy	LBf	3 118	1	5	3½	3½	72½	8	Nakatani C S	33.10

OFF AT 3:08 Start Good. Won driving. Track fast.
TIME :21³, :44², 1:09², 1:16² (:21.78, :44.46, 1:09.50, 1:16.41)

$2 Mutuel Prices:

5–ICANTGOFORTHAT	12.00	4.40	3.00
2–SAINT BERNADETTE		3.40	2.40
6–NO TURBULENCE			3.80

$1 EXACTA 5–2 PAID $20.60 $2 QUINELLA 2–5 PAID $16.20 $1 TRIFECTA 5–2–6 PAID $121.70 $1 SUPERFECTA 5–2–6–8 PAID $666.00

B. f, (Mar), by In Excess*Ire–Texinadress, by Copelan. Trainer Knapp Steve. Bred by Michael E Pegram (Cal).

ICANTGOFORTHAT had speed between horses to duel for the lead, battled along the inside on the backstretch and turn, kicked clear past midstretch and held sway under a strong hand ride. SAINT BERNADETTE a bit crowded between horses at the start, saved ground chasing the leaders, steadied briefly early on the turn then waited off heels, came out leaving the bend, split horses brushing a foe into the stretch and rallied gamely. NO TURBULENCE settled outside, went three deep on the turn and four wide into the stretch and just got the show. TWICE AS GOLDEN was in a good position chasing the pace three deep to the stretch and was edged for third. LIL MISS HOLLYWOOD broke in a bit, tracked the leaders along the inside to the stretch and lacked the needed response. SEPTEMBER SECRET angled in and dueled three deep early then alongside the winner until past midstretch and weakened. DUEL close up chasing between horses on the backstretch, dropped back into and on the turn and gave way. WILD AND ICY sent along inside to press the early pace, stalked along the rail, came out on the turn, steadied into the stretch while weakening and also gave way.

Owners— 1, Broberg & Knapp; 2, Stronach Stable; 3, Grenier Dennis & Norine & Lewkowitz; 4, Lewis Robert B & Beverly J; 5, Seagle Dennis M; 6, Lo Hi Stable; 7, Kuelbs J M; 8, Siemon Margaret T.

Trainers—1, Knapp Steve; 2, Headley Bruce; 3, Kruljac J Eric; 4, Baffert Bob; 5, Mitchell Mike; 6, Machowsky Michael; 7, Mitchell Mike; 8, Baker D Wayne

Okay, did you get all four horses in order? Did you identify the winner? On the other hand, the exacta? How did you do overall? If you got all four horses in order, and possibly were able to tell how far apart they were in lengths, my personal opinion is that you do not need to read the rest of this book. For the rest of you, if you feel that being a little more "on the Zen" will help you with your handicapping, I encourage you to read on to determine how Zen can be a positive factor in your horseplay.

For your information on how I would have handicapped the race, I only would have been confident of the first two top finishers, Icantgoforthat and Saint Bernadette. However, I would have scored well in this race because I also gave the horse No Turbulence a significant chance to run third or fourth. Therefore, using this horse that I would have expected to go off at long odds due to his recent loss at a second tier track such as Turf Paradise, I would have also been able to secure the superfecta which paid $666 for a one dollar ticket.

Here is my betting analysis of each of the horses in postposition order. Remember this analysis was done before the race, and without the benefit of seeing the horses on the track or being able to observe the race time odds.

Horse number one, Wild and Icy, appeared to be somewhat over-matched for me in this race, because he was going from turf to dirt and had broken his maiden for a claiming price of $62,500. Additionally, while this horse was moving from turf to dirt, its prior dirt Beyer Speed Figure had been somewhat low, not even breaking 70. I would have only used this horse on my "all" tickets.

Horse number two, Saint Bernadette, was obviously a quality animal that was improving with each race. The Beyer Speed Figures were a solid 91 and 92, and while the horse had recently broke it's maiden, it had done so in maiden special weight company, and with a good time at six and a half furlongs. My only significant knock on this horse is that it appeared to be a deep, or relatively deep closer, which might compromise the animal's chances. The horse was a must use, however was able to be beaten due to its extreme closing style, and I intended to use him in the first and second spots.

Horse number three, Lil Miss Hollywood, appeared to have a little bit of back class, having previously won in the Grade I Del Mar Debutante, a closer look showed that the horse had only broken it's maiden in maiden claiming ranks ($50,000) the race before. While Mike Mitchell as a trainer and Gary Stevens as a jockey are a popular combination, my feeling was that Lil Miss Hollywood would get over bet. While she might get up for a piece (third or fourth), I did not feel that it was a particularly good betting opportunity (accordingly, this horse would be only included in my "all" tickets).

Horse number four, Duel, was the other Mike Mitchell horse ridden by Mike Smith. My feeling on this "hidden entry" of Mitchell, is that Duel, a Laurel Park (Maryland Track) horse in it's last start, was heavily overmatched in this race, and would be used as a "rabbit" to insure an honest pace. I considered this horse an obvious throw out, but would probably use him in the "all" tickets, in that it would have been the only horse that I would have thrown out of this particular race (so in other words he will be used on the "all" ticket)—as a note I was right regarding his usage in this race, he immediately went out to the front and then dropped back and gave way.

Horse number five, Icantgoforthat, I immediately liked, and I also liked the fact that I knew it would be under bet ridden by J. J. Steiner and trained by the relatively unknown Steven Knapp. The horse had speed, had a top recent Beyer Speed Figure of 83, and could obviously go the distance as shown by the race on January 25, 2002, where it won a similar state bred race. The horse was, in fact, eligible for this race because his previous wins had been in restricted state bred starter company, and a claiming race. Additionally, the horse had originally broken it's maiden at the maiden special weight level, and had been running consistently since that time. Additionally, the jockey Steiner was familiar with this animal, having ridden him in his last four starts. Finally, and possibly most importantly, the horse seemed to have an increasing Beyer Speed Figure, having previously gone from 55 to 65 to 75 to 83 in its last four starts. I also felt that this horse was the only real speed in the race. The only other horses that appeared to have legitimate speed were Duel (a phony), No Turbulence (that I felt had a chance, but was slightly outclassed), and September Secret (that was coming off a long layoff and would be extremely over bet). For these reasons, my impression of the race was that Icantgoforthat would go out somewhere near the lead and then hold on, hopefully to win to a likely fast closing Saint Bernadette. Icantgoforthat was my hero.

Horse number six, No Turbulence, had recently been running with some speed, and was additionally dropping back in distance from a mile and sixteenth, to six and a half furlongs. Eric Kruljac is an excellent trainer who often trains at Turf Paradise. I have discussed previously the possibility that sometimes when a horse goes to a second tier track the Beyer Speed Figure received may not be legitimate. On paper, I considered the possibility that the 69 Beyer Speed Figure that No Turbulence had received at Turf Paradise had not been commensurate with its actual previous efforts which generally were around the mid to high 70s. Additionally, this horse had shown one other feature which none of the other horses showed; versatility to come from off the pace as it had done in some of the previous maiden special weight races running a mile at Santa Anita. I considered the possibility that Kruljac might request the jockey Kent Desormeaux to either take this horse to the lead, or on the other hand, take this horse back and try to make a late run. I consider Kent Desormeaux to be one of the best jockeys in the country, and the fact that he was riding this horse for Kruljac indicated that this horse was very likely to show up somewhere in the top four. However, I felt it was somewhat under-matched compared to Icantgoforthat and Saint Bernadette. I would utilize No Turbulence in the race's lower tiers (third and fourth on my superfectas).

Horse number seven, September Secret, had obviously been a good horse on June 10, 2001 when winning with a 91 Beyer Speed Figure going five furlongs at Hollywood Park. Five furlongs at Hollywood Park in June is much different from six and a half furlongs nine months later at Santa Anita. While there were no noted gaps in the workout line, I did not feel that this horse would do much in this race, especially off the long layoff. Additionally, while I thought it was possible that this horse could be ready, and could win, I felt it would be extremely over bet and was a poor betting opportunity. I was willing to accept the possibility that this horse would beat me and I would lose. I would use this horse only on my "all" tickets underneath my selections.

Horse number eight, Twice As Golden, had a chance, I felt, though his Beyer Speed Figures were relatively low compared to the other animals. Still, this horse was now going to be running his third start off the layoff, and also dropping sharply in class from the Santa Ynez Grade II. The animal had outstanding connections by being trained by Bob Baffert, ridden by David Flores, and owned by Bob and Beverly Lewis (who obviously had the deep pockets to purchase the horse for $535,000 at the Keeneland sale). While I felt that this horse had a chance, I felt her most likely position would be in the third and fourth spots, and I was not confident enough to key off this horse, and only used her on the "all" tickets.

Okay, so there you have my analysis. What I would have bet in this race is that I would have played Saint Bernadette (2) and Icantgoforthat (5) in an exacta box (probably a $10 or $20 box). Additionally, in that it was only an eight-horse field I would have played a superfecta partial wheel the two five, with the two five, with the six (No Turbulence), with all (2,5/2,5/6/all) and then protected myself with the two five, with the two five, with all, with the six (2,5/2,5/all/6). On these two bets, the winning $1 price was a $20.60 exacta, and a $666 superfecta.

The basic point of my analysis on these horses is to show you how I would have assessed that race. That is not to say that I do not make significant errors when I assess other races, just that I honestly selected this race as an example for you to look at to see if your handicapping would have seen the winners. I believe the handicapping techniques I have discussed in the previous chapters will help you with all your handicapping. However, I hope that the most useful part of the book is to follow, when I explain how the concepts and the way of Zen will allow you to see your winners more easily, and also to enjoy your time at the track more. I intend to show you that the way of Zen can be your path to more successful horseplay, as Kid Rock would say:

"If it looks good, you'll see it.
If it sounds good, you'll hear it.
If it's marketed right, you'll buy it, but…
If it's real you'll feel it."
— Kid Rock, Musician, and CEO of Top Dog Records

Bet With the Best, All New Strategies
from Americas Leading Handicappers
(A book published by the DRF, which includes outstanding sections written by Andrew Beyer, Steven Crist, Lauren Stich, and others).

Section 2
Zen as the Way to See Winners and Be a Winner

12
What is Zen?
An Introduction

"Yield and overcome;
Bend and be straight;
Empty and be full;
Wear out and be new;
Have little and gain;
Have much and be confused.

. . .

Be really whole,
And all things will come to you."
— Lao Tzu, from the *Tao Te Ching*

Zen is not a religion, or a philosophical theory. Zen is a view of the universe and life that does not fit easily within the rigid categorizations of Western thought and belief. To demystify Zen, the reader must see Zen as a path to liberation or enlightenment. It is about experience and practices that will allow self-development and increase your capacity to see life with clarity and act with that same clarity. It is a way that teaches compassion, wisdom, calmness, and other practices that create a consummate whole or oneness.

Zen, quite literally, means meditation (Zazen being the more technically correct term for meditation or quiet sitting); the practice of meditation is central to Zen. More generally, however, Zen must be seen as a path, or a way. Zen has as its forerunners various types of Mahayana Buddhism and Taoist practices. Mahayana is the great vehicle that allows followers to locate the spiritual path to enlightenment; Taoism is a path of enlightenment and liberation, based on freeing oneself from needless conventions.

There are certain distinctions concerning how Zen fits in specific eastern cultures:

- *Japan*—where Zen was greatly influenced by Bushido and the warrior status of the well-known Samurai.
- *China*—where Zen was colored by Confucianism and Taoist philosophy.
- *India and Malaysia*—where more mysticism and tantric philosophy in some Buddhist sects made Zen appear "out-worldly" and almost cultist.

For basic purposes (and for most Western adherents), these distinctions can be somewhat minimized. If the reader wants a detailed discussion of the history of Zen and how it differs in various locales, and specifically its early roots in Taoism, Mahayana, and Buddhism, the authoritative book is Alan Watts' *The Way of Zen*.

For our purposes, I will discuss the way of Zen in general, in order to demonstrate how it can be of invaluable assistance in horse wagering and in one's overall life.

Whenever I try to explain Zen in a conceptual way that people can quickly understand, I draw a big circle on a piece of paper like this:

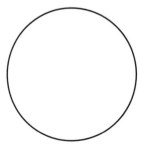

That circle is Zen. It is a path that encompasses the whole: it ends at the beginning, and it begins at the end. It is all and yet it is nothing. Even more so, it is not only the circle, it is the "empty" spaces both inside and out. One of my favorite Zen quotes is the following:

> **"Thirty spokes share the wheels hub;**
> **It is the center hole that makes it useful.**
> **Shape clay into a vessel;**
> **It is the space within that makes it useful.**
> **Cut doors and windows for a room,**
> **It is the holes, which make it useful.**
> **Therefore, benefit comes from what is there;**
> **Usefulness from what is not."**
> — Lao Tsu, from the *Tao Te Ching*

The way of Zen is not a means of being pushed to enlightenment. Instead, when much of the worldly clutter (much of which is within our own minds) is cleared away, we find ourselves enlightened because we finally see things as they truly are.

In Zen, koans are often used between master and disciple to illustrate what Zen is (and what it is not), and how the master gained enlightened knowledge. A koan can loosely be translated as a parable or a story, offered to make a point. Often koans are in the form of a question and answer, and are sometimes humorous. Every horseplayer in the world knows the value of a sense of humor, and every successful horseplayer I have ever known was a comedian at heart. Throughout the remainder of the book I will toss in some koans which I hope will lead you to understand how Zen exists. Hopefully, some will let you see how your handicapping can also be positively affected.

How about this one to invoke thought:

> **"Absence of evidence**
> **is not evidence of absence."**
> — Anonymous

Zen is traditionally seen as enlightenment or awakening, and finally, as ethics and a means of conducting oneself. As we will see, all three have a great tie-in to horseplayers.

An enlightenment or awakening will allow us to clearly see through the needless clutter in a race and feel the winner. Appropriate meditation techniques will clear our mind, allowing us to use our acquired handicapping tools correctly. Finally, the ethics of Zen (briefly summarized as compassion, honesty, generosity, clear mindedness, and humbleness) will make us better human beings and more likely to be welcomed at our track or OTB.

Just as a brief summary of upcoming chapters: We will see how calmness and centering (essential Zen attributes) will allow the mind to relax and let go, so we will not be knocked off our methods of handicapping by outside forces. We will see with clarity of purpose and focus. We will learn that modesty and humbleness are the way of Zen, and all successful horseplayers know that there is never a place for arrogance or overconfidence. We will find that Zazen or Meditation is the way to enlightenment. Meditation is not only about relaxing the mind, it is about insuring that the mind is clear and crisp so it can be utilized to its greatest potential. We will see the bigger picture of where we fit in the universe, where a horse fits in a race, a race in a career, and our handicapping in a race. We will find that there is a possibility of collateral damage, or harm to others and ourselves, if we focus too narrowly or inappropriately on horseracing. Zen is the way of moderation, and we must use moderation in our play and in our lives. We will learn means to get into "the zone", or more on the Zen; those wonderful times when ten horse fields are handicapped as easily as Secretariat in the Belmont. Conversely, we will know that when we fall off the Zen, it may be time to go to the bar, or just to play a round of golf. We will find out about the karma of a betting establishment, and learn that anger and superstition affect the Zen. Finally, we will learn about the concept of Warrior Zen and Bushido, and how aggressive actions (and non-actions) can be your keys to winning at the horses.

I believe that the way to victory at the horses, and the path to Zen enlightenment, go hand-in-hand, or hoof-in-hoof, if you will. Throughout time, horses have been seen as mystical in and of themselves. If you have spent any time around horses, you will know that they are Zen creatures of the highest order, and for us to try to understand them, we need to be more Zen ourselves. Remember, it is all about how our path to learning can lead to a more enlightened horseplayer. You may be surprised that this is not as difficult as we may make it seem. Often as horseplayers, we get in our own way. Zen will steer us away from these negative forces. Before we go on in detail in the upcoming chapters, read this final quote, and realize what potential we all hold (horseplayer or not).

"It is not just an arbitrary idea that the world is good, but it is good because we can experience its goodness. We can experience our world as healthy and straightforward, direct and real, because our basic nature is to go along with the goodness of situations. The human potential for intelligence and dignity is attuned to experiencing the brilliance of the bright blue sky, the freshness of green fields . . . the beauty of the trees and mountains (and I would add the beauty of the thundering miraculous horse in full gallop)."

— Chogyam Trungpa [with a little addition from your friendly author] in *Shambhala, The Sacred Path of the Warrior*

The Way of Zen
By Alan Watts

NOTES:

13
Calmness and Centering

"Heaven and earth are impartial;
They see the ten thousand things as straw dogs,
The wise are impartial;
They see the people as straw dogs.
The space between heaven and earth is like a bellows.
The shape changes but not the form;
The more it moves the more it yields.
More words count less.
Hold fast to the center."

— Lao Tsu, from the *Tao Te Ching*

One of the most important concepts to Zen is the idea of finding one's center. This center could loosely be described as one's place in the world and the universe. As will be discussed later, Zazen and Meditation should clear the mind of the flotsam and jetsam, to allow us to see our place more clearly. In this chapter, I will demonstrate how nearing a position of centeredness can help you be successful at the racetrack, and how the resulting sense of calm will make success more and more frequent.

One of the most important ideas in Zen is to see things as they are, not anything more, nor anything less. Finding one's center will insure that we see things as they are. This concept entails not forcing one's perception on what is actually going on. Zen would ask when you look at the mountains, what do you see? The answer, in simplified terms, is you see the mountains, and with great clarity and without distraction. It is exactly the type of clarity we want when we handicap and analyze a race.

Being centered insures we do not taint our handicapping and analysis with extraneous factors. The logic of this is so simple it is almost staggering. The closer we stay to our center (our true place), the more clearly we will see, and the better we will do. An outgrowth of this is we will also know we are seeing (handicapping) better and so we will be calmer. One of the true hallmarks of someone who is centered is an almost eerie sense of calm. You will see this in the best of horseplayers as well—a calm that shows through even on the worst of non-winning days.

The concept of centeredness and calmness are inexorably intertwined. They complement each other, specifically feed off each other, and magnify one another. Additionally, the concept of centeredness is not as abstract as it may first appear to some Western readers. It is explainable, attainable, and directly applicable to horse wagering.

> **"He who stands on tiptoe is not steady.**
> **He who strides cannot maintain the pace.**
> **He who makes a show is not enlightened.**
> **He who is self righteous is not respected."**
> — Lao Tzu, from the *Tao Te Ching*

What will make us centered? Specifically, what will make us centered in our efforts in the wagering realm? The answers are not complex, and all are inherently Zen concepts.

TAKE THE LONG VIEW

We are each one part of the process of the universe. We are an endless piece of an ongoing puzzle. We must see all things in the biggest scope possible. Each individual race is only one in a long series of races. The successful player does not worry over one loss, or two, or many. The player knows that the loss is just an opportunity to learn more about the universe of how races can be won (and lost). The key to winning is very simple: knowing how to lose. The successful player remains dispassionate about losses. In the book *Zen and the Art of Poker* by Larry W. Phillips, the author accurately talks about the "smiling, ironic indifference to the vicissitudes of fate" (p.51) shown by the best poker players. I believe this stands even truer for great horseplayers. The wry smile after a particularly bad beat is common; sometimes a nod, a smile, a sigh, and a tip of a hat. The key is that the great horseplayer really feels this way.

The line, "It would be funny if it was not happening to me!" comes to mind. Yet the true horseplayer knows more. It really is funny, even when it is happening to me, perhaps especially when it is happening to me. Why stress the bad beat? Take the long view, and remain dispassionate. The horrible ride Frankie Dettori gave on Swain in the Breeders Cup Classic was still only one loss. One race in many thousands you will play; learn from it, and see it as a step in a process. One link in a chain, or better yet, one link in the armor of your handicapping skill. Soften and learn.

> **"Markings in dry clay disappear**
> **only when the clay is soft again.**
> **Scars upon the self disappear**
> **only when one becomes soft within."**
> — Deng Ming Dao, from *365 Tao*

DO NOT GET ANGRY OR TAKE IT PERSONALLY

Good players know that anger is the bane of winning play. Anger encourages the impulsive, poorly thought out wager. It is imperative that the successful player knows that in the last race, Horse A, and Jockey B, did not run stupidly to make you, the gambler, lose. They did not do it to you—they just did it—it happened—do not get mad. Do not allow yourself self-pity or anger; it will only cloud your vision in other races that day, or that week, or that year.

> **"Some say the world will end in fire,**
> **some say in ice.**

From what I've tasted of desire,
I hold with those who favor fire.
But if it had to perish twice,
I think I know enough of hate
that for destruction, ice is also great
and would suffice."
— Robert Frost, from the poem *Fire and Ice*

Anger and hate have no place in a successful player, but likewise, overreaching or pressing has no place in our repertoire. We should not "desire" too much either. We cannot force our will on the horses; we can only take what they offer us. Pick our opportunity selectively and we can win, but try to force a race and we are sure to lose. Anger, and taking races personally, are outside the realm of Zen. Every player has had the misfortune of having a "bad beat", and then deciding he will win the next race come hell or high water. The next win does not come because it is being forced by the desire to win. After a bad beat, we must return to the tried and true handicapping techniques, and work for the next opportunity, but we must let it happen, we cannot force it. We can control our anger and ego by becoming more dispassionate; even the most "on their Zen" horseplayers must realize that anger exists in them, but we must sense these negative passions arising and dissipate them.

"I was no less angry than I had been,
but at the same time. . .I [recognized]
that anger can blind human vision."
— Malcolm X

As a horseplayer, when you feel anger rising, remember to smirk a little, knowing the horse and jockey did not conspire to ruin your bet. One of the most difficult aspects of horseplay for me initially was controlling my angry and negative emotions. Before I was able to personally incorporate Zen into my conceptualization of horse handicapping, I did very un-Zen like things—tearing up tickets, knocking over chairs, yelling, etc.—very boorish, and very negative.

Beyond the fact I was ruining others legitimate enjoyment of a wonderful pastime, I was also virtually guaranteeing further defeats for myself when I let my anger get the better of me. I would bet to catch up, I was too emotionally involved, and I lacked the necessary detachment to be successful and find the way of the winner at the betting window. Let the bad beats go and turn the page because there is always a next race.

I find that when my anger tries to well up I have two primary positive options:

- Turn the page and redouble my handicapping on the next target of opportunity (the upcoming races for that day or the next day's card).
- Do something unrelated to horses—go home, have a beer, listen to music, or take a walk.

Both options are positive—do not let negative emotions pull you into bad bets. We are all part of a wonderful world and a bad beat should not set us back. While no one ever promised you a rose garden (or a rose from the Kentucky Derby winner's blanket), you can always lighten up and go buy your significant other a dozen American Beauty roses. Nothing that happens to you at an OTB is ever so terrible that you should be depressed for long.

"Don't worry—Be happy"
— Bob Marley

STRESS INDUCES BAD WAGERING

Stressors are manifold, but all will negatively affect your wagering. As any doctor can tell you, not all stressors are negative stressors; getting married or having a baby is stress, though most would say positive stress. Negative stress in the wagering realm might include:

- Not bringing enough money (under funding or playing with scared money).
- Playing in proximity to others whose presence is not conducive to pleasant play (such as whiners and complainers).

☯ Playing with time constraints (not taking sufficient time to handicap).
☯ Playing in an environment that you are not familiar with.
☯ Playing after a number of days when you have lost.
☯ Placing wagers of larger size than normal.

Stress should be eliminated via relaxation techniques (which we will discuss in the meditation section) and by eliminating the stressor itself.

Eliminating the stress is very important. As a SWAT team leader in the FBI, I can state authoritatively that stress induces inaccuracy in all areas. During tryouts for SWAT candidates, we induce stress via physical exertion prior to pistol qualification. Candidates who would usually shoot in the mid-90s (on a 100 percent score scale) routinely shoot in the low-90s or lower. The importance of this for the horseplayer is readily apparent. When stress decreases performance (in SWAT tryouts during shooting, or in horse wagering during handicapping), there are two ways to combat this:

☯ Remove or limit the stressors, and
☯ If the stressors are not removable, know they exist and that they may be affecting your decisions.

To return to the SWAT analogy, while stress (both real and simulated via physical exertion) decrease performance in shooting and decision-making, this is not a closed-door process. If we train under stress, we begin to perform better while under real stress. If we train shooters after inducing stress, and if trained correctly they begin to shoot better while being stressed. As they shoot more while experiencing the stress, the stress begins to affect them at a decreased rate. This is applicable to us horseplayers as well.

Let us assume that it is a major racing day like the Breeders Cup, and we intend to make some sizable wagers (more than on a normal race card): we may feel stress. If we do this multiple times, we should be able to assess if our play is changing based on the source of the stress. Good "feel" in this area will lead to greater success as stakes are increased. One way to judge if you are over-reacting to stress, is if you are making bets that you normally would not. If you are universally a pick six player, but at the end of one particularly difficult day you find yourself playing superfectas at a second tier track, you are probably outside your comfort zone.

Finally, regarding stressors: Know that positive stressors can also negatively affect your play. Some positive stressors include:

- Having just scored a sizable win (do you then bet more heavily, or too little, not wanting to lose a winning day?).
- Being in an environment where others are betting extravagantly (or miserly).
- Being with someone whom you feel is a good handicapper (do you want to impress this person?).
- Having a few too many libations.

The key with positive stressors is similar to negative ones—closely monitor how you are playing, and stay close to that center, and that calmness that you know is in you. Do not let the good or the bad affect you unduly; be dispassionate.

> **"Fortune smiles upon the man**
> **who can laugh at himself."**
> *— 14,000 Quips and Quotes*

SENSE OF HUMOR REQUIRED

A sense of humor forces you into your center, and is essential for a good gambler. When we laugh at our mistakes, we gain perspective on ourselves. Many Zen koans demonstrate the Zen master's style of self-depreciating humor. In actuality, the world is funny—truth is funny, sometimes sadly so, but darn funny none-the-less. Many martial arts Sensei and instructors have this same humor. One very talented Tae Kwon Do instructor, with massive bow-legged legs, was an instructor of mine for a period. He was unhappy about how the class was training and said "we go run now" (I leave the accent to your imagination—but my immediate thought was how hilarious—this person could snap many necks with those legs, but he could not run 200 yards). Ha, Ha, Ha . . . until he ran with us on those stumpy, little bent pegs for more than three miles (leading most of the way, I might add). Funny, yes, a little sick definitely, but hey, he was right on.

Every good horseplayer is funny; whether dry or slapstick, laughs abound. The way jockeys mess up races is funny, it has to be, or you would cry. If you look hard, you will see the humor in many of your "beats." The ability to laugh will allow you to see things more as they are. A huge additional benefit is laughter soothes any rising anger and greatly increases calm. As we have already seen, calm helps handicapping and clarity. If things go awry, use the following schematic concept to find your way back to the center and to wins:

☯ Tough beat? Find the joke (likely in the jockey's ride), laugh, turn the page, you are back at the center.

BE PESSIMISTIC, WHICH IS REALISTIC

Good gamblers are realistic, which entails a healthy dose of pessimism. If you expect the worst possible alternative, anything else will be victory. The worst in a series of losing races (or days) is merely a blip in the process of racing. Pessimism insures the reality that when we lose, we will immediately look to the learning possibilities of a loss. Besides, even the worst luck can be followed by clarity and a return to the zone.

BALANCING AND CENTERING INVOLVES MORE THAN JUST GAMBLING

Many gamblers (and horseplayers in particular) do not take care of their whole being. Instead, they inappropriately concentrate only on wagers, winning, and losing. The true followers of Zen (and all Eastern doctrines) know that balance and centeredness involve spiritual, mental, and physical concepts. Wagering is not only a cerebral concept, it also is helpful to have physical activity to maintain a clear mind. Take care of your physical side as well. Zen followers created fantastic martial art disciplines (Kung Fu, Aikido, Karate, etc.) which involve mental, spiritual and physical discipline. This is advice the gambler can heed.

"Exercise nurtures the body,
The body nurtures the mind,
The mind nurtures the soul."
— F. M. Donner

A successful horseplayer knows that a healthy body will enable a player to more adroitly manipulate the mental gymnastics that a long racing card demands. On difficult days like the Breeders Cup, which tax the mind (and the body), the strong are likely to will out and find more winners later on the card.

Centeredness and balance are also physical concepts. Most people involved in Eastern style martial arts have what I would describe as physical balance. They walk lightly, they move efficiently and with what I would describe as a latent (or dormant) ability to move quickly and decisively when needed. These are amazingly pertinent attributes for the horseplayer too—a "readiness" shall we call it. Great horseplayers have something similar, like the movement of a cat.

Another side to physical Zen and martial arts training is that in addition to centering and lightness, others on the outside often view the physical Zen as a sign of danger. While the reader will see in the later warrior Zen chapter that the way of Bushido (the Japanese Zen warrior code) is the path of compassion, often the cool detachment, bearing, and mien of Zen martial art advocates creates fear in others.

True horseplayers also have an aura of long term invincibility. The true players may lose battles, but they have the physicality to win the war. Take care of yourself physically, and the physicality will help take care of your mind and soul: This is a major step toward balancing the seesaw that can be horse wagering.

A FINAL CONCEPT ON CENTERING, CALMNESS, ZEN AND ANIMALS

In an animal on which you wager (whether it be horse, dog, or even human), you want physical strength, an insightful brain, and a strong willful heart and soul. As a gambler, should we also not aspire to some of these same qualities? If we want our animals to be Zen, calm and centered, we should be, too. I can prove this to you by showing you how the hypothetical "dog Zen master" might provide guidance.

"If a dog was your master, you would learn stuff like:

When loved ones come home, always run to greet them.

Never pass up the opportunity to go for a joy ride.

Allow the experience of fresh air and the wind
in your face to be pure ecstasy.

When it's in your best interest—practice obedience.

Let others know when they have invaded your territory.

Take naps and stretch before rising.

Run, romp, and play daily.

Thrive on attention and let people touch you.

Avoid biting, when a simple growl will do.

On warm days, stop to lie on your back on the grass.

On hot days, drink lots of water and lay under a shady tree.

When you're happy, dance around and wag your entire body.

No matter how often you're scolded, don't buy into the guilt
thing and pout; run right back, and make friends.

Delight in the simple joy of a long walk.

Eat with gusto and enthusiasm.
Stop when you have had enough.

Be loyal.

Never pretend to be something you're not.

If what you want lies buried, dig until you find it.

When someone is having a bad day, be silent, sit close by,
and nuzzle."
— Anonymous

Now that is my kind of Zen doggie—you can change a few words to find that Zen pony. If the animals can be that Zen, we can find it, too.

The Complete Book of Zen
By Wong Kiew Kit

14
Arrogance and Confidence

**"If you have the idea of superiority, and are proud of
your ability, this is a disaster."**
— Zen Disciple Yuanwu

The way of Zen is not the way of ego, pride, and arrogance. Zen is by nature ego-less. Ego is a false affectation and destructive by its falseness. Ego can also wreak havoc on the horseplayer; it will distort perception and induce bad (often overly reckless) play. Zen is about reality, as is horse handicapping; ego has no place in either. The opposite of ego, arrogance, and pride is humility and humbleness. While those looking from the outside may see Zen adherents as confident and sure of purpose, they will also feel the true humility as well. When we come to understand that we are one speck in the cosmic now, how could we be arrogant or self centered? It is not about "me," it is about everything else, and where "me" fits in. Humility is real.

"When you are fully gentle, without arrogance
and without aggression, you see the brilliance
of the universe. You develop a true perception
of the universe."
— Chogyam Trungpa

One must be humble, gentle, and genuine. One cannot be compassionate and genuine when one holds on to arrogance. Arrogance actually comes from holding on to the idea of "me." "I" or "me" is not important in Zen or horse wagering. What is key is how everything fits together in a unified (sometimes chaotic but related) whole. Nothing you accomplish is important if you are proud of what you do. One should not open a door for someone else because you want to hear "thank you"; you open the door, pull out the chair, or donate to charity because it is what should be done. Good behavior is genuine and not a show. We are not proud of our good acts; we do them because we are genuine.

The other main cause of arrogance is what Chogyam Trungpa refers to as a reliance on "habitual tendencies." It is essential for Zen, and successful bets, to never blithely rely on habitual patterns. You must always learn and use your established skills, but blind reliance on what occurred in the past is the death knell of Zen and winning wagers. We must always be open to new ideas, new handicapping techniques, and new ways of finding the answer to the horseracing puzzles. Habitual reliance is arrogance in a different form. It is like saying, "I know the answers so why learn a new handicapping method—mine works well enough."

Zen is about an open mind. I like to think of a cartoon horseplayer with a door in his head into which we can pour techniques and knowledge, even if there is already great knowledge within. Would it not be foolish to lock this door so that it never allows new knowledge in? You might think also about the person who shuffles through life looking down at his or her feet. You might pick up a quarter occasionally, but you will never see the sky, the trees, or even the horserace for that matter. Look up and open your mind to the delightful fabric that is your world. Your world involves horseracing—Can you think of a more colorful, dynamic palette of beauty and energy than racing? Do not get into blind habitual patterns or ritualized arrogance; be honest, humble, and open to the ideas, concepts and methods which can help you in your life and handicapping. You are going to risk your money to get more money, so risk some soul to get more soul.

> **"As a warrior, you are willing to take a chance;
> you are willing to expose yourself to the phenomenal
> world, and you trust that it will give you a message,
> either of success or failure. . . you trust not in success,
> but in reality. You begin to realize that you usually fail
> when, action and intellect are undisciplined or
> unsynchronized, and that you usually succeed
> when intelligence and action are fully joined."**
> — Chogyam Trungpa

Being ego-less and gentle will make the world an even more wonderful place. It also will have direct positive impact on your handicapping and enjoyment of horseracing. Here is why:

HORSE WAGERING NEEDS BETTER SPORTSMANSHIP

Being arrogant is a growing scourge on many sporting events. I am personally not an "I love you and you love me, and we're a happy family" Barney (the purple dinosaur) kind of person, and yet the sporting world could use more sportsmanship. Football has gross taunting end zone displays, basketball has routine technical and flagrant fouls, baseball has bean balls and players spitting on officials, and we will not even speak about hockey. Horseracing has jockey room fights, and stupid trainer comments, but the horses pretty much run hard and ask for very little.

The horses are the truest of Zen athletes, no troublesome lawyers for contract talks, no choking their trainers/coaches (though maybe a kick here or there), and no refusing to play/run. If the horse can be so "stand-up" (as we would say in law enforcement), can the fans be just as squared away? Many outsiders view horseplayers as foul mouthed, arrogant, loud, uncouth, obnoxious vermin, because many are. Zen gamblers can alter this perception of players in general by being courteous, cordial, warm, humble, and nice. Good conduct on our part can make the wagering experience better for all involved. This is an attainable goal for all of us in horse wagering. Let us each make an effort to contribute to a positive environment by providing our own measure of goodness each time we are at an OTB or racetrack.

When we win, let us be humble and appreciate the luck involved: Buy a round of drinks, tip the teller, smile.

When we lose, congratulate the winner. Even if the winner made a "numbers play" or got lucky on a questionable DQ (disqualification), be happy for the winner.

When we act similarly to the descriptions above, we are acting in a Zen way. This is ridding yourself of ego; you should truly feel happy for the other players. Beyond the good sportsmanship, it will have the secondary benefit that if you treat others well you may gain information that will help you in later races. If you congratulate the player who just hit a $4,500 superfecta, perhaps he will tell you how he or she did it, and perhaps you can use this information when a future opportunity presents itself.

> "Let no one be deluded that a knowledge of the path
> can substitute for putting one foot in front of the other."
> — M. C. Richards

It is important to realize that even small actions affect the whole. Good sportsmanship and consideration from the horse bettor is not difficult, and it allows the environment which you frequent to be a better place. We get to make the world (OTB and track included) a better, more enjoyable place. We learn at the same time. Maybe the purple dinosaur was more on path than I had assumed. Good job, Barney.

HUMILITY KEEPS ONE CENTERED

In the last chapter, we discussed extensively the value of balance and finding one's center. Humility is an integral part of maintaining one's balance. If we become arrogant or overconfident in our ability, we will lose our center. Pride pulls us to make foolish wagers and to bet with our ego and not our thoughts and ability. Pride knocks us away from our center.

One of my favorite comments to make after a significant win when congratulated is, "Even a blind squirrel finds a nut once in awhile." For me, this minimizes any skill involved and emphasizes how much luck is necessary to win. This statement is not just an empty catechism either, I know that in any victory a great amount of luck must be involved—even with the most adept, flexible, and adroit handicapping, one needs good fortune. While I want to let myself be a well-trained, skilled, diligent, intuitive, blind squirrel, I will always be a blind squirrel nonetheless. The horseplayer must remember that everything is a process and humility assists in centeredness and clarity.

> **"If the horse is good enough,**
> **he'll win with the rider facing his tail."**
> — Dorthea Donn Byrne

ARROGANCE SEEMS TO CREATE BAD LUCK

I can state with absolute certainty that arrogance creates bad luck. This is just one of the few facts that is an absolute truism in horse wagering (and all forms of gambling). The truly humble player knows that bad luck may lurk just around the corner—do not tempt it.

One of the more common themes discussed by serious horseplayers is "angering the Gods of gambling". While I do not believe in a "superfecta deity"—similar to a God of wine, like Bacchus in mythology—I know arrogance breeds bad luck. Why does it breed bad luck? While you may observe some later discussions that are explanatory of the arrogance equals bad luck theme, I offer that regardless of the reasons it happens, it just does. Why fight it? Just get down from the arrogance pedestal.

EGO AND PRIDE CAUSE GAMBLERS TO INAPPROPRIATELY NARROW FOCUS

Zen itself is ego-less, since it is not about oneself. Wong Kiew Kit, a master of Shaolin Kung Fu, describes this by advising that the initial (non-fighting) stance is the "non-ego stance." Obviously, a master of Kung Fu has every ability to tear you limb from limb, and yet an overriding concept remains: non-ego.

The reason pride, ego, and arrogance have no place is that Zen is based on compassion for everyone, and because ego gets in the way of enlightenment and broader understanding. If we are too concerned with how important we are, and how much sway we hold in our world, we will never see how we are really just a small piece of an intricate, beautiful, universal puzzle. We are each a little bit yin, a little bit yang; when all the parts fit without being forced, the "universal puzzle" has no missing pieces. It is much the same as the analysis of the race—if we are so arrogant to believe that say "speed figures are the universal key" to racing, we will then miss the importance of breeding, the fitness of the animal, the competence of the connections, etc. There are no keys, no easy outs in racing. We must check our arrogant pride and narrow mindedness at the OTB door. We must see openly, and use all of our skills, not become overconfident, and use only a few.

WHAT YOU SUCCEEDED AT BEFORE
IS IRRELEVANT IN THE BRAGGADOCIOS SENSE

Each race is a separate entity unto itself. While it may have taught you something to win the last race, it does not mean you are "better" and therefore more likely to win the next one. Why brag about your last win, when there are more races ahead. Your time spent bragging can better be spent analyzing the next race, or analyzing the appearance of the horses on the track.

I realize how accurate this is every time I go to the track. While I place many different types of bets as opportunities arise, I generally bet pick 3's and pick 4's. I have found these wagers provide an opportunity for significant gains. Arrogance and bragging have no place in the middle of these multi-race bets. It makes no difference if I catch a $40 winner in the first race, if I do not hit races two and three. This is even truer in pick 4's. I have had many days when I got three long shots but did not hit the fourth race. You obviously want your longest horses to win each leg of the pick, but never allow yourself smugness if you get a shooter (long shot)—it isn't over until the fat filly whinnies!

HUMBLENESS EXUDES THE EXPERIENCE
OF BEING THE VICTIM OF BAD BEATS

Everyone feels like they have gotten the short end of the stick sometimes (and they probably did). Get over it. I like what Andrew Beyer said in *Beyer on Speed:*

> **"Of course it is human nature to remember vividly the bad luck responsible for a set back; we think of our triumphs as fully deserved instead of remembering the good luck that may have made them possible."**

The non-ego players realize beats come and go, and our job, as a successful player is to limit the frequency. All good horseplayers experience the frustration of incompetent rides, but Zen allows us to see it in context because our next lucky win is undoubtedly someone else's bad beat.

Another positive technique, which will create a genuine humble spirit, is that of "doubling your losses." Here is what I mean:

- *Doubling your wins.* Every gambler (at any level and in any pastime) has won. Let's say a bet is made for $5 to win on a $40 winner and in return, you receive a brand new crisp Ben Franklin. You thought (or worse yet said), "How stupid, I could have bet $20 and won $400." You could have, but you did not. Be happy with the win, look back, and see what handicapping "feel" got you the winner in the first place. Another opportunity like it will come along again, just insure you see it next time; you can bet more then. Mentally doubling your winnings (or in my example, quadrupling them) is ego thinking and is not conducive to positive events.

- *Doubling your losses.* Example: you love the 5 to 1 shot on the top of a trifecta, so you play him over everyone in an eight-horse field ($42 for a $1 bet—your horse/all/all). He wins, beating two of the longest shots on the board, only to be disqualified and put last for interference down the stretch. As you reach for your beer (hopefully, not to hurl at the screen), remember how much you liked this horse, and that maybe you really should have done a $2 trifecta wheel or also used this horse in pick 3's and exactas. You would have lost more money, but humility is telling you this is the way, and it could have been worse—a whole lot worse.

MACHO KILLS GAMBLERS

**"I lost the last race,
but I will bet more next race, because
I am better than most players and I will win."**

While the above is a philosophy that many gamblers adhere to, it is a losing one. No one is ever "due" to win. When someone gets into this type of mind-set, they are almost certain to lose.

Getting ego involved creates bad decision-making. Any seasoned horseplayer knows how narrow one's handicapping edge is in any given race. We cannot afford to let anything diminish our clarity of purpose by being blinded by getting macho. Think of it like when you were younger, and out in bars and people would get drunk and mouthy, and put their "beer muscles on", as we used to say. Wager because you feel it is the right wager, never because you are trying to feel important or make up for a previous slight (loss).

THE MORE EGO-LESS YOU ARE, THE MORE EMOTIONLESS YOU WILL BE

Ego and pride create strong emotional set-ups. No-ego creates less emotion, which creates more neutral clarity and more cogent handicapping. Clarity and the ability to see through the clutter are major factors in handicapping. It is important to acknowledge that emotion gets in the way of clarity, and pride is a very strong emotion. I will give you an example, I believe, demonstrates this clearly. Someone states (with pride), "I picked the winner of the Kentucky Derby."

Congratulations, buy a rose for your date and have a mint julep. The above statement, while clearly factual, is a very egocentric statement. While my gambler side wants to know how you played the derby winner, the reality is, it is only important in the context of how it was played. If you picked the derby winner, and you only play win money, you won, but if you play trifectas or superfectas, you better have found some other horses (or have very deep pockets with all's).

Many players feel the need to identify the winner (and then say that they did so). Allow me to identify the second and third horses in a few derbys and Breeders Cup races and I will make you a few bucks, and admit I could not single a winner. Hmmmm.

EGO AND PRIDE CAN LEAD TO WHINING

Every gambler of every sort has had unlucky beats. The Zen player knows this will happen, so they smirk, turn the page, and go on. Ego can create the situation where after a bad beat someone complains and whines—"I should have won that race if only for . . .," or "I got screwed by jockey X because . . ."

The above person is venting about how bad they lost. Without ego constrictions, we instead know it was not our fault, and that in fact our handicapping was probably right on. If in the face of incompetence by a jockey, trainer, etc., we could still observe that the positive outcome we as a Zen handicapper foresaw almost became a reality, we are probably handicapping very well.

Whining, bitching, and complaining are very negative components that will almost certainly throw you off the Zen. After a bad beat be ego-less, smile, take a sip of your beverage, admit you were on in your handicapping, sigh and get over it.

In regard to complaining, you should limit it not only because it will likely lead you off the Zen path of winning, but also because it creates a negative environment for everyone around you. Everyone who plays the horses loses. Therefore, I do not particularly need to hear you complaining about your bad beat. If you wish to comment that you got a bad ride and it cost you the race, I will probably nod my head in sympathy. If you rant and rave and throw your tickets, I will most likely ignore you, or if I am in a playful mood, I might make a comment like, "That horse would not have gotten up even with a perfect trip," just to watch the fireworks.

I used to be one of the worst complainers and screamers in the horse-playing contingent until I understood how boorish and negative my behavior was. When I was doing research for this book, I came across a book dealing with poker playing and Zen. I never played too much poker, but boy, when I did, I saw most players bitch, throw their cards, act very boorish just like many horseplayers. In his book, the author identified "Eight Final Reasons not to Whine or Complain in Poker." You can be sure they apply to horseplay:

- You look somewhat silly when you do win.
- Not whining adds to your Personal Invincibility Quotient.
- Complaining implies that you have problems in the game, but other players do not.
- What is the "whinee" supposed to do? (i.e. you are not going to acquire a lot of sympathy from the people trying to win your money in a mutual pool.)
- Whining practically shouts lack of experience.
- Your opponents do not care.
- It can set off a chain reaction. (i.e. "you thought your beat was bad, buddy that was nothing, listen to this . . . .")
- It is a waste of energy.

I was able to limit my own boorish complaining behavior by realizing that it is completely outside the concept of the path of Zen. I had intricately woven Zen into all facets of my life, and when I observed my bad behavior at the OTB, I realized how incongruous it was. Once I saw this, I saw that whining and complaining had no place in a Zen approach to horseplay.

Do not whine.

Zen and the Act of Poker
By Larry W. Phillips

15
Zazen (Meditation)

"Empty yourself of everything.
Let the mind become still.
The ten thousand things rise and fall, while the self
watches their return.
They grow and flourish, and then return to the source.
Returning to the source is stillness, which is the way
of nature.
The way of nature is unchanging.
Knowing constancy is insight."
— Lao Tzu, from the *Tao Te Ching*

Zen is a release from the constriction that every action must be painstakingly thought out. There is no paralysis of thought; actions take place naturally as needed. Zazen, or sitting meditation, is the primary means to cultivate concentration and clarity. Through meditation, we can empty ourselves and let go. Meditation is not only about relaxing the mind, it is also about honing the mind to its keenest edge so it can be used for complete understanding. If we are able to keep the mind sharp and acute as horseplayers, we will greatly increase our likelihood of identifying winning horses. Clarity allows us to see the race for what it really is. Meditation clears the mind for the upcoming handicapping tasks; it also leads us to a freer way of seeing and opens our mind to possible racing and handicapping permutations, which a cluttered, narrowly focused mind would miss.

To many Westerners, the idea of Zazen or sitting quietly in a lotus position seems obscure, odd, and mystical. It really is not any of these things. It is merely a means to rid ourselves of useless clutter. No one from the West believes it odd to spend significant amounts of time every day tidying the house, going to the restroom, or going to the health club to rid the body of physical toxins. All three are examples of activities that discard things we no longer need or desire. Zazen is no different; it is a tool to help us rid ourselves of mental toxins and the minutiae of thoughts we no longer need. The most direct outgrowth is a greatly increased acuity for whatever activity we wish to engage in. After meditation, we can more easily focus on physical activities (all of which involve mental concentration), artistic endeavors, or purely mental exertions such as writing, formulating business solutions, and (most importantly to us) handicapping.

> **"I want to make myself an empty room:**
> **Quiet whitewashed walls with slant sunshine**
> **and a fresh breeze through open windows"**
> — Deng Ming-Dao, from *365 Tao*

In its most simplistic form, meditation is the practice of sitting quietly, with good posture and proper breathing, and just letting go. One does not concentrate on anything; you are trying to gradually still the mind. Some Zen and Buddhist disciplines concentrate on counting breaths or on the manner of breathing. Other ideas are to concentrate on one simple koan (i.e., what is the sound of one hand clapping?). Personally, I find if I concentrate, I lose the purpose, and keep coming back, instead of letting go. If I need a mantra or something similar to allow myself more letting go, I concentrate on a sound (which obviously is not there) such as waves on the shore, or horses' hooves pounding the turf.

The traditional types of meditation are designed to create an atmosphere conducive to enlightenment. Sitting Zen usually involves sitting in a traditional (or modified) lotus position, with good posture, with palms up, breathing naturally, with eyes partially closed, gazing downward though fixed on no particular object. The eyes should not fixate, much in the same way that the mind should not fixate. The entire technique is designed to purge the mind, via naturally letting go of built up mental toxicity, detritus, and debris.

I have a bad back and bad knees from playing football and rugby, so most of my personal mediation I do in a quite dark room in a sitting position; sitting erect with good posture following all the breathing and non-concentration techniques. I will also sometimes be supine and concentrate on breathing techniques, though this is more a generally accepted relaxation technique than a meditation venue. There are many outstanding books and instruction on meditation. I feel that each individual's meditation methods need to be personalized by each person for best results.

If meditation seems too obscure and mystical for you as a Westernized horseplayer, consider the alternative of coming home and relaxing in a quiet, darkened room listening to music (preferably without vocals) for twenty minutes before you begin your handicapping. Do not think about the handicapping task at hand and if you find you must think of something, think of the names of your favorite horses (Citation, Cigar, Ruffian, etc.), or of the beauty of a blanket finish.

> **"After silence, that which comes nearest to expressing the inexpressible is music."**
> — Aldous Huxley, as quoted in *Harper's Book of Quotations*

I pledge that if you at least take the first step, and relax with some music and try to empty your mind that way, you will immediately see positive results in your handicapping. You will begin to see how just this initial relaxation will create clarity when you handicap. As you determine how this helps your handicapping, consider how the positive benefits may be greatly magnified with more ritualized and formal meditation techniques.

Based on the methodology and concepts behind Zazen, let's examine how this is directly applicable to your success as a horseplayer.

MEDITATION OPENS THE MIND
SO IT CAN SEE MORE BROADLY

Meditation clears the mind of the dust and silt, which can clog our observational skills. Handicapping and observation of horseflesh are skills that can be greatly enhanced by clarity of mind (and clarity of purpose). I believe strongly that the human mind is wonderful beyond our own understanding of its operation. The mind processes millions of pieces of information in an instant, though we are only consciously aware of a minute part of what we observe. Is there a way for us to increase this awareness so we see and "feel" more? Absolutely—Zazen.

As we clear our minds, we are able to consciously (and more importantly subconsciously) process more data. Everyone who picks up a racing form, or sees a horse move on the track knows what a vast amount of informational bits are present. If we can subconsciously process more of these "bits," we will find more winners. This is the aspect where it gets a bit tricky for the uninitiated. If we are processing the racing information at a level other than the purely conscious state, we may sometimes "feel" the winner, more than just handicap him out in concrete terms. To secure these "feel" winners, it is essential the mind is not tainted by garbage. Zazen insures this clean slate.

"Feel" winners are not hunches, guessing, numbers plays, or luck, they are real. It is important that when we are on the Zen, we play these horses. These horses will be some of your greatest winners (in term of odds); horses that you feel and others cannot see. It is important, essential in fact, that players not see this as mumbo jumbo. You are still using your handicapping techniques obtained through training and experience, but you are just using them at a conscious and ultra-conscious level.

The capacity of the human mind is vast. Parts of the brain that are dormant can be forcibly actualized and wakened if needed. Many writers other than Eastern philosophy authors have understood this. Paddy Chayefsky in his novel *Altered States*, dealing with isolation chamber experiments (isolation chamber—Zazen mediation—similar-hmmm) and their ties to the origins of consciousness, writes:

"He saw an image of a cluster of neurons, sleeping neurons, actually curled up in postures of sleep, lying in subdued shadow. The implication was clear. These

**were stored neurons, stored in some bank of our
mental computers, perceptions picked up somewhere
in life and selectively filtered out of our rational
consciousness. . . They were waiting
to be activated, to be fired."**

Zazen will help enlighten us and activate the neurons to which Chayefsky so eloquently refers. If you have any doubts about these concepts, you need go no further than the feelings people get even without meditation. Law enforcement is replete with examples of getting that strange feeling, the hairs on the neck, the tingling, whatever, and then having the armed fugitive being there, the bad person having a gun under the seat, etc. I will give you an example that happened to me in my job as a FBI agent.

We were completing an arrest of two fugitives with drug and weapons backgrounds outside a hotel in the Phoenix area. Some of the SWAT components (including myself) were to jump from a van and make the arrest just prior to the subjects arriving at their vehicle. The signal was given, and as always happens due to Murphy's Law, the two subjects were already in their car when we exited the van. I trained my MP-5 (a type of machine gun) on the driver through the rear window, and commands were given to get out of the car and on the ground. The passenger complied immediately, but the driver looked in his mirrors and assessed what he wanted to do. After what seemed like an eternity (though it was only 20-30 seconds), the driver slowly exited the vehicle and gave up. I was speaking to the case agent immediately thereafter, and I commented that the driver was deciding whether to grab the gun he must have had in the car, but the case agent replied that he did not have any weapons other than a pocketknife. The case agent added that in fact the driver was not the dangerous one of the two (the passenger had been wearing a shoulder holster with a 9mm handgun in it). I "begged to differ" as they say, and told him to check the car again to find the weapon. He returned and said there were no weapons other than a second knife. I *knew* what the driver was thinking, because of the visual clues, body language, my experience, etc. I *knew* he had a gun and was deciding whether that was the day to "try law enforcement." I *knew*. I sent a SWAT-trained agent over to check the car more thoroughly and there was a .45 semi-automatic tucked beneath the seat. I *knew*—I felt it.

Trust those hidden neurons, because when they are trained correctly, they will fire, and you will feel what you may not automatically see. I could not have identified to you each individual visual and auditory cue which I observed that told me that the subject had a gun, and was considering exercising his option to have me or someone else kill him. The clues were there, but it would be impossible to put it into words.

The point here is you do not have to put it into words. You just have to know that the ability is there. With handicapping, all the various permutations of speed figures, pace figures, trips, condition, breeding, etc. are astronomical, especially when we might be considering twelve horses or even more if it is the Kentucky Derby. It would take reams of paper to cross-reference all the numbers and qualifications, some of which are complicated visual interpretations involving horse condition. The key is that we do not have to write it all down, and in fact, we should not even try. Zazen and its resulting clarity enables us to process much more than we could verbalize or write down. When we are on the Zen, we will be consciously and ultra-consciously using all our techniques, and putting it together in a way beyond mere verbiage. You will feel the winner.

ZAZEN HELPS YOU SEE WHAT *IS*

Zen is based on seeing what actually is. It is not about preconceptions, or made up concepts about reality. It is about "true." Many horse races turn on separate multiple factors. The key is determining which factors will be determinative. We need to see what is, not what is unimportant. Zen allows us to sift the wheat from the chaff.

"Moon over water, sit in solitude."
— **Deng Ming Dao, from *365 Tao***

The above is a wonderful analogy, and very meditation specific. Neither the water, nor the moon strives to achieve a reflection. In much the same way, meditation and Zen are natural, and not forced. We should not strive to find the contenders in the race, we should see what is. The important factors will seem more heavily weighted in our analysis as we see things more clearly. An immediate positive by-product is that we will be able to dismiss false reliance on a singular style of handicapping that can lead us down narrow, overly restrictive paths.

What is—is. This is why we need to see it from all angles, not just one or two. Many times one handicapping technique, breeding for example, may point to an opposite conclusion than all other handicapping techniques. Do we then throw out the breeding information and go with all the other overwhelming information? The short answer is no, we use it all, because we have the ability to do so. There will be races when the value of just one technique may outweigh everything else. A horse with great turf breeding may have shown nothing in multiple races on dirt; bad speed, slow pace figures, weak jockey/trainer combination, etc., but now switched to turf and voila, a high priced winner.

We must see things as they are, not how we want them to be. We may want to rely on our techniques, and put only numerical values on them, but we cannot. It is too simplistic to expect a numerical value to give an answer. We must see in totality, using our intuitive experience as a means of finding inherent value.

MEDITATION IS ABOUT LETTING GO

Zazen and koans, and all of Zen, are about the concept of letting go—letting go of preconception and one-dimensional thought. The universe is a process, and we are all small parts of that process. When we stop worrying about each individual piece, we can begin to see and grasp the whole. When we let go of the pain and anger of losing one race, we can gain by acquiring wisdom that can help us understand the process of wagering on horses. We let go of the loss and we win. Conversely, if we hold on to the dismay and disappointment of the loss, we are not Zen, and we lose doubly (our money and our Zen).

It is key to note here that we must let go of our wins as well. We already know ego is out. Wins, losses, wins, losses—it is only a process. One horserace does not a career make. Zen is able to demonstrate to us that if we win, we win and if we lose, we can still win because we use it to our overall, long-term, advantage.

WOW, DOES MEDITATION HELP WHEN YOU LOSE

Even though it is a process, losing streaks are not fun in any traditional sense. We can learn from them yes, but fun, no! Meditation and relaxation techniques will quiet the angry, fiery, non-Zen like devils that arise after frequent losses. Calm is good.

"A parting word?
The melting snow is odorless."
— Bokusui, noted Japanese Haiku poet,
as quoted in *Japanese Death Poems*

MEDITATION IS ABOUT TRUTH AND HONESTY

Many horseplayers are disingenuous, or at worst, dishonest. Sometimes if you ask a player which horse they like, they tell you a horse they do not like to "talk you off" the horse they are wagering on. This is not the path of enlightenment. Honesty is paramount in Zen. If someone asks me which horse I like, I always tell him or her. I never lie; that is not the way of Zen.

There are important caveats to the concept of honesty, and about seeing what is, and telling the truth. I provide you my selection in a race, with the assumption that you will use him with dignity and honor. If I give you "Trotting Thomas," in the third race, and I am going to key him in the trifecta, Trotting Thomas with all with all, and you then make the exact same bet, I would be miffed (or some such perhaps more potent phraseology). In essence, you just took money from my pool, betting my exact same bet. I would never give you another pick. If you asked subsequently, I would not mislead you; I would remind you of what you had done before with Trotting Thomas, and tell you, "You are on you own."

The converse is also true. If I ask you whom you like and you respond by giving me a cogent analysis that I find valid, I would ask you if I could include your horse in my trifecta or pick 3. If you agreed and it assisted me, you can be sure there is a beverage coming your way.

Honesty and integrity are the highest of Zen virtues, and unfortunately often absent from many horseplayers. I will relate one story to give you an example. I was asked which horses I liked in a race and responded I was going to play a $10 exacta using one horse over two others. I stood in line and made my bet. At the betting window nearby, I overheard my inquisitive "friend" play a $40 exacta with the exact same horses. The race went off, and in a thrilling finish, my top exacta key was caught at the wire by one of my underling picks. I therefore netted myself (as well as my bet thieving friend) a big fat zero. I believe that was about the happiest I ever was to lose money, especially when he came by after the race and complained how it had been foolish for him to key my top pick.

ZAZEN CAN BE MINGLED WITH KOANS

Sometimes while meditating, if a koan or puzzle is introduced, it can be interpreted with extreme clarity. I believe a koan can best be viewed as a signpost, a signpost to enlightenment. When a koan is seen with lucidity and clearness during Zazen, it points a way.

Koans like, "What does it sound like to clap with one hand?" are interpreted clearly while in meditation; you consider the koan, you do not dwell on it. So while sitting and empty you have a flash of enlightenment or the enlightenment comes in waves, and you know what the sound of one hand clapping is. (Not a whole lot in actuality).

This koan/Zazen tie can work with racing analysis, too. I do not meditate or sit quietly while mulling speed figures, but in major races I will "concept" those horses during meditation. If I like two or three horses, I do not add in Beyer Speed Figures and Tomlinson Ratings; I just let the horses run the races in my mind. I do not know that it brings enlightenment, but it does often give me clues and insight. The races in my mind are beautiful and never involve DQs and bad rides.

Tao Te Ching
By Lao Tsu

NOTES:

16
Collateral Damage

"May the force be with you."
— Obi-Wan Kenobi, from the movie *Star Wars*

In the last few chapters concentrating more directly on Zen, I have emphasized what could simplistically be seen as the positive ways in which Zen can facilitate a better environment, particularly for the horseplayer. Yet, just as Zen is a path to what is actual, real, and true, it would be wrong to focus only on the positive aspects of horseplay. In this chapter, I will address some of the aspects of gambling, which many perceive as negative.

Zen is all about seeing what is, not what we want, or what we expect to see. Accordingly, it would be inappropriate to fail to acknowledge the negative ways in which horseplay can affect the process that is our life. In this chapter, I will make an effort to provide a small sign post (yield sign if you will), to guide the horseplayer away from what can be the negative influences of horse wagering. We are in the process of enlightenment! We need to discard the negatives, though we need to realize the negatives exist because it is all about locating a clearer and cleaner path. Negatives are part of the process, but skipping around them clearly cannot hurt us.

In *Cold Zero*, former FBI Special Agent Christopher Whitcomb, in his often times compelling, and spectacularly well-written book about the FBI's elite Hostage Rescue Team (HRT), describes the ambush technique for locating a moving target (human being, bad person) through the scope of a high powered sniper rifle, and taking a killing shot. As a SWAT Team Leader, though not HRT trained, I relate strongly to the loneliness he describes.

"Make the right decision and you save the day. Make the wrong decision and you spend the rest of your life fighting administrative, civil, and possibly criminal charges, tangling with people who have no idea in the world what this (taking a shot) is like. Less than a tenth of a second either way and it is all over. Less than a tenth of a second window of error to kill a human being. . . there are no second chances."

Regardless of the wrong decisions we make in our horse wagers, there are many things more important, as Mr. Whitcomb eloquently illustrates. Yet, oftentimes gamblers want to believe that every wager they make is life and death. It is important that we do not let our wagers have that much impact. Everything is a piece of a puzzle. In the huge concept of reality even life and death are minute. Many of the Zen Japanese death poems illustrate the concept that even the death of a Zen Master is not extremely important in the grand scheme.

**"Man is Buddha—
The day and I grow dark as one"**
— Ryusai

**"Round a flame
two tiger moths race to die"**
— Kaikai

**"Fall, plum petals, fall—and leave behind
the memory of scent"**
— Minteisengan

The concept to all of this is not brain surgery. Even what we perceive as truly very important is not too serious in the overall scheme. One racing loss, or a very bad day at the track is infinitesimally small in the concept of the world. More pointedly, a loss is minimal even in the concept of your gambling life. Do not allow horseplay to ever negatively affect your overall being. Balance in everything is the key. Horseplay is one small (very small, in fact) piece of your own puzzle. Many horseplayers miss this concept entirely. They begin to feel that their wagers are what is important, which is inaccurate. What is important is EVERYTHING, this completely beautiful all in which we exist. As a player, if we begin to over-emphasize our gambling, we are bound to unbalance our lives. As with humbleness, it is not about us, it is about fitting ourselves into our world.

We must never use our gambling as an excuse to diminish the responsibilities in all our other realms. Horseplay must fit comfortably within the social, personal, business, and financial obligations that we live with. All gamblers have horrible tales of associates whose lives and relationships have been ruined by wagering activity. A key here is perspective and realism. Horseplayers must be realistic about goals, objectives, and reasons for play. The most important concept, without doubt, in this area is BALANCE. We have the ability to fit horseplay within our overall lives, and if we fit it carefully, we can be successful at our wagers and at our own lives. We can also consciously insure that our gambling does not negatively affect our broader life. More importantly, we can have our horseplay positively affect our expanded view of the process of the world. We can choose, because we can choose how to play the game of life.

**"Life is like a game of cards,
The hand that is dealt you
Represents determinism,
The way you play it is free will."**
— Jawaharlal Nehru

While we cannot control all the factors in our lives, we can have a positive impact on many of them. We do not have to allow our feet to fall off the path. We can make an effort to keep ourselves toward the center.

What is collateral damage? Collateral damage is generally defined as a military or law enforcement term meaning losses to civilian and innocent personnel as a direct result of a legitimate offensive action.

Col•lat•er•al—secondary or incidental

Dam•age—

A) harm

B) the estimated monetary equivalent of loss or injury sustained

As a FBI agent, and SWAT Team Leader, I do not believe that the military terminology definition of collateral damage has any place except in the worst-case scenarios. The world has periodically shown us that such realities exist. While we must understand there are arenas where such losses occur, we must try to use our natural compassion to limit such occurrences. This is the broad concept of Zen. Cruelty, viciousness, and random harm have no place, and we must do all we can to combat these tendencies.

In the more narrow sense, Zen should keep us balanced, and secondary harm and monetary injury should not be prevalent because of our horse wagering. We can allow our lives to proceed down paths, which will not create collateral damage.

Let us look at some issues (positive, negative, and neutral) which have a relationship connection as to whether, in the gambling and horse-playing sense, we are destined to be wedded to collateral damage.

"Between love and madness lies obsession."
— From the perfume "Obsession"

PICK YOUR PARTNERS AS WELL AS YOU PICK YOUR PONIES

One of the true anathemas of the horseplayer is the scrutiny the player gets from their spouse or significant other. Most spouses look at gambling as a waste of time and money. Whenever you win, they may want a share, and when you lose, they provide an angry retort. If you are in a serious relationship (or are married), it is essential that your significant other understand your commitment to horse wagering.

If your partner does not understand this commitment, it will force a giant wedge into your personal life. Worse yet is hooking up with someone who is opposed to gambling in general. It is truly amazing to me that a large percentage of heavy players have spouses who despise gambling. This produces a significant amount of unneeded stress on the horseplayer. The happiest (and most successful) horse-players have spouses that understand and support their horse wagering. This support should not be underestimated. If you intend to make a sizable wager (whatever is sizable for you), and your partner cannot accept this, you will be increasing the likelihood of negative feeling, both in your handicapping and in your relationship.

In his book, *Beyer on Speed*, Andrew Beyer comments that while he had previously felt that "women and gambling don't mix," he changed his mind when he found his wife. Instead of knocking his wagering efforts, she made comments such as, "If you're going to take a shot to hit it, then bet what you've got to bet. You don't want to miss this because you cut corners to save a few hundred dollars. Don't wimp out!" This is absolutely, 100 percent correct. The support for the player is key, and understanding that losses happen is essential as well. Just as in all aspects of a relationship, gambling must be seen as a partnership. While one may do the handicapping, both must realize the risks and potential gains. Many horseplayers try to separate their gambling from the rest of their lives. This is an idealistic, simplistic and inaccurate view. Just as the world is a process, so are we, and wagering is a piece of the whole that is each individual horseplayer.

I am fortunate to have found someone who is supportive of my horseplay (and the time it takes away from other things). To be successful at wagering, significant time and concentration must be expended, and your partner must expect and understand this commitment. Choose your partner knowing she or he will have to accept your wagering as part of *you*. If they are to love you, they must understand (or even better, support) your wagering. If you are lucky, you might get close to the ideal.

"We're the bridge across forever, arching across the sea, adventuring for our pleasure, living mysteries for

the fun of it, choosing disasters, triumphs,
challenges, impossible odds, testing ourselves
over and again, learning love"
— Richard Bach, from *A Bridge Across Forever, A Love Story*

BE HONEST ABOUT YOUR BETTING

This is a direct corollary to point number one about picking your partners as well as you pick your ponies. You cannot pick your partner successfully if you are not truthful about how you gamble. You must be honest with them about how much you win, lose, and wager. Zen is the way of honesty, sometimes-brutal honesty, but honesty nonetheless. If I do not tell my partner how much I win, or lose, how can I assess whether or not she can accept this?

Many horseplayers lie about how much they bet. This is not the way of Zen nor of the successful horseplayer. Dishonesty is the path to long-term defeat in relationships, and in gambling. Honesty allows your partner to pull for you, and increases your positive karma. If you say you are betting $10 a race and are really betting $100, your partner cannot make an accurate assessment of the support to provide. Be honest.

GAMBLING IS NOT ALL THERE IS

Zen is intimately woven into the concept of balance. We must balance gambling into the broader spectrum that is our entire life. Many horseplayers are overly focused on gambling, and can, in the worst-case scenarios allow it to ruin their lives. We must never overemphasize our horse wagering at the cost of family, finance, and health.

It is a beautiful, wonderful world out there; do not limit it to reruns of old races to locate bad trips. Go to a play, ride your bike, or take a trip to Utah (Utah does not have gambling. Well, maybe the trip to Utah is too big a step).

Too many players allow horse wagering to become too large a focus in their lives. Balance is the key.

I will provide you a clue here to determine if you have lost your perspective. If you have had a bad wagering day, and you come home and your beautiful wife is there in a negligee, with a bottle of champagne, with massage oil and incense nearby, and all you think of is that disqualification that knocked you out of the pick 6, you've got problems. Enjoy your life, and realize horseplay is just a part of it.

DO NOT GRIND—TAKE A BREAK

If you have gone through a series of tough days at the track, take a break. Do not handicap, nor bet for a period of time. Go run, do some physical activities, go play golf. Do something else. Besides, golf is also very Zen, and you can learn things that will help your horse-play. Horseplay is much like golf and Zen—you cannot force it. If it's going bad for a while, do not grind at it, do not force. Here I will use the Zen pastime of golf as an example.

> **"Great golfers do not will the swing into being, they use their will to find the swing that is already there, that was there before they were born and will continue to exist through eternity. Then they surrender their will to it. . .The knowing is everything. . .you are your knowing. The knowing finds the swing and the swing is you."**
> — Steven Pressfield, from *The Legend of Bagger Vance*

All great golfers know that practice is the key (much like horse handicapping), but sometimes you can burn out, practice too much, get frustrated and need time off. I look at it as a "freshening" time. When we are playing great golf (or handicapping with expertise), we should feel how we are doing well and compete often. Conversely, if we play poorly for no explicable reason (and practice does not seem to help), hang it up for a while. Freshen yourself and do some other things. You will come back with a more positive attitude, and correspondingly do better.

I think taking a break makes particular sense after inexplicable, strange, and expensive losses. As I write this section, it is one day after the most bizarre, ridiculous, and for me costly, Kentucky Derby's of my career. The first three horses in order were War Emblem (ugh), Private Citizen (no way), and Perfect Drift (not a chance) that lead to a $9,000 trifecta and a $90,000 superfecta. I will state honestly that I did not consider any of these horses to have a legitimate chance to win the Derby. After drowning a few sorrows, I took the love of my life (who understands gambling losses and how I bet) and her son to watch a movie, and vowed to not pick up a racing form for two weeks until the Preakness.

GAMBLING NEED NOT BE INHERENTLY SELF DESTRUCTIVE

After a series of bad and unfortunate beats, some players engage in what I call the self-fulfilling prophecy. In other words, they try to lose. They seem to purposefully continue to lose. A classic example is to continue to play against a track bias, then argue that the best horse (the one they had) lost. Who cares if the "best horse" lost, if he could not win because of the track bias?

Certain horseplayers (most at one time or another) wallow in their own misery of losses. This type of self-defeating behavior is a death move in horseplay. If we are losing inexplicably, we must wager less, not more. Do not try to get your money back in one race. Horseplay is a game for the patient and longsighted. The tiger strikes periodically, he does not chase after each item of prey. He picks his spots, just as a horseplayer must. Do not wallow in pity after a loss (or losses). Do not multiply a loss by forcing and playing badly—this only guarantees more losses and could be termed ritualized, gambling suicide.

Within the concept of Bushido, or the Samurai's Warrior code, Westerners have always been fascinated by the concept of Hara-Kiri (ritual suicide) or Seppuku (self-murder). The concept was that in that time period of warrior states, there was no overriding criminal code to insure all injuries were recompensed with justice. Instead, if someone committed an act egregious enough, he must then pay with his own life (by his own hand). The key here is that this concept no longer has a place in the current world of Zen because there now is an overriding criminal code, which should maintain honor and justice.

Whenever I think of Seppuku in terms of gambling, I cannot help but think of the player who thinks he deserves to lose, and as a result, makes continued bad bets trying to lose. I posit here that while ritual suicide now has no place in the Zen world, wallowing in losses (and adding more) have no place in the successful horseplayer's repertoire. It is hard enough to win at this game; why force more losses?

CENTERING ELIMINATES WHAT THE MORAL MAJORITY SEES AS THE NEGATIVES OF GAMBLING

Much of the moral majority in the world sees gambling as a sin (at worst), or an evil (at best). This is an overly narrow perspective and far outside the realm of Zen. Gambling is neither good, nor bad, it just is. We are the facilitators of its motivation, we can allow wagering to be a positive, exhilarating, and possibly lucrative pastime, or we can let its more insidious side overwhelm us.

The reality is, that if we remain balanced and centered in all our activities, the negatives associated with wagering cannot harm us. We must exercise, love our family, professionally accomplish our job, and realize horseplay is just a piece in a marvelous matrix. We need to have fun to enjoy our world, it is a wonderful place; the color and majestic pageantry of horseracing is a wonderful addition.

> "Paint. . . catch the sunrise on your canvas! Take the light of it on your face, through your eyes, spread it into art! Swiftly now, swiftly! Live the dawn with your brush!. . .The sunrise is reality, the painting is what we make of it. . .Reality has nothing to do with appearances, with our narrow way of seeing. Reality is love expressed, pure perfect. . . Unbrushed by space and time."
> — Richard Bach, from *ONE*, a novel

Some horseplayers fall victim to financial problems, excessive drinking, and family strife. Horse wagering should just add spice, and perhaps a little money, to an already full and complete life. If we balance our lives, and experience the broad joy in this world, we will not allow ourselves to be victimized by the negatives. One of the things I continually emphasize to new FBI agents, is to do the very best you can at all the things you do. When at home, be the best husband and father; when at work, be the best agent; and when in recreation, be a positive force there as well.

When we strive to be the best we can in all aspects, we set our goals high, and we should. Our ultimate goal is to make a positive impact in our world. We can surely do so by trying hard and remaining in balance. All the little positives, when summed up in total, can have a major impact. We do not need to let a loss of focus force us off the path into bad habits like excess drinking, financial problems and family carnage.

As they say in golf, balance is good.

Japanese Death Poems
Written by Zen monks and Haiku poets
on the verge of death—compiled by Yoel Hoffmann

17
The "Zone" and Concept Handicapping

"(One) aspect of the warriors discipline is that it also
contains discriminating awareness, or skillful intelligence.
Therefore it is like the bow and arrow. The arrow is sharp
and penetrating; but to propel, or put into effect that
sharpness, you also need a bow. Similarly, the warrior is
always inquisitive, interested in the world around him.
But he also needs skillful action in order to apply that
intelligence. . .(then) the arrow of intellect is joined
with the bow of skillful means"
— Chogyam Trungpa, *Shambhala The Sacred Path of the Warrior*

Many schools of Zen and Buddhist thought describe flashes of
awareness, and the corresponding moment of enlightenment. Others stress a more gradual path to enlightenment. The distinction may be moot, in that even in the gradual methodology
schools, there will be instances of brilliant breaking through at specific points on the enlightenment road. While horse handicapping is

only a narrow bandwidth in the realm of what is, these flashes of enlightenment can occur in horse wagering as well. Every good hand-icapper has looked at a race and *known* that they have the winner. Here I do not mean a short priced favorite that everyone can see. Instead, I mean a horse that is covered (hidden to the vast majority of other players). The Zen handicapper has been able to lift the various veils, and see exactly how the race will unfold. The player absolutely knows he has a winner. Note here that "winner" is a relative term, and understanding this as a correct gambling concept is essential. If I uncover a horse that I am certain will run in the top three finishers, and he is 25 to 1, I have a horse I can win on regardless of whether he runs first, second, or third.

Occasionally, these flashes of spectacular horse handicapping insight may arrive in bunches. We see four or five races where we feel the outcomes are certain, or as certain as things can be with human beings involved. Our animals are outrunning their odds at huge prices, and no one else even seems to have a clue. We are IN THE ZONE.

The zone is not some metaphysical moment when all our planets are aligned. It is a real, periodically visited kingdom of gambling happiness and quietude. It exists, and you will periodically find yourself there, if you allow it to happen. To get into the zone, you should follow the doctrines of Zen and good handicapping, and follow whatever path gets you there most frequently. When you are on the Zen, and in the zone, you are not unbeatable, but you will be damn tough to play against. The key to being in the zone is realizing when you are there, and when you are not. The easiest way to know you are in the zone is that handicapping good horses will seem very "easy." They will literally jump off the page for you. There will be enormous clarity of your resolve.

One way to test if you are in the zone is to do something I would call "concept handicapping." Concept handicapping is to scan and analyze the past performances of a race very rapidly. Do not pour over a race; let the information in the past performances seep into whatever corner of your mind it chooses. Then see if you can feel the winner (remember that winner is not necessarily the first horse across the finish line—it may be a high priced second, third or even forth). What you are doing in concept handicapping is using the tools of handicapping you have previously perfected, but using them in a very Zen way. You are seeing more than just the surface that everyone can see; you are delving deeper instinctively, by using more of your mind's capacity.

> **"Great understanding is broad,**
> **and lesser understanding is picky.**
> **Great words carry strength and little words**
> **are petty and quarrelsome"**
> — Chuang-Tzu

The above quote is from one of the three classic foundations of Taoism, and illustrates what it is to be in the zone.

How can we get to the zone? What should we do when we are there? What can we do when we cannot find the zone even with a Geiger counter, microscope, and meditation?

Let's analyze some concepts that affect our relationship to our horse-wagering zone.

IN HORSE BETTING, USE ACCUMULATED EXPERIENCE BUT LIVE/HANDICAP IN THE PRESENT

Alan Watts, in *What is Zen*, admonishes that the first thing the Zen trainee must do is "get the feeling of the obvious." It is all about right now. While the past may provide some historical guidance, we (particularly Westerners) tend to think that what happened in the past is determinative of what will occur in the future. As Watts explains, exactly the opposite is true. The past follows the present like the wake follows a sailing vessel, eventually disappearing. It is the ship causing the wake, not vice versa. The important puzzles are about this sailing ship known as "now," not the past. We need to unlock a race, we have the keys, but we must focus on the lock directly in front of us.

As successful Zen horseplayers, we must concentrate on the present race. We need to open our mind to the possibilities of this race we are looking at, not erroneously focus on a horse's past efforts. We must assess the horses past performances (absolutely), but the last race was completed weeks ago. We must assimilate the past performance information (pace, breeding, Beyer Speed Figures, jockeys, etc.) into the completely new context (clean slate, if you will) that is today's race. What the horse (and rider) did three weeks ago is only pertinent to us in that it may provide suggestions as to how today's race may play out. Unfortunately, many horseplayers over-emphasize the last few races without seeing how this race may be run, often completely differently. When we handicap "in the present," we will more often find ourselves in the Zen zone of knowing exactly how today's race is destined to unfold.

THE ZONE IS ABOUT USING EXPANDED CONSCIOUS AND ULTRA-CONSCIOUS AWARENESS

Everything seems to have crystal clarity when we are in the zone, because we are seeing/feeling more than we normally do. Zazen is about creating a peaceful mind, which is then a more open vessel to the stimuli that exists in the world. When we are extremely clear of mind we look at the world, and it is sharply and pointedly in focus. This is why the winners jump off the page at us. We are processing more of the information that is available to us. Moreover, we are processing it at both conscious and ultra-conscious levels.

It has long been a known empirical fact that humans consciously assimilate only a small portion of the data the brain holds. The eyes, ears, and other senses obtain many times the information that the conscious mind can process. Therefore, we must trust that our ultra-conscious or supra-conscious mind will collate and correlate these extra data particles for us. This is why when we are on the Zen, winners seem to scream out in our brain. Our mind tells us the winners, though we do not know exactly why. It is important here to know we are still using our handicapping skills and assimilating the data more coherently because we are using parts of our mind that we sometimes do not.

I have always desired to find exactly the right quote to illustrate our vast mind capacity. The penultimate quote is in Larry W. Phillips's, *Zen and The Art of Poker,* where he quotes the dust cover of a book by a Danish Scientist named Tor Norretranders. The quote is starkly and insightfully accurate:

> **"During any given second, we consciously process only sixteen of the eleven million bits of information our senses pass on to our brains. In other words, the conscious part of us receives much less information than the unconscious part of us. We should trust our**

> **hunches and pursue our intuitions because they are
> closer to reality than the perceived reality of
> consciousness."**

Say no more: I am listening, hearing, and knowing because I will be trusting my unconscious or ultra-conscious picks.

> **"Nothing is so simple that it cannot be misunderstood"**
> — Freeman Teaque Jr.

YOU CANNOT FORCE YOURSELF INTO THE ZONE—BUT YOU CAN FORCE YOURSELF OUT

One of my goals in this book is to serve as a guide toward Zen concepts that will lead you toward the zone. All the concepts of balance, humility, calmness, openness, etc., should lead the handicapper toward the zone. Still, an essential component is that you cannot force your way into the zone. This is true much in the same way you cannot exert your influence on the arrow after it leaves the bow, or muscle a perfect golf shot; you will never be successful foisting your will onto your wagers. You should use your positive principles of handicapping, open your mind and the path will lead you to the zone from time to time. As you relax more and gain confidence in your instincts, you will find your way down this path more frequently.

While you cannot force yourself on Zen, you can force yourself out. It you are in the zone, do not overanalyze it. You are using the most of your perceptions and your mind. If you try to use your conscious mind to figure it all out, you are doomed to lose the Zen. It is relatively simple; you are in a good spot, a place where the sun shines brightly or the stars twinkle mightily, and you know which stars will twinkle in which race. Is it essential that you can consciously know why each star (horse) will twinkle just at that instant? Of course not! What matters is that you bet the twinkle. Have faith and be victorious; overanalyze and you will not be in the zone for long.

CONCEPT HANDICAPPING WILL SOLIDIFY YOUR SPOT IN THE ZONE

Concept handicapping is my terminology for looking at a race quickly and feeling the winner. While you might initially see this as mumbo jumbo, it works when you are in the zone. When it is operating effectively, you can be assured of your position squarely in the Zen. Conversely, when concept handicapping does not show you any winners, instead rely more on your conscious mind and your overt handicapping tools.

If you are not even in the same area code as your "good zone," use the handicapping skills and tough it out. Alternatively, if far enough away from the zone, hang it up for the day. The real deal here is concept handicapping. It can show you where you are in relation to the zone. Be humble enough to listen to the cues.

> **"The person with true humility never has to be shown
> his place, he is always in it."**
> — From *14,000 Quips and Quotes*

Listen to what concept handicapping hints at, listen to what your wagers are telling you, and if you are in the groove, swing hard.

HUNCHES ARE NOT GUESSES

You have done your handicapping and your feelings are telling you the long shot is a lock to hit the board. Just a guess? Hopefully not, your hunch may be right on.

Experienced horseplayers are veterans of the horse wars; they have seen tens of thousands, or hundreds of thousands of past performances, post parades, and paddock activity. Our hunches may be the accumulated awareness of horseflesh we have seen over decades. Our unconscious side observes things our conscious side misses:

A dappled coat on a long shot or an almost invisible awkward step on a false favorite.

Allow your "hunch" to correctly steer you toward the long shot and away from the favorite. Hunches are not guessing when you are near the zone.

BEING IN THE ZONE IS NOT AN EXCUSE
TO HANDICAP SHODDILY

Just because all indications (including concept handicapping) are telling you that you are in the zone, this is no excuse to handicap poorly. You still need to see all the information in the past performances. You are never "bulletproof," even when you are on the Zen;

keep those feet on the path. Take heed to what Larry W. Phillips says in *Zen and the Art of Poker:*

> **"Your goal as a player is to reach a point**
> **where a great many things will have to go wrong**
> **for you to lose badly. They will have to go wrong in**
> **bunches, repeatedly for an extended period of time.**
> **Once you have reached this point you won't**
> **give it as much weight because you know**
> **such occurrences are relatively. . .rare."**

Keep handicapping well, keep learning from your mistakes, keep humble, and open your mind and you will spend more time closer to the epicenter of the zone. When you fall off the Zen, you will know you can find your way back.

Thorsons Principles of Zen
By Martine Batchelor

NOTES:

18
Karma and Superstition

"You unlock this door with the key of imagination.
Beyond it is another dimension—a dimension of
sound, a dimension of sight, a dimension of mind.
You're moving into a land of both shadow and
substance, of things and ideas. You've crossed over,
the sign post up ahead—The Twilight Zone"
— Rod Serling

Karma is most readily accepted as a Buddhist concept. It is clearly related to Zen, but probably at a more basic intuitive level. Some schools of Buddhism see Karma as the "force" which continually molds the person into similar entities day after day (and life after life—due to reincarnation). Less metaphysically, reincarnation is not a necessary element, and "reincarnation" is more a personal rebirth from moment to moment. Where Karma controls, it does so through the ego of the individual. Because the ego is grasping, bad Karma is created, and no personal growth (enlightenment) occurs. The individual is destined to replay over, and over, and over, the same ignorance and narrowness. With this narrow ego focus there is no possibility of awakening or attaining enlightenment.

Clearly, in the horse-wagering arena, "Bad Karma" is the grasping for winners. Grasping or attempting to over control life virtually necessitates losing, because we are not letting go and seeing the races for what they are. Positive endeavors are necessarily spontaneous; we must go beyond our Karma, or mere consequential action. Karma is in essence a force that tends to make us repeat ourselves, and if not particularly enlightened, we will repeat our mistakes.

For the gambler, Karma is inexorably linked to superstition. Horseplayers are notoriously superstitious. When they win, they do not change pens for weeks, they sit in the same seats and drink the same noxious drinks.

**"See a penny pick it up,
all day long you'll have good luck"**
— Unknown

Superstitious activity makes players feel like they have positive Karma. I do not believe that acting superstitiously can help you, but if you must be superstitious, do not let it hurt you. If you must change pens, wear green, or drink pink grasshoppers, have at it, if it makes you feel better, but still handicap professionally. Do not believe that every Tuesday you must play the gray horse in the last race.

Someone I consider a close friend and a wonderful handicapper is a San Francisco 49er fan. He repeatedly plays 4-9 quinellas, and exactas, and even pick 3's. I wish I could buy him a 4-9 quinella in every race, so he would use his great handicapping skills and forget about his beloved 49ers.

**"We used to play poker with Tarot cards,
but stopped when four players wound up dead"**
— Comedian Steven Wright

The point of the 49er story is that my friend (let's call him "Steve" Young, the former 49er quarterback) is too outstanding a handicapper to superstitiously cling to playing numbers. If Steve must be superstitious, I would rather buy him a pink grasshopper (though he prefers Coors Light®), and let him tell me his true handicapping selections.

To avoid wedding ourselves to bad Karma and superstition, we must embrace an openness, a freedom that allows us to expand beyond the limits of our Karma and superstitious tendencies. Spontaneity is the key. We must play whole-heartedly, but not attach ourselves to diehard methodologies. As a handicapper, we must always be attuned to new ways to handicap, and new techniques, which can identify winners. We must never continue to replay methodology, which facilitates us losing time after time.

One concept of Buddhism (particularly reincarnation schools of Buddhism) is that dishonesty, alcohol abuse, exploitation, useless expediency and other negatives will invariably create bad Karma. These negatives are inherently ego full and nothing close to letting go. When I was a young child, I adored the conceptualization that if you were very good (honest, helpful, courteous, respectful, humble, etc.), and you died, you would be reincarnated as someone or something wonderful such as Albert Einstein or maybe a dog. If you were a lying, heartless, spiteful jerk, and you passed away, you would come back as a sea slug. Your Karma followed your soul throughout your reincarnated existences. I have grown up some since my youth (though not as much as you might believe), but I still believe your Karma follows you. While I do not believe obnoxious, vociferous, arrogant horseplayers will be reincarnated as sea vermin, I do believe bad luck, and an inordinate amount of beats will haunt them.

In Western terminology, Karma has sometimes come to be defined as the positive or negative aura one seems to carry around with them as in, "He's got good Karma." The gambler with good Karma seems to win, while those with bad Karma seem to lose often.

A major key here, is when we open up and let go, we will realize the inherent value in doing good, compassionate things. We will not be reincarnated as sea slugs, not because we are afraid of slithering through the seas of our future lives, but because we are truly trying to make everyone's world a little better. The Golden Rule of "Do unto others as you would have them do unto you" is not even Zen enough. You do the right thing because it simply is the right thing. Still, both the Western and Buddhist concepts of Karma will lead the Golden Rule folks to wagering advantages over the sea slug brigade. If we are to be successful horseplayers we must foster good Karma, and disengage ourselves from the bad. Additionally, while superstition is not as negative as bad Karma, it is still generally useless for the horseplayer.

In *Zen and the Way of the Sword,* by Winston L. King, it is noted that Zen is inexorably linked to the Buddhist teaching of "Karmic Destiny." Karmic predetermination states that "the individual is required, *even fated* [emphasis added] to accept the role that has been given to him." If as a horseplayer, we accept that we are a negative or superstitious player, bad Karma will invariably fate us to losing. While we cannot fight our Karma and fate, we can affect it in a positive way. When we look at others, observing their Karma is not exceedingly difficult. Can we feed off others good Karma? Can we break the cycle of our own negatives through positive energy? Absolutely! Do not be a sea slug in life, nor at the track.

IF YOU FEEL NEGATIVE OR ANGRY WHEN YOU BET YOU WILL PROBABLY LOSE

Many gamblers (in all wagering endeavors) speak about making a bet, but being certain, it will not come in. We have all done it; the horse may look like a certain winner, and yet we are confident it will lose. This is a two-fold negativism concept. If we are completely certain we are going to lose, we must not bet on the horse. This is a moment when even negative Karma can help you. Listen when your "bones" tell you it is a loser. Do not make the play, or at the very minimum, cut back.

When you are angry and negative you will almost certainly lose. This is the time to redirect you energies. Listen to music, cook dinner, go to a play, have sex, walk the dog, whatever it takes to redirect your negative energy into a positive focus. I believe strongly that when you are negative and angry you are so far off the Zen you need to refocus before you can win. A sense of humor is required. If you must continue to wager when you are down, try laughing at yourself. We all know our own idiosyncrasies are great fodder for humor. You may come a little closer to the successful gambling path with some self-depreciating comedy.

**Question: What made that horse good
on a sloppy track?
Answer: His "muddhah" was a mudder!**
(Note: No one would take credit for this awful joke)

SOMETIMES A DICTIONARY CAN TELL MORE ABOUT WHAT IS IMPORTANT THAN A RACING FORM

Ok, you are imagining I somehow fell off the wagon and started sniffing glue as you read the last heading. No, there is no huffing going on. My point is that pure superstition has no place in wagering. In the *Random House Webster's Dictionary, Fourth Edition* three definitions are of interest:

Su•per•la•tive: of the highest kind or order
Su'per•sti'tion: An irrational belief in the ominous significance of a particular thing, circumstance, or occurrence
Sup•ple: Bending readily without breaking or splitting; flexible

Using those exact definitions, I will now include Zen commentary.

- ☙ *Su•per•la•tive:* of the highest kind or order *(Somewhat Zen)*
- ☙ *Su'per•sti'tion:* An irrational belief in the ominous significance of a particular thing, circumstance, or occurrence *(Not even slightly Zen)*
- ☙ *Sup•ple:* Bending readily without breaking or splitting; flexible *(Very Zen)*

As they would say in horseracing, I guess the two is a "throw-out."

CLOTHING MAKES THE MAN (OR WOMAN)

While Zen is extremely minimalist in its approach to garments (the Buddhist monk, and his robe being familiar to Westerners), clothing can have an effect in your approach to wagering. Martial Arts training is universally done in clothing suitable for the purpose. The horse handicapping you do should be done in clothing that makes you feel the most likely to win. For many, comfort is the key, while for others, it is a successful, high end, well-groomed appearance.

In every cinematic extravaganza about gambling, losers and "down and outers" are depicted as shoddy and badly attired; winners tend more toward the Grace Kelly and Fred Astaire looks. I always envision Sean Connery as James Bond at the Baccarat table. Clothing is a personal issue, but it can set a mood for you even before you set foot in the OTB. Do what feels right for you, and it can give you some positive energy, which you can build on.

GAMBLING ROOMS HAVE THEIR OWN KARMA

The Buddhist concept of Karmic Destiny holds that your frailties (and strengths) follow you across lifetimes. It is cause and effect. You reap what you sow. Still, man has the "rare good fortune to be born a human being and thus [be] the possessor of special faculties and perceptions, [which with] proper use of will and mind [can show us where we are] in the scheme of things" *Buddhism, A Way of Life and Thought,* Nancy Wilson Ross. As sentient beings, we can see where we are in our world.

As a horseplayer, frequently our "worlds" will be an OTB room, or a racetrack clubhouse, or grandstand. I believe that such venues have Karmic Destiny, which follow them. The phrase, "The room is cold/hot," is extremely telling. Cold Karma in a room can seep into the most Zen of players; "good heat" can warm the unluckiest of bettors.

There are different ways to play in hot or cold locales. If the room is absolutely "dead" and you have already handicapped your wagers, consider making your wager and leaving. You can watch the races elsewhere (or go online or call in for the results); the bad Karma cannot affect you this way. If you must stay to watch the races, be quiet, be sympathetic to those who are losing, but overall be quiet. If you start participating in the pain, it will absorb you, and you will likely begin to play poorly.

If the room is "hot," jump in, be gracious, laugh, and buy drinks. Play with the others. This is no excuse not to handicap, but listen to others when they seem hot and add their selections into your pick 3's and superfectas (after you ask if it is Okay to do so). When the room is "on fire," enjoy the roll.

A question immediately presents itself: If rooms can be torrid or frigid, and this affects our chances of winning, (and it does), can we, as an individual gambler, light a fire for our preferred gambling den? While I do not think you single-handedly can turn an iceberg into a whistling teakettle, you can nudge an OTB into warmer hemispheres. The commentary, "It is always darkest just before the tornado hits" is no way to brighten a room. Make some jokes, poke fun at yourself (never others), buy a round, complement the waitress on her legs, or the waiter on his butt, although the last two options present their own risks. The bottom line is if you lighten up, the room may as well.

**"I have some very rare photographs, including a photo
of Houdini locking his keys in his car."**
—Comedian Steven Wright

I know a very sizable horse bettor who has an effect on his betting establishment that is extraordinary. Dr. Detroit is a howler; his yelling expertise is renowned. When I first ran into Dr. Detroit, he annoyed the hell out of me. I attempted to peacefully enjoy the races. As the horses came down the stretch, Dr. Detroit stood up and caterwauled for some "no chancer" to "pass these pigs." This yelling always took place at full volume, race after race.

What I came to find out, as I learned more about Dr. Detroit was that sometimes he had bet the horse he was yelling for, and sometimes he had not. He just wanted to excite the room. He always bought drinks regardless. Dr. Detroit was there to have fun, and wanted his OTB to have just as much enjoyment as well. I have grown to like Dr. Detroit and his outlandish screaming. Having fun is good.

ACQUIRE SUPERSTITIONS THAT DO NOT AFFECT YOUR CHANCES OF WINNING

Superstition is not in any way similar to Karma. Superstitions are irrational silliness. If you must have irrational concepts when you play, do not allow them to force you into losses. Some people play numbers, but this is no more than superstition. If it is essential that you play the 1-4-6, play quinella boxes on these numbers, do not add them into your legitimately handicapped horses. Acquire idiosyncrasies that will not affect you. I admit that I have a superstition that when I am paid winnings I do not want $50 bills. Where I acquired this stupidity I have no idea, but when the teller tries to pay me in 50s, I request 100s or 20s. Absolutely insane, but it does not affect my winning or losing. If you believe you only win when you handicap with green pens, buy extra green pens (i.e., if your superstition is dumb but the cost is minimal, what the hell!).

Just always remember that "Luck is a lady" so be especially nice to women (there may be some bonuses to this anyway). Note: you lady players will have to come up with a corresponding theory.

"Horseracing is the sport of kings and the trap of fools."
— Anonymous

GOOD DEEDS CAUSE GOOD KARMA

While the goal of Zen is to reach enlightenment, or even nirvana, it is clear that in Buddhist doctrine, good deeds generate positive purified Karma. While good karmic destiny is not the ultimate goal of Zen, it can absolutely help the gambler on his way to the zone. Creating good Karma is not the ultimate objective, merely an intermediate stop off.

Every horseplayer who wants to be successful should donate to charity, kiss babies, pet dogs, tip tellers, give to the poor, help ladies across the street, whatever. Remember that good acts increase the likelihood you will be reincarnated as a tiger and not a tiger moth over a candle flame. In addition to positive Karmic influence, you will help make the world a better place. Even if I do not win each day at the track, making the universe better is a damn nice ancillary benefit.

KARMA CAN AFFECT YOU WHEN YOU HANDICAP

Because you should not bet while angry, guilty, or negative, you should also not handicap while in these moods. The atmosphere in which you analyze the DRF has a great deal to do with success.

I prefer to handicap the evening before, with low music, or in silence. If you like opera, country, or rap you will probably select that type of music. It is up to the individual player as to what calms him or her most effectively.

One common mistake is to try to handicap during the day's races while within the scurry and noise of the OTB room. The day of the races is the time to finalize minor details and look for changes of riders, medication, and horse condition. The majority of your handicapping should have been completed previously with minimal distractions. Remember "music soothes the soul of the savage beast," and there are no beasts more savage than an unsettled horse bettor.

DO NOT LET YOURSELF BE YOUR OWN WORST ENEMY

Know thyself, and Karma and superstition will not stand in the way of enlightenment. The greatest possibility of Zen is that through letting go, we can surpass all superstition and Karma through enlightenment.

**"In all the colors of the rainbow there is one light.
That's unity. In this sage-like view, you see the
oneness throughout, and you are serene and**

unaffected. When that realization comes to you, you
are enlightened."
— Swami Amar Jyoti
Dawning, Eternal Wisdom Heritage for Today

You can lift yourself from the smoggy cloud of bad Karma by continuing on the gradual (and periodically rapid and spontaneous) stairway to enlightenment. When Karma is bad, play more studiously, or not at all. Realize you can lift up from the Karma and reincarnate not as a sea slug, but maybe as the most royal of all, the horse.

Buddhism, A Way of Life and Thought
By Nancy Wilson Ross

NOTES:

19

Warriorship and Zen

"In order to be a good warrior, one has to feel. . . The
warrior is sensitive to every aspect of Phenomena—
sight, smell, sound, feeling. He appreciates everything
that goes on in his world, as an artist does.
His experience is full and extremely vivid. The rustling
of leaves and the sounds of raindrops on his coat are
very loud. . . Because of his sensitivity, the warrior can
then go further in developing his discipline."
— Chogyam Trungpa, *Shambhala, the Sacred Path of the Warrior*

One of the concepts of Zen most readily applicable to horse
wagering is the concept of Warrior Zen or Samurai Zen. One of
the classics in all of literature is *The Art of War,* by Sun Tzu. The book
delineates Zen methods of being successful in battle. The lessons provided are easily adaptable to all areas where confrontation and skill
are prerequisites. Horseplay obviously involves combat in the sense
of doing battle to win a share of the betting pool, and clearly is a

skill/concentration endeavor. In much of the Samurai culture the primary "skill" involved was swordsmanship. In Winston L. King's book *Zen and the Way of the Sword,* the author demonstrates the link between Zen warriorship and swordsmanship: "The great purpose of swordsmanship study and practice [is] the development of the mental/spiritual person." This continuum proceeds both ways—many skills can be a tool to enhance one's Zen-ness and increasing one's Zen ability leads to correspondingly improved skill. The skills or dexterity involved can be manifold—golf, music, archery, painting, martial arts, swordsmanship, motorcycle maintenance, or horse handicapping. One of the most fulfilling aspects of a Zen view is that your broadened perspective will allow you to have wins, losses (and dead heats), provide more information to make you a better player. The more you play, the more clarity you attain, and the more clarity you attain, the better you play. It is a nice upward spiral.

> **"And God took a handful of southerly wind, blew his**
> **breath over it and created the horse."**
> **— Bedouin legend**

There are a number of specific concepts identified with warrior Zen, and linked to Bushido (loosely translated as the samurai's warrior code of honor) which explain the overall nature of the warrior style of Zen. Bushido is basically the ethical requirements of the Japanese warriors known as samurai. It is a code of moral principles which these warrior knights were required to observe. One of Bushido's primary underpinnings is Zen, and applying human effort beyond traditional methods to define excellence. Knowledge and skill were assimilated by the samurai to allow wisdom to grow. Knowledge was exemplified by the character of the warrior. The warrior mentality was the key to the samurai's Zen.

Listed here (with brief notational explanations) are the credos of Bushido. These values are just as essential in the repertoire of the

successful horseplayer as they are in the samurai's mastery of his swordsmanship. I believe these moral principles could establish an outstanding standard for everyone—not only bettors and samurai.

- *Courage*—the bravery and fearlessness to do what is right.
- *Benevolence*—to be brave we must be tender and caring for all, particularly those we vanquish.
- *Politeness*—the outward manifestation of the sympathetic regard for the feelings of others. (Politeness here includes the concept that manners, gracefulness, and deportment also include power in repose—latent strength).
- *Veracity*—honesty is Zen and lying is cowardly and dishonorable.
- *Honor*—honor was an integral credo of the Bushido code. (Seppuku or ritual suicide could be the result if one's own honor was forsaken).
- *Loyalty*—loyalty under the code was to the family and to one's feudal lord.
- *Education*—the samurai must continually strive for wisdom and enlightenment. The role of teacher was seen as a developer of the soul and was a sacred position.
- *Self-control*—the samurai must exhibit a stoicism of character, and never display his emotions by overtly showing joy or anger.

Based on these principles, the Samurai would be an outstanding horse handicapper, would he not?

> **"Betting the ponies is done
> in various methodical ways by professionals,
> haphazardly by some enthusiasts,
> and often in a rather bizarre fashion
> by others just out for a day's lark."**
> — Cooky McClung, *Horses are Different*

Now that we have a good idea what warrior Zen and the Samurai are all about, let's examine some specific ways it is applicable to horse wagering.

WHEN IN THE ZONE, AND ON THE ZEN,
PLAY FEARLESSLY LIKE A WARRIOR

Aggression is a key success attribute in wagering. Wagering on horses is very similar to a battle or war; you must pick your times to bet and then strike firmly and quickly. When it is right, attack rapidly and with large bets. When no opportunities are present, retreat, and await a more opportune chance. Bet aggressively and heavily when the advantage is largest—be focused and ultra aggressive.

> **"One defends when his strength is inadequate,**
> **he attacks when it is abundant."**
> — Sun Tzu

BET LITTLE OR NOTHING WHEN
NO OPPORTUNITY ARISES

This axiom is universal: Why bet when you cannot find the horse? Still, even the best players seem to be drawn to periodic bad play—be better than even the best players—**do not play when no opportunity exists.** Realize here that "opportunity" is a broad concept; opportunities can occur with short priced horses, but they are less likely.

YOUR ONLY GOAL IS TO WIN
THE HORSE PLAYING WAR

One battle does not make a war. The key to success is to be ahead in the end. Your choice of wager here may be key. The player who wins multiple "win" wagers on 3 to 5 shots will overall lose money if this is the only way he plays. Many small "chalk" victories can easily be outweighed by one overwhelming pick 6 or superfecta win. You may win your yearlong handicapping war of dollars with one single large payout, but you will not crawl ahead in the long run on small odds.

> **"Losers walking around**
> **with money in their pockets**
> **are always dangerous, not to be trusted.**
> **Some horse always reaches out**
> **and grabs them."**
> — Bill Barrich, *Laughing in the Hills*

BEING ZEN IS NOT AN EXCUSE TO HANDICAP HAPHAZARDLY

Regardless of your proximity to the zone, handicapping is based on good skill. Great handicapping skills are an essential start. We must carry our force with us in war, and we must always carry our handicapping skill with us in horse wagering. As much as some of our wins may seem to outsiders as metaphysical magic, it is still based on our heightened perception and good methodology.

> **"Not everyone understands what a completely rational process this is, this maintenance of a motorcycle (read handicapping a race). They think it is some kind of a "knack" or some kind of "affinity for machines" in operation. They are right. The knack, is almost purely a process of reason. The troubles are caused by what old time radiomen called a "short between the earphones" failure to use the head properly. A motorcycle functions entirely in accordance with the laws of reason, and study of the art of motorcycle maintenance is really a miniature study of the art of rationality itself."**
>
> — Robert M. Pirsig, *Zen and the Art of Motorcycle Maintenance*

THE CALMNESS OF ZEN COUPLED WITH GOOD HANDICAPPING WILL ENABLE YOU TO MAKE LARGE WAGERS WITHOUT FEAR

When you have the calmness and intimate sureness of Zen, you will not stress high dollar plays. Many of the best handicappers still have anxiety when they make a bet that is outside their normal range. If a player handicaps a pick 4 and he is normally a $100 player but the bet as handicapped is $250, he may feel stress and be afraid to play it. When one attains more of a Zen state, he or she will see it not as a risk, but as an even greater opportunity. There will be the sureness to strike with speed and confidence. I should explain here exactly why making a larger bet might present a smaller risk instead of a larger one.

If we look at a pick 4 (or superfecta—or any of the multiple horse wagers), and only favorites are likely to run, a minimal opportunity exists. Many bettors (even bad ones) will hit the bet. Conversely, let us assume the four horses are very difficult to see, because of many possibilities in each spot. If our Zen player can see the potential winners, the cost of the ticket is realistically unimportant because very few will even play the $250. A large windfall is possible. Once good handicapping and Zen are utilized, the choice is clear (almost ordained): Make the bet because you see it as correct.

THE LION/TIGER MENTALITY

Animals are Zen. Inaction is action.

> **"The momentum of one skilled in war is**
> **overwhelming, and his attack is precisely regulated."**
> **— Sun Tzu**

Lions and tigers do not strike at each item of prey that passes, they strike selectively. They wait for the right opportunity. Some of your largest wins will occur when you save your cash and wait. Do not waste money on stupid wagers just for "action's sake." Wait to bet aggressively on the races that you see and feel with crystal clarity. Wait, and then strike with a surgeon's precision. If you absolutely must have action, merely play one-dollar exacta boxes on your top three picks in each race until the race you came to play. The six dollars wagered in each of these races will appease your bad side, but not deplete your funds when opportunity awaits.

> **"All the soldiers taken must be cared for**
> **with magnanimity and sincerity**
> **so that they may be used by us."**
> **— Chang Yu**

TREAT YOUR VICTIMS (VANQUISHED FOES/OTHER GAMBLERS) WITH COMPASSION

Since gambling is a mutual pool endeavor, when we win, others lose. You must always treat others with respect, dignity, and honor. Beyond the absolute Zen-ness of this, there is an added benefit. We can always learn. The vanquished and losing bettor, if treated with respect, can educate us by demonstrating how they handicapped and why they lost.

> "For the samurai, the application of Zen
> was used as a calming influence to center himself
> before battle, thereby allowing the perfection
> of the mechanics of aggression."
> — Sun Tzu

CALMNESS, CENTEREDNESS, AND HEIGHTENED PERCEPTION WILL TELL YOU WHEN TO BE ULTRA AGGRESSIVE

Overall calmness allows you to detach yourself from misgivings, and play correctly with ruthless aggression. Do not out think yourself; absorb all the extra information your mind is capable of feeling and then act. Be most aggressive when you see the path most clearly. It will be apparent to you. All the practice and signals will show you the way.

It is when the horseplayer is able to leave the conscious side behind that he can play aggressively and with sureness. He intuitively interprets all the race data with a scanning glance. It is akin to the effortless artistry you see in Zen athletes like Michael Jordan, Tiger Woods, Babe Didricksen-Zaharias, Walter Payton, or even Secretariat. Use that often underutilized grey matter, and your horse picks will be as quick and surefooted as Walter Payton.

> "You experience a vast realm of perceptions
> unfolding. . . the realm of perception is limitless,
> so limitless that perception itself is primordial,
> unthinkable, beyond thought. There are so many
> perceptions that they are beyond imagination. . . There
> are feelings that you have never experienced before."
> Chogyam Trungpa, *Shambhala, The Sacred Path of the Warrior*

In Trungpa's book, he writes of the Tibetan concept of "Drala" or natural wisdom—wisdom of the cosmic mirror, a self-existing wisdom reflected in our power of perception. "Drala" literally means "above the enemy." In horse handicapping we are utilizing the realization of our wisdom to move beyond the enemy—the enemy of poor play.

GREAT WARRIORS AND GREAT HORSEPLAYERS MUST REMAIN FLEXIBLE

Choose your type and size of wager based on the opportunities presented. Never be wedded to a certain type of wager. Never be fixated on one handicapping angle. The way to success is through flexibly selecting options.

> **"When confronted by the enemy respond to changing circumstances and devise expedients. How can these be discussed beforehand?"**
> — Sun Tzu

Sometimes your wagering opportunity will not appear until the race itself. You may have handicapped a horse you believe will win, but he is a low priced morning line favorite and a DRF handicapping pick. Therefore, he is probably not a great key as the last part of a pick 3 or double. Yet amazingly, when his race goes off, he is at 5 to 1. Once you insure the horse is sound, he may now be a wonderful win play or very usable in trifectas, exactas, and pick 3's going forward. When did this opportunity occur? Not until your race was close to post time.

TO BE SUCCESSFUL YOU MUST KNOW THE WAGERING GAME AND YOUR OPPONENTS, BUT MORE IMPORTANTLY YOU MUST KNOW YOURSELF

If you are tired, grumpy, angry, or out of sorts, your likelihood of winning is infinitesimal. Conversely, when sharp and clean from meditation, the world of horse betting may seem as simple as tic-tac-toe. If you can determine when you are in the zone and handicapping well, you can insure frequent success, regardless of what other players do. Know yourself, and everything else will fall into place. If in addition to knowing yourself, you know your opponents (the other gamblers and the mutual pool), you will be successful with remarkable regularity.

> **"If ignorant both of your enemy and of yourself, you are certain in every battle to be in peril."**

"When you are ignorant of the enemy but know
yourself, your chances of winning or losing are equal."

"Know the enemy and know yourself; in a hundred
battles you will never be in peril."
— Sun Tzu, *Art of War*

Bushido, The Warrior's Code
By Inaz Nitobe, compiled and edited by Charles Lucas

NOTES:

20
Conclusions

"We gaze upon the horse's quiet beauty, their natural
elegance, and we are captivated. They see us softly in
gentle light. . .rewarding human companionship with
strength, grace, and intelligence. As they run through
arenas and open fields, past mountains and seas,
moving like the wind toward heaven, we travel
with them—if only in our hearts."
— Anonymous

There are no absolute conclusions in Zen because it is a continuing process. We know that the starting point is mastery of the handicapping techniques and from there, we follow the path of Zen. We must be calm, avoid anger and arrogance, and find our center. We must locate the zone via meditation and utilization of heightened perception, and then we must bet our winners decisively with a warrior's heart. Yet, even beyond this we must continue to educate ourselves, we must continue to move forward. We must let go, and remain open to ever newer, and ever more perfected visions and techniques. Finally, we know that being a "successful player" is much more than picking winning horses; it involves balance, being happy, and enjoying the beauty of the horses and the horse people. Being successful involves laughter and love.

As long as we live, we are on a road. Accordingly, we should keep growing and bettering our horseplay, our world, and ourselves. We may be able to someday open a new passageway to enlightenment. We all must have goals, whether it is the upcoming trifecta, or nirvana, but we cannot grasp too hard for the brass ring or it will surely slip from our hands.

In a book called *Touchstones, A Book of Daily Meditations for Men,* a Dutch proverb is quoted:

"He who is outside the door has already a good part of the journey behind him."

The author continues:

"Today, I will remember it is the reward of the journey itself, not the destination, that I seek."

Keep to the path, and enjoy the scenery along its twisting route. Good luck in life and at the horses.

"May all your chosen horses be long of nose when the photo finish sign flashes."
— F. M. Donner

Appendix 1
List of Zen and Eastern Philosophy Books Which May Provide Insight

The Art of War; Sun Tzu (Translated by Samuel B. Griffith)

Buddhism, A Way of Life and Thought; Nancy Wilson Ross

Bushido, The Warrior's Code; Inazo Nitobe (Compiled and edited by Charles Lucas)

The Complete Book of Zen; Wong Kiew Kit

Dawning, Eternal Wisdom, Heritage for Today; Swami Amar Jyoti

Japanese Death Poems; Written by Zen Monks and Haiku Poets on the Verge of Death (Compiled by Youel Hoffmann)

A Little Book of Zen; Edited by Katherine Kim

The Pocket Tao Reader; Selected and Translated by Eva Wong

Shambhala, The Sacred Path of the Warrior; Chogyam Trungpa (Edited by Carolyn Rose Gimian)

Tao Te Ching; Lao Tsu (Translated by Gia-Fu Feng and Jane English)

Thorson's Principles of Zen; Martine Batchelor

365 Tao; Daily Meditations; Deng Ming-Dao

Touchstones, A Book of Daily Meditations for Men; (Edited by Hazelden Information and Educational Services)

The Way of Zen; Alan Watts

What is Zen; Alan Watts

Zen and The Art of Motorcycle Maintenance, an Inquiry into Values; Robert M. Pirsig

Zen and The Art of Poker; Larry W. Phillips

Zen and The Way of the Sword, Arming the Samurai Psyche; Winston L. King

Appendix 2
List of Specific Handicapping and Equine Books and Publications Which May Be of Help

Ainslies's Complete Guide to Thoroughbred Racing; Tom Ainslie

American Turf Monthly; Published Monthly by Star Sports Corporation, 306 Broadway, Lynbrook, NY 11563

Beyer On Speed, New Strategies for Race Track Betting; Andrew Beyer

The Blood Horse; A weekly publication of the Thoroughbred Owners and Breeders Association, PO Box 4367, Lexington, Kentucky 40544

Class in Thoroughbred Racing; Chuck Badone

Daily Racing Form; A daily publication, 821 Corporate Drive, Lexington, Kentucky 40503

Forty Years of PEB, The Racing World in Sketch and Caricature; Pierre Bellocq

Handicapping Speed, The Thoroughbred and Quarter Horse Sprinter; Charles Carroll

Horses Talk: It Pays to Listen, The Paddock and Post Parade; Trillis Parker

The Quotable Horse Lover; Edited by Steven D. Price

The Race is Pace; Huey Mahl

Thoroughbred Champions: Top 100 Race Horses of the 20th Century; Produced by the Blood Horse Inc., PO Box 4038, Lexington Kentucky, 40544

Turf Overlays, How to Handicap Grass Winners That You May Be Missing; Bill Heller

The Winning Horse Player, An Advanced Approach to Thoroughbred Handicapping and Betting; Andrew Beyer

Bibliography

Ainslie, Tom. *Ainslies's complete Guide to Thoroughbred Racing, Third Edition.* New York: Simon & Schuster Inc., 1986.

Bach, Richard. *The Bridge across Forever, A Love Story.* New York: Dell Publishing Co., 1984.

Bach, Richard. *Illusions, The Adventures of a Reluctant Messiah.* New York: Dell Publishing Co., 1984.

Bach, Richard. *One, A Novel.* New York: Alternate Futures Incorporated (Silver Arrows Books), 1988.

Badone, Chuck. *Class In Thoroughbred Racing.* Glendale, Arizona: AT Press, 1987.

Batchelor, Martine. *Thorsons Principles of Zen.* London: Harper's Collins Publishers, 1999.

Bellocq, Pierre. *Forty Years of PEB, The Racing World in Sketch and Caricature.* New York: Daily Racing Form Press, 1995.

Beyer, Andrew, Tom Brohamer, Steven Crist, Steve Davidowitz, Dave Litfin, James Quinn, Alan Shuback, Lauren Stich, and Mike Watchmaker. *Bet With the Best, All New Strategies from America's Leading Handicappers.* New York: Daily Racing Form Press, 2001.

Beyer, Andrew. *Beyer on Speed.* New York: Houghton Mifflin Company, 1993.

Beyer, Andrew. *The Winning Horseplayer.* New York: Houghton Mifflin Company, 1983.

Blood Horse Inc. *Thoroughbred Champions; Top 100 racehorses of the 20th Century.* Lexington Kentucky: The Blood Horse Inc.1999.

Carlson, Richard Ph.D. *Don't Sweat the Small Stuff at Work.* New York: Hyperion, 1998.

Carroll, Charles. *Handicapping Speed.* New York: The Lyons Press, 1991.

Chayefsky, Paddy. *Altered States, A Novel.* New York: Harper & Row Publishers, 1978.

Deng, Ming-Dao. *365 Tao, Daily Meditations.* New York: Harper's San Francisco, 1992.

Fang, Gia-Fu, and Jane English. *Lao Tsu: Tao Te Ching.* New York: Vintage Books, 1972.

Fitzhenry, Robert I., Ed. *The Harper Book of Quotations, 3rd Edition.* New York: Harper Collins Publishers Inc., 1993.

Griffith, Samuel B. tr. *Sun Tzu: The Art of War.* London: Oxford University Press, 1971.

Haley, Alex. *The Autobiography of Malcolm X.* New York: Ballantine Books, 1977.

Hazelden Informational and Educational Services. *Touchstones, A Book of Daily Meditations for Men.* Center City Minnesota: Hazelden Foundation, 1991.

Heller, Bill. *Turf Overlays.* Chicago: Bonus Books Inc., 1998.

Yoel Hoffmann, ed. *Japanese Death Poems Written by Zen Monks and Haiku Poets on the verge of Death.* Boston: Tuttle Publishing, 1986.

Jyoti, Swami Amar. *Dawning, Eternal Wisdom, Heritage for Today.* Boulder Colorado: Truth Consciousness Inc., 1991.

Kim Katherine. *A Little Book of Zen.* Kansas City Kansas: Andre McMeel Publishing, 1998.

King, Winston L. *Zen and The Way of the Sword.* New York: Oxford University Press, 1993.

Lathem, Edward Connery, and Lawrance Thompson ed. *Robert Frost: Poetry and Prose.* New York: Owl Books, Henry Holt and company, 1984.

Lucas, Charles, ed. Inazo Nitobe: *Bushido, The Warriors Code.* Santa Clarita California: Ohara Publications Inc, 2001.

Mahl, Huey. *The Race is Pace.* Las Vegas Nevada: Gamblers Book Club, 1983. www.gamblersbook.com, 1-800-522-1777

Martin, Steve. *Cruel Shoes.* New York: G.P. Putnam's Sons, 1979.

Parker, Trillis. *Horses Talk: It Pays to Listen.* Las Vegas Nevada: Parker Productions, 1989.

Phillips, Larry W. *Zen and the Art of Poker.* New York: Plume, Published by the Penguin Group, 1999.

Pirsig, Robert M. *Zen and the Art of Motorcycle Maintenance.* New York: Bantam Books, 1984.

Pressfield, Steven *The Legend of Bagger Vance*. New York: Avon Books, 1996.

Price, Steven D, Ed. *The Quotable Horse Lover*. New York: The Lyons Press, 1999.

Ross, Nancy Wilson. *Buddhism, A Way of Life and Thought*. New York: Vintage Books, a division of Random House, 1981,

Sartre, Jean-Paul. *No Exit*. New York: Vintage Books, 1955.

Trungpa, Chogyam. *Shambhala, The Sacred Path of the Warrior*. Boston: Shambhala Publications, Inc., 1984.

Watts, Alan. *The Way of Zen*. New York: Vintage Books, 1989.

Watts, Alan. *What is Zen?* Novato California: New World Library, 2000.

Whitcomb, Christopher. *Cold Zero, Inside the FBI Hostage Rescue Team*. Boston: Little Brown and Company, 2001.

Wong, Eva, TR. *The Pocket Tao Reader*. Boston: Shambhala Publications, Inc., 1999.

Wong, Kiew Kit. *The Complete Book of Zen*. Great Britain: Element Books Limited, 1998.

Acknowledgments

Initially I would like to thank my parents for their love and financial support during this project. Without my parents' assistance, this book could never have been completed.

While this book was a "labor of love" for me, my girlfriend Kathy finished the majority of the labor during the process, while I continued to receive her unconditional love. Thanks Kathy, I love you!

I would like to acknowledge *The Daily Racing Form* and *The Blood Horse Magazine*® for expeditiously providing the charts and additional information I required to complete the book. For my readers, I have attempted to identify other writings, on both Zen and handicapping, which some may find illuminating. I recommend these additional resources, which are more in-depth and better written than my own.

A talented young artist named Brandon Brown produced the beautiful pen and ink artwork included here. His skillfully rendered artwork lends much to this book, and helps to interweave and commingle the concepts of Zen and horses in a striking visual format.

I would also like to thank Bruce Large for proofreading the original manuscript and correcting numerous errors. Ron Hansen, a former professional horseplayer and close friend, provided me outstanding ideas from someone I consider a " gambling emeritus."

Thank you Michele DeFilippo, at 1106 Design, for your dedication and help to my project. We couldn't have finished it without you.

Finally, I wish to acknowledge all the interesting, unique, and innovative horseplayers I have met during my wagering career. It would be impossible to individually comment on every "character" I have interacted with and learned from, in my wagering travels. I acknowledge you all! Hopefully, some of that vast accumulated expertise I gleaned from others, I have been able to semi-cogently relate back to you, my reader. ☯